To

16/1/07

To one

best for

21 st Birthday.

Audrey
J.

CERVANTES

Sebastian Juan Arbó

CERVANTES

Adventurer, Idealist and
Destiny's Fool

THAMES AND HUDSON

London · New York

Rendered from the Spanish by
Ilsa Barea

Contents

PART TWO

Translator's Foreword

In this biography Juan Arbó not only tells the story of Cervantes as far as it is known, and paints a vivid picture of the times in which he lived, but also offers the reader an interpretation of *Don Quixote* in the light of its author's psychological development.

Whilst *Don Quixote*, the novel, and the legendary figure of its hero, the Knight, belong to the heritage of all civilized nations, they must always remain of particular significance to Spaniards. In the literature and civilization of his country, Cervantes, or rather his *Don Quixote*, plays a rôle as important as does Shakespeare in this country. Practically every generation of Spaniards has produced its own assessment of the twin figures of Don Quixote and Sancho Panza, which have become part of the national myth. At the same time, a great number of scholars have been collecting documentary evidence which might shed light on the life of Don Quixote's creator. The documents that have been published are, however, frequently obscure or ambiguous. Long periods in Cervantes' life are still a blank. A number of conjectures have been made, and some of them have led to heated controversies, particularly about the shadier aspects in Cervantes' family history.

Juan Arbó, who is the first Spanish writer to present a popular biography of Cervantes since the publication of important new documents, has had to take all of this into account. He had to argue, at least indirectly, with other opinions, which would be available in print to a Spanish reader, though not to an English reader. He had to count on his readers' familiarity with the main episodes in *Don Quixote*. This does not mean to say that every Spaniard has read the great novel, any more than every Englishman has read all Shakespeare's plays. It does mean, however, that a number of Don Quixote's adventures have become part of Spanish popular tradition. Any child brought up in Madrid must have seen the bronze monument of Don Quixote and Sancho Panza in the *Plaza de España,* Spain Square; the Knight and his squire are more than mere fiction. In this atmosphere, the author of a Cervantes biography cannot but refer to many mental associations and notions which would inevitably come into the minds of his readers. Juan Arbó has done all this. Moreover, he wrote his biography within a definite Spanish tradition; anyone who knows Spanish periodicals or conversations among Spaniards will remember that quickness and terseness of comment are counterbalanced by repetition, by variations on the same theme, which are used to bring the point home to a somewhat self-absorbed audience.

For all these reasons, bearing in mind the great differences between the Spanish tradition and approach and the English, I have found it advisable to convey Juan Arbó's portrayal of Cervantes in a free rendering. Without in any way falsifying the original, I have omitted certain passages and condensed others, as far as this could be done without distorting the meaning and without losing any new aspect or fact necessary to the narrative. Here and there a section has been summarized, a sequence rearranged, and in a few instances a linking phrase has been inserted to restore the continuity. I have taken great care, however, not to introduce, as it were on the sly, my own opinion, interpretation or style.

I have, however, added a few small details to the text, and this needs justification. Where an allusion would have been understandable in English only with the help of long footnotes, I have preferred to extend the quotations from documents Juan Arbó used. So, when Juan Arbó merely referred to the dedication preceding Part One of *Don Quixote,* I inserted a passage from this dedication, in the belief that it would be clearer for readers who did not have *Don Quixote* at their elbow. Of course, I have done nothing of the sort where an added detail would have distorted Juan Arbó's line of argument.

Finally, I must confess to having taken the liberty of using my own versions of quotations from the works of Cervantes and of documents relating to his life, even where translations already exist. Whereas I have no illusions about the value of my English verses, I believe that a new direct translation suits the tone of this modern biography; I hope that it may help to illustrate points of Cervantes' complex personality, which Juan Arbó portrays with so much sympathy and imagination.

ILSA BAREA

Faringdon,
January, 1955

*I have seen servants upon horses, and princes
walking as servants upon the earth.*

ECCLESIASTES X, 7

I

Birth and Adolescence

OCTOBER had come and the evenings were growing shorter. The first cold winds were sweeping across the grey uplands of Castile and through the streets of the old town of Alcalá, huddled on the flat banks of the river Henares, in the shelter of its range of hills. In those years Alcalá de Henares was a famous place: famous for its university, which had risen to greatness in Queen Isabella's reign, famous for the princes and sons of the great who came to study there, for its churches and palaces, but also for the industriousness of its peasantry.

Towards nightfall, heavy carts laden with grapes returned to the town on the road along the river, between rows of acacias. In the dusk, the students still walked up and down under the arcades, embroiled in political or theological discussions, or planning their next noisy pranks.

Silence and cold began to creep over the town. Alcalá withdrew into itself. Fires were kindled on the hearths; mothers counselled their children while the old men recalled wars of long ago; and before going to sleep, everyone said a prayer for absent friends, for there was hardly a home which did not have a member of its family away in foreign lands.

One day, when the acacias were shedding their sere leaves and an autumn sadness lay upon town and fields, a boy was born in a modest little house near the kitchen garden of the Capuchin monastery. The house belonged to a bitterly poor family of gentlefolk who already had three children; the father was an apothecary-surgeon, and deaf. A few days later the fourth child was christened Miguel in the church of Santa María la Mayor.

Nowadays Alcalá leads a quiet existence. Its university has closed long since, and the bustle and gaiety departed with the students. The greatness of the times of Queen Isabella lies confined in tombs. The church of Santa María la Mayor, too, is in ruins, its bells silent, its great windows empty, kestrels wheeling round its mutilated spire. If the name of Alcalá still has the power to thrill, if its deserted streets still cast a spell on the visitor, it is on account of that little boy who was born within these city walls, who made his first uncertain steps on these flagstones, and who first learnt about beauty from the tints of this sky, the gentle undulations of these fields. The ruins of the church in the vast market place enshrine the memory of a brief scene, on Sunday, October 9, 1547, when in the dim light of votive candles the godfather, Juan Pardo, held Miguel de Cervantes towards the font.

*

He was a fair-haired boy, thin, lively and nimble, with wide-awake merry eyes that held a glint of mischief and irony—the legacy of his mother who, many years later, was to don a widow's weeds while her husband was still alive, so as to move the Duke of Sesa to pity and obtain his help for the ransom of her sons in captivity.

From his father he inherited a goodness of heart which was never impaired throughout his hard and stormy life. And there were also in him an enthusiasm for the good and the beautiful, and a spiritual restlessness which held great promise. Resolute of mind, he possessed an intelligence acute enough to make him perceive and understand each fresh situation and to rectify, if belatedly, the blunders of his heart; yet his heart was so passionate that it always blundered anew.

As a child he went to school like all the other boys of his age, first in Alcalá, later in Valladolid and in Madrid. Doubtless he played in the streets on his free days, or on the river-banks under the poplars. He may often have stopped in the market square to listen to a local ballad-singer, stirred by the old man's beautiful tales of love and gallantry. The walls of the city must sometimes have appeared oppressive, while the paths leading from the town lost themselves all too soon among the hills which bounded the horizon. But beyond those hills were other cities, there was the wide world where wars were waged and reputations made; beyond the hills were Flanders, Italy and America.

That Miguel's character and cleverness secured him a privi-leged position in his family is obvious from the number and the quality of the schools to which he was sent. His parents clearly endeavoured to give him an education more in keeping with his talents than with their means.

By then there were seven brothers and sisters. Though mutual affection united the family, their talk when they were together at nights cannot have been very cheerful. "Where there's no flour, all things turn sour", says the Spanish proverb. No doubt Miguel often heard Leonor de Cortinas, his mother, complain about their hardships or hint at the slackness and irresolution of his father, whose deafness made him luckily impervious to reproaches.

Such scenes, and the books he read at a time when Spain was still living—as though in a feverish dream—through the heroic exploits of her Conquistadores, drove Miguel to seek refuge from petty domestic misery in bright day-dreams of the future. His father, too, sought to escape from current ills, but he preferred to dwell upon his own family's prosperous past. On those sad evenings, after a scant supper, the tired and disheartened old man who had never possessed much spirit would evoke the glittering times when, as Diego de Alcalá recorded, the people of Alcalá stopped to gape at the brothers Cervantes in all their finery, silks and furbelows, riding past on handsome horses with their retinue. Or he would talk of his uncle Juan, who had been magistrate and governor on the estates of the Count of Ureña in distant Andalusia. . . . And even while his feeble, indolent father con-soled himself with memories of what once had been, Miguel was dreaming, perhaps, of how he would restore the lost splendours of his family.

Among his sisters Miguel seems to have had two favourites,

Andrea and Luisa, the Martha and the Mary of his home. Or rather, one embodying the worldly, the other the mystical element —the twin impulses which from the outset contended for mastery in Miguel's person. He gave his love to the meek Luisa who, on a bleak February day when the timid young shoots in the corn, fields round Alcalá heralded the spring, let the doors of a Carme, lite convent close behind her for ever. And he admired Andrea, who was always entangled in love affairs, halfway between expe, diency and sentiment, which never led to an open scandal and invariably brought some advantage for the family.

They were both intimates of his, but particularly Luisa. From Andrea, Miguel may have received shrewd practical advice, expressed with an amusing mixture of impudence and charm. Of his dreams in which he saw himself as a poet and fighter, however, he could only have spoken to Luisa. The name she adopted as a nun, Luisa of Bethlehem, sounds like an echo of Miguel's peculiar feeling for the Holy Night; it might have cropped up first in one of their conversations. "You'll be an Abbess and I'll be a Captain . . . and they'll call you Luisa of Bethlehem"—that was the way people talked in the old tales.

Luisa de Cervantes entered the convent while her brother was in Seville, and it is not known whether he ever saw her again. Luisa came to be a Prioress. Miguel never became a Captain.

2

Seville

WE seem to see the hand of Providence behind the fact that the Cervantes family had to move incessantly from one place to another, enabling Miguel to explore the country and the cities of Spain to his heart's content, so that one day he could bequeath us the fruits of his vision, matured in the clear light of his creative mind.

The boy was scarcely more than twelve when his family was forced to move house, at first, it seems, to Valladolid; later, they went to Cordova, where the paternal grandfather was still living, and from there to Seville, always driven on by the same urge, the vain hope that a new city would offer greater professional scope to the paterfamilias. (After two years they were to leave Seville for Madrid, thinking, like the knight in the old ballad, that "fortune changes with a change of house".) Thus, ever-hopeful, did Don Rodrigo de Cervantes move from city to city with his load of children and worries.

It was on a spring day of 1563 that Miguel arrived at Seville with his father, brothers and sisters. His mother had stayed behind in Alcalá with her two younger children, to wait till prospects were such that she could join her husband. The good lady had every reason to be wary, but for once the new place of residence gave solid grounds for hope.

At that period Seville was rich and prosperous. The discovery of America and, as a result, the intense maritime traffic between the port of Seville and the Spanish possessions overseas had brought great wealth. Seafarers, merchants and adventurers from all parts of Spain poured into Seville, which grew apace. Commerce was given a new impulse, arts and letters flourished. Not only because of its beauty, but also because of its expanding industry and its intellectual life, Seville was one of the foremost capital cities of Spain, if not the foremost.

Beneath a limpid blue sky, the city's many towers, spires and great buildings spilled over the confines of the ancient town walls into a wide and pleasant vale. So must it have appeared to the bewildered eyes of young Miguel as he rode up to the Macarena Gate. But rather than feeling a stranger he may have felt a young knight destined to unlock its magic secret. There was in him something akin to this land and sky—was his grandfather not a native of Cordova?—and something of the spontaneous gaiety, the ready affection of the Andalusians, perhaps even a trace of their happy-go-lucky revelry.

But it was not until he got within the confines of Seville itself that he received the most important impression of all: the quays of the river Guadalquivir with their suggestion of the sea. There the great sailing-ships of the world were moored, thence they set sail. Heavy galleons loaded with the treasure of the New World rode at anchor after their long, slow journeys by sea routes which Columbus had first traced on the map.

Miguel spent long hours by the quays, on hot mornings and on mild evenings, when merry-making started in Triana on the opposite bank of the Guadalquivir and the last sunlight glinted on the Golden Tower. Then the river awoke to quicker life. Small boats decked with green branches came and went on the smooth waters. Music, songs, and the laughter of young people filled the air. Tall ships drew slowly near with the tide and dropped anchor, while the whole waterfront shouted greetings. Miguel would watch the sailors disembark, with something strange and distant in their voices and in their eyes. They would talk of perils, wars and great deeds, of fabulous riches, of won-derful landscapes and magnificent cities. It would excite his imagination and crowd his dreams with fantastic visions, inter-mingled with reminiscences from his books of chivalry.

Meanwhile his sisters stayed at home to look after the household and the necessities of life. At that time, many Italians lived and traded in Spain, and it is thought that some of them were frequent guests at the home of the Cervantes in Seville. Perhaps they had business deals with Don Rodrigo. Perhaps, however, they were attracted by the lively charms of the sisters, particularly of Andrea, who must have combined rare beauty with an exceptionally shrewd insight. There is also the possibility that an Italian lived in their household as a lodger, which would have helped to keep them afloat in spite of the difficulties of their new existence, and in spite of Don Rodrigo's apathy.

However meagre their means might be, Miguel again went to the best schools in Seville. There he made friends with the sons of families of high standing, among them possibly with Mateo Vázquez, the future Secretary to King Philip II. They may have talked of their hopes and prospects. They may have discussed poetry, for the atmosphere of Seville was favourable to the Muses. If so, they will have commented on the poems of Herrera, in those days undisputedly the leading poet, who shut himself up in proud solitude and wrote songs about his disdainful mistress or about actions on the battlefield. Perhaps they dreamed of following in his footsteps, and read their first verses to one another.

For all that, we imagine Miguel to have been more intent on walking through the streets of Seville, filled as they were with a motley throng such as he could never have seen in any other town he had known. There was the open market, all bustle and noise, on the flight of stairs in front of the Cathedral. There were the high balconies of the Giralda, the Moorish tower, commanding a great view of the teeming city, its garden-lands, and away to the wide horizons. He might amble through the patrician quarters of San Martin, San Vicente and Santa Catalina, might go with his brother Rodrigo to the Junk Market, paradise of street arabs and pickpockets, or visit the Mancebia where ruffians, pimps and panders had their haunts. The rich and variegated life of Seville was spread out before his eyes: bullies fighting in the street while the onlookers hovered between fear and amusement—a drunkard holding forth in the gutter—a condemned man on his way to the

B

gallows, straddled on a donkey, a rope round his neck and a swarm of urchins running alongside—a gay and sumptuous wedding procession—people gambling—people quarrelling—in one street an improvised fiesta with singing and dancing—in the next alley a beggar exhibiting his hideous sores. Here Miguel may have laughed, there his eyes may have filled with tears of pity: intense conflicting emotions must have shaken him. Nowhere could life have shown itself in cruder and more violent contrasts than in Seville, nowhere could he have seen the face of mankind so naked in all its moods. Sorrow and pain cheek by jowl with pleasure; abject misery hard by luxury; men dying in the streets, abandoned, starved or ailing; others living in magnificent palaces, rich and sheltered; boisterous singing in taverns, and moans issuing from the ordure in the street—the young boy saw and absorbed it all. Each thing struck its own chord in his retentive mind, though the riverside and the tall masts with their fluttering pennants cast the greatest spell. Yet if he dreamed of the open sea, the way to it was soon to be closed to him, at least for the time being.

In spite of Andrea's resourcefulness, the situation at home had steadily worsened. The hope that in Seville Don Rodrigo would find a better field for his abilities had once again proved false. While the gloomy old man was thinking nostalgically of Alcalá where Doña Leonor had always kept things going somehow, they heard the news that the Court had moved its seat from Toledo to Madrid.

If this venture had been another sad disappointment, the fault lay no more with Seville than it had earlier lain with Alcalá or Valladolid; it was due to Don Rodrigo's incurable fecklessness. Each time they had chased a new phantom of hope. This time Madrid, a transformed Madrid, rose before them as an alluring mirage. Perhaps they saw prospects of Miguel finding a position at the Court. Also, Madrid was less far from Alcalá, where Doña Leonor was still valiantly struggling to keep a home for herself and those of her children who lived with her. This was another strong reason why they should leave Andalusia and return to Castile. From whatever final motives, the Cervantes family decided after much havering to move to Spain's new capital. One fine day in 1566 they rode away from Seville towards their new goal, their new illusion.

3

Madrid

WHEN he came to Madrid, Miguel was nineteen years old, a slim, spruce young man with a most engaging manner and an enthusiastic gleam in his intelligent eyes, not yet dimmed by the shadow of his first disappointments.

Since its elevation to capital of Spain, the city had rapidly spread across the hills on both sides of the river Manzanares. New streets, straight and spacious, were laid out, old streets lengthened, gullies filled in, slopes levelled. From one day to the next, as it seemed, monasteries and palaces rose where forests had been. In the lowlying districts, the park of El Prado took shape with wide avenues, tall poplars and leaping fountains.

This new Madrid hummed with zest for life like a huge beehive. Fiestas were celebrated, literary circles organized, people met and gossiped, the first playhouses were opened. They were stages not quite worthy of the name of theatre, yet the figures of Lope de Vega, Tirso de Molina and Calderón were already looming ahead. Spain's entire intellectual life began to concentrate itself here where the Court was established. Migration to the capital assumed unexpected proportions.

Although life in Madrid was austere compared with Seville, its intense, restless quality cannot have failed to arouse Miguel's interest. Artists from all over the world had come to the city to contribute to the completion of the Escorial, Philip II's great monument, on which work was already far advanced. Madrid was the centre, heart and brain of the Spanish Empire; whatever happened there had worldwide repercussions. There were issued the orders which were executed on the other side of the globe;

there all the pulsations within the vast realm were recorded and co-ordinated.

The change in Miguel's existence was marked by a greater seriousness and a stricter sense of purpose. Under López de Hoyos he resumed his studies in grammar and composition. Once again his personal qualities gained him affectionate appreciation; his teacher, an old humanist, writing in praise of some of his verses, called him "my dear and beloved pupil".

All the same, Miguel's intellectual development was destined to remain incomplete. It was based mainly on books read at random and on such lectures as his itinerant family's mode of life permitted him to attend, always under different teachers. There were two factors, then, which in his case stood in the way of an integrated education: the basic instability of his life, and his unquiet temperament. Neither in his studies nor in his actions was he ever able to submit to an orderly discipline and to a fixed method. He was not the man to spoil his eyesight poring over texts old or new; no doubt he preferred a walk through El Prado to listening to the most accomplished lecturer on philosophy. If López de Hoyos loved and praised him, it was certainly more because of his lively intelligence, goodness, charm and human warmth than because of any scholarly zeal.

It was good so. He learned more from life than from books. Not that he despised these, but he read only what spoke to his mind and responded to his urge for freedom. In this sense he read even torn scraps of paper he picked up in the street, whatever people might think of it. We may be sure that he preferred the romantic chivalry of *Amadis of Gaul* to Doctor Villalpando's learned *Súmulas*. Some of the earnest scholars who were then the shining lights in Spain, such as the clever Suárez de Figueroa, were to denigrate him for this reason. Indeed, they themselves produced most erudite treatises, whose virtues we willingly accept so long as we are not forced to read them. He, however, wrote *Don Quixote*.

In Madrid Miguel tasted the sweetness of his first triumphs, but the honey quickly turned to gall. His impetuous nature and his

ardent love for poetry made him seek the friendship of young poets
—future celebrities—who then congregated in the capital, making
their first essays at creative writing and reading them to small
circles. Fate, however, was to drive him far away from this group.

Love had crossed his path. At one time it was assumed that
he had met a lady of high rank; this was later refuted, together
with an entrancing legend of duels and adventures, well worthy
of him and his temperament. Certainly some woman played a
rôle in his life in those days. And what is more probable than
that a young man of his stamp, greatly susceptible to women and
attractive to them, passionate and ambitious, should have raised
his eyes—and his thought—to the lady of his dreams? There may
be no evidence in the documents, but there is in his books. He
was brave, noble, a poet and in love. He was aware that his verse
was praised, perhaps even a little too aware of it. This lady lived
a remote existence, shut up behind high, thick walls like the
princesses in the books he liked to read; he had to win her
through his gallantry. What could have restrained his desires?
Cervantes was one of those beings who always fall in love with
the distant, beautiful and inaccessible, to whom reality is never
immediate, but something woven of impalpable matter, the stuff
dreams are made of, and as elusive as dreams so soon as they try
to grasp it. He was a true child of his epoch, which favoured
exaltation.

Let us therefore assume that she was a lady of high rank, as the
old tradition had it; that he was separated from her by his poverty;
and that he was ingenuous enough to believe that he could win
her through his fame as a poet, his nobility of mind, and his
bravery. Thus it happened in the books. There was no reason
why it should not happen in real life. How could the language
of his dreams lie, when he felt its truth in his whole being?

It may be that memories of this time of his youth were alive in
him when, much later, he fashioned the figure of Dulcinea out
of dreamy tenderness and bitter disenchantment.

*

In Madrid, the whole Cervantes family was again living together, with the exception of Rodrigo, the brother next in age to Miguel, who was possibly even then serving with one of the Spanish regiments in Italy. As in Seville, Italians used to come to their house, presumably some of them stayed there as boarders. At all events there is a document which shows that a certain Locadelo made a gift to Andrea, consisting of clothes, pieces of furniture and cash, all listed in a letter of donation which says that they were given in recognition of her care and nursing of Locadelo during an illness, and "so that she should be in a better position to contract an honourable marriage".

Inevitably, the family discussed with their foreign friends not only business, current difficulties, news of battles, and the happenings at Court, but also Miguel, for whose future they had great hopes. "The Church—the Sea—the Court" were, in the slogan of those times, the three roads open to ambitious young Spaniards of more or less noble birth. The Italians must have spoken in praise of their country, although Miguel's parents would have disliked anything which would have taken the son away from them, preferring the idea of a position at Court, where young Mateo Vázquez of Seville was already safely entrenched. But Miguel wanted to see the world, and Italy offered him the best opportunity of doing so. To the bolder spirits of his generation, Italy seemed a country of unlimited possibilities. For one who was interested in Letters, there were the brilliant courts of Cardinals, the palaces of Spanish Viceroys, and—Rome. In Rome Juan de Encina had made his home, and had earned applause with his pastoral play *Auto del Repelón*, which was performed at a festival in Cardinal Arborrea's mansion. Rome had helped to make the names of Cristóbal de Mesa, Rey de Artieda and Cristóbal de Virués, and of many others who had attuned their lyres to the rhythm of Tasso's stanzas. It was in Italy, too, that the greatest of them, Garcilasso de la Vega, had gathered the sweetness with which he imbued his songs.

To those attracted by a military career—and Miguel was undoubtedly tempted by the idea—Italy could boast great war lords.

There were the famous Spanish Tercios garrisoned at Naples and in Sicily, always held in readiness to go into action either in Flanders or the Near East, the two storm centres where glory and fortune beckoned.

In Seville, when watching the galleons sail down the Guadalquivir, Miguel may have felt the lure of America. Once in Madrid, however, the enchantment waned. America seemed no longer a shining goal for those with noble dreams of fame, adventure and freedom. It had become the province of reckless, ambitious careerists with their eyes on riches rather than glory; in short, of desperadoes.

Many years later, Cervantes was again to think of America—when his fortunes were at their lowest ebb, and his mind hagridden, darkened, and harassed by misery.

Now he set his heart on Italy.

4

Historical Interlude

A SOMBRE tragedy in the private life of King Philip II was nearing its climax: the tragedy of Don Carlos, heir-apparent to the throne, an enigmatic figure whose story to this day belongs as much to legend as to history.

Eccentric, irritable, hypersensitive, given to violent changes of mood and racked by continual bouts of fever, the Prince had, from infancy on, been a source of concern to those about him. His early years were overshadowed by a lack of tenderness and affection. He was only four when his mother died, eight when the Infanta Juana, his aunt, who had taken him under her wing, left for Portugal to be married. This caused the Prince to cry bitterly for days on end, and afterwards he complained of loneliness. Some of the twists in his character may have been due to those early impressions, but the principal trouble was a mental instability inherited from his great-grandmother, the mad Juana, which only grew worse with the years. His emotions swung from one extreme to the other; his love and his hate were equally unbridled and violent.

When Cardinal Espinosa, one of the mightiest men at Court, banished a comedian whom the Prince befriended, Don Carlos insulted him in public and threatened to kill him. He was capable of sympathy for the poor, on whom he would shower money with open hands; at the same time, he would order children to be whipped and torture animals for his amusement. As a small boy, it was an effort to make him uncover his head in the presence of the King. The Duke of Alba once forgot to kiss the Prince's hand at a ceremony, whereupon Don Carlos proclaimed his

15

eternal hatred for the Duke. On being reproved by the King, he had to be taken to bed with an acute attack of fever. Overween, ing pride and cruelty were his most striking characteristics, and his cruelty in particular asserted itself when he had one of his tantrums. No wonder a foreign Ambassador predicted, at an early stage, that Don Carlos would come to a bad end.

In 1562 the King sent him for reasons of health to Alcalá de Henares, where he took up his studies jointly with his uncle, Don Juan of Austria, the future victor of Lepanto, and his cousin, Prince Alessandro Farnese. Soon, however, he plunged into an intrigue with the young daughter of one of the gate-keepers at the palace. One Sunday in April, having arranged to meet her in the garden at noon, he gulped his meal, dismissed his atten, dants, and dashed down a dark staircase. He missed a step, rolled down the flight, and crashed into an iron door at the bot, tom. There he was found, moaning, with a deep wound in his head which was bleeding profusely.

At first the injury was not considered dangerous, and the King, who had hastened to Alcalá, felt hopeful enough about it to return to Madrid. But on April 30th, Don Carlos had a high fever; his condition grew quickly worse, and on May 2nd he received the Last Sacraments. There was scant hope of his recovery.

All Spain shared in the King's sorrow. Special prayers were said, processions arranged, the best doctors called in, and even quacks were mobilized. In Alcalá, the remains of a Franciscan friar who had died in the odour of sanctity were disinterred and taken to the palace, in a procession made up of a clamorous multitude. The door of the Prince's bedchamber stood wide open and he was seen lying in a coma in the middle of the room. As the remains of Fray Diego were laid on the bed beside the dying Prince, the people outside sank to their knees in supplica, tion.

The Prince recovered. Again there were processions every, where, this time of joy and thanksgiving. Miguel de Cervantes and his young friends were probably among the crowds that watched the great procession in Madrid and saw King Philip walk past, his head bared under the scorching sun, clad in black, and very pale.

Pleasure at the Prince's recovery was soon marred, for he proved himself more reckless, ungovernable and intemperate than ever. His gluttony got beyond control, his licentiousness and violence increased. He used to walk in the streets of Madrid and insult any woman he happened to meet, by mauling her and paying her the grossest compliments. He slapped Don Diego de Acuña's face on the pretext that he had dared to make a comment when he saw the Prince listening behind a door. He slapped Don Alfonso de Córdoba on the pretext that he had not come quickly enough when the Prince called for him, though he later admitted that he had, in fact, "felt a burning desire to do so during the past six months and was entitled to have his wish fulfilled". Once, when he found that a shoemaker had made a pair of shoes too tight, he ordered them to be cut into small pieces and stewed in the manner of tripe; then he forced the hapless shoemaker to swallow the dish in his presence. Not only did he want to kill Cardinal Espinosa, he also threatened the life of the Duke of Alba, and, later on, even that of Don Juan of Austria. In short, Don Carlos had reached a stage when no one could bear with him and he could bear with no one.

There were three or four exceptions to this. There was, above all, the one human being for whom Don Carlos showed the deepest affection: Queen Isabella, his stepmother. And the depth of his love for the Queen was the measure of his hatred for his father. We cannot but believe that the two feelings were interconnected. Isabella of Valois and Don Carlos were of the same age. Originally a marriage between them had been planned. She was lovely, kind and compassionate. In her, Don Carlos found the tenderness and sympathy his mother was not there to give him. The Queen was possibly the only person who knew how to soothe him in his attacks of rage. On her he centred all the affection of which he was capable.

When the drama had run its course, a list written in the

Prince's own hand was found among his papers. It enumerated first his friends, then his enemies. The name of Isabella of Valois headed the list of friends, "the King, my father", the list of enemies. Certainly Don Carlos had been absent from the wedding ceremony of the royal couple, on the excuse that he was ill; even then, many had believed that it was deliberate. "When he first saw her, he fell head over heels in love", people said, and remembered that she once had been promised to him. If this event had not been the cause of his hatred of his father, it had at least added fuel to the fire. Isabella of Valois, on the other hand, though she may have felt pity and affection when she first saw him, no doubt counted herself lucky in that the original project had been abandoned. Don Carlos was a sickly lad, emaciated by the quartan-fever, one shoulder higher than the other, making him almost a hunchback, and with a limp. In addition he had an impediment in his speech. As a historian has pointed out, one could not even begin to compare Philip II, a relatively young man at that time, with his son, who was not only luckless but also unlovable.

The relationship between father and son was poisoned, and there was nothing to stop its worsening. Don Carlos began to make haphazard plans to free himself from his father's tutelage, in the conviction that he was old enough to marry and govern. The chronicler Cabrera says that the Prince had not come to this decision on his own, but that it was insinuated to him by the Count of Egmont—whom the Duke of Alba soon afterwards sent to the scaffold at Brussels—during his stay in Madrid. Cabrera also maintains that the Prince kept in touch with certain Flemish representatives at Court who carried on Egmont's work and encouraged Don Carlos in his idea of going to the Low Countries, "where they would be his obedient servants".

Be that as it may, the Prince at about this time decided to choose a bride without first consulting the King. His choice fell on the Austrian princess Anne. Of this he informed the King, at the same time asking to be made Governor of Flanders where he intended to reside after his marriage. Though Philip II appeared to acquiesce, he was in reality outraged at his son's lack of respect. Don Carlos, however, felt appeased by the assurance he had obtained from his father, and happy at the prospect of a marriage which he hoped would bring him his freedom. It was then that unrest flared up in the Low Countries. The King, who had planned to go there with his son, cancelled the journey; the wedding was postponed; the Duke of Alba was appointed Commander of the Army in Flanders.

This appointment inevitably provoked deep resentment among the Flemings in Madrid who were only too well aware of the Duke's harsh methods. Thus it is not difficult to credit Cabrera's report that in Flemish circles they did their best to convince Don Carlos of the danger to his own plans implicit in the Duke's mission. Certainly the news enraged the Prince beyond measure. When the Duke called on him to take his leave, Don Carlos cut him short and shouted that he, not Alba, should go to Flanders and "it would be the Duke's death if he denied it". With these words he drew his dagger. The Duke easily held him at bay until servants intervened. He thereupon informed the King of the incident. A few days later, the Duke of Alba departed for Flanders.

From then onward the Prince's hatred for his father was the ruling passion of his life, and it bred within his sick mind fantastic plans which all had the same ultimate aim: to go to Flanders, proclaim himself King of the Flemish Provinces, and set the country free. Whether it is true or not that these ideas were secretly fomented by the Flemings who cherished their country's liberty, the fact remains that Don Carlos pursued them with unreasoning recklessness, driven by his desire for revenge and his urge for personal freedom. Step by step, from one imprudent act to the next—acts of a desperate and unbalanced man—he blundered towards final ruin.

Don Carlos spoke of his Flemish projects to his uncle, Don Juan of Austria, who had always shown him sympathy. Don Juan had recently been appointed Captain-General of the Mediterranean area and so was the only person in a position to grant

Don Carlos the ships he would need. Yet Don Juan was aghast at his nephew's proposals. First he tried in vain to dissuade him, then he asked for time to consider. The matter was so grave that he informed his half-brother, the King, of all the Prince had told him.

The King kept silent. Days passed. Don Carlos sought another interview with his uncle, but Don Juan of Austria avoided any further encounter. As his difficulties mounted, so did the Prince's state of panic: he turned wildly from one expedient to another. He wrote letters to grandees, demanding money "for a most important journey he had in mind", but most of the letters ended up in the King's hands. He confided in his friend Ruy Gómez, the man he most loved and trusted, but no sooner had Don Carlos put his secrets into words than the King learnt of them. Alone in his madness and unaware of his isolation, Don Carlos was reeling as though in a vacuum. He called at every door behind which he hoped to find help, and at every door loomed, invisible, the stern and silent figure of his father, the King. Unseen, the net was closing round him and he began to be assailed by unnamed fears; perhaps it was the very silence that roused a sense of menace in his shuttered mind. Terror soon became overwhelming. His bedroom was turned into an arsenal. He slept with his sword, his dagger and a loaded musket always at hand; he tried to secure his door with a device which he could manipulate from his bed by means of pulleys.

Philip II said nothing. He waited in silence, and his silence was the most terrifying thing of all. Not one of his son's steps escaped his vigilance.

Inexorably the final crisis drew nearer. The King had gone to the Escorial. Don Carlos wanted to exploit his father's absence in order to launch the latest version of his project; this entailed going to the port of Cartagena, where he expected to find ships assigned to him by his uncle, and setting sail for Italy. From Italy he would travel to Flanders by land. But Don Juan of Austria was nowhere to be seen.

Then Don Carlos indulged in yet another insane act. On the

eve of a church function when he would have to take the Sacra/
ment in public, he went to Confession and told his Confessor
that there was a man whom he hated and was unable to forgive.
The priest thereupon refused him absolution. In his perturbed
frame of mind the Prince consulted no less than fourteen other
clerics, whom he called in from the convent of Our Lady of
Atocha—a new proof of his derangement. While they were un/
able to allay his doubts on a point of theology, they themselves
grew suspicious and in the end wrested his secret from him: the
man he so hated was his father and "he wished to kill him if he
could". We may take this for an outburst of fury rather than the
expression of a set intent, but he did utter the words. And the
King learned of his confession.

Don Carlos believed that he had settled everything at last, but
in truth nothing was settled. All he had done was to build a
castle in the air which was bound to collapse at the King's first
gesture, but which was also substantial enough to bury him under
its ruins. He had asked the Director of Posts to keep eight horses
at his disposal the following morning. The official, warned of
the Prince's intentions, made excuses and hurried with his report
to the King, who had gone from the Escorial to El Prado, his
residence near Madrid. On the same day, Philip II returned to
the capital.

In the evening, they all met in the Queen's apartments. Isa/
bella, in complete ignorance of events, welcomed Don Carlos
with her usual kindness. Don Carlos kissed the King's hand,
and the King received him graciously.

The following day was Sunday. King Philip heard Mass
together with his son, "with the greatest calm in the world and
without the least show of emotion". For the last time father and
son knelt side by side in prayer. Immediately after Mass Don
Carlos succeeded in steering his uncle, Don Juan, to his rooms
where they spent two hours behind closed doors. It is not known
what happened between the two of them, but it can be conjec/
tured. The Prince was no more able to persuade Don Juan than
Don Juan was able to dissuade the Prince. In the end Don

Carlos drew his dagger and assaulted his uncle. Don Juan had to ward him off with his own sword till attendants came to his assistance. Soon afterwards he asked to see the King. Don Carlos, realizing that this time the scandal would not be hushed up, pretended to be ill; it may be that rage, fear and desperation had really exhausted his body. Late in the evening, when the King sent for him, Don Carlos begged to be excused on the grounds of indisposition.

By then the Prince had but a single thought—to flee, to get away from his father, never mind how and where to. Again he gave orders to have horses in readiness for the early hours of the morning. Once more the King immediately learnt of it. He did not need this information, however, for his mind was made up.

It was the night of January 18, 1568. The King summoned the four most important personages of his Court, Ruy Gómez, Antonio de Toledo, the Duke of Feria and Don Luis Quijada. It was after eleven o'clock when they entered, singly, the room where the King was awaiting them. They were followed by the King's two chamberlains, Don Pedro Manuel and Don Diego de Acuña. In silence they listened to the words of their sovereign. Afterwards one of them wrote that on that night Philip II had spoken to them "as no man has ever spoken before".

Towards midnight those six men and the King descended the inner staircase of the silent palace, guided by the feeble light of a torch. Wordlessly they made for the apartments of Don Carlos. First came the Duke of Feria, then the King. Philip II wore armour over his clothes, an iron helmet on his head, and beneath his arm he carried a naked sword. The others, too, carried drawn swords. At a respectful distance followed the King's two valets, Bernal and Santoyo, with hammers and nails.

The two gentlemen on duty in the Prince's antechamber were ordered to let no one pass. Don Carlos was asleep, trusting in his armoury and in the mechanism which locked his door. But this mechanism had already been dismantled by order of the King, without the Prince's knowledge, and the door was easily opened. Taking every precaution, they entered the bedchamber. The

Duke of Feria stepped to the head of the bed and removed sword and musket. Don Carlos was startled out of his sleep and reached for his weapons. He found only his dagger, and even the dagger slipped from his fumbling grasp. Ruy Gómez took it. The Prince was defenceless.

So far the room had been dark. Now lights were brought. And Don Carlos found himself face to face with his father. In terror he exclaimed: "What is this? Does Your Majesty wish to kill me?" This the King denied, telling him to calm himself, and adding that all he was doing was for his son's good. He said it slowly, "with great gentleness". Then he ordered his valets to nail down the shutters of the windows.

The Prince comprehended at last. He leapt from his bed, threw himself at the King's feet, sobbing: "Kill me, Your Majesty, but do not imprison me, or I shall kill myself!" "You will do no such thing," the King answered, "it would be an act of madness." "Not of madness, but of despair because Your Majesty treats me so badly", said the Prince. He rose to his feet —so it is reported—his teeth chattering, his whole body trem-bling, and made as if to hurl himself into the fire blazing in the hearth; but Don Antonio de Toledo grabbed him in the nick of time. Between them they managed to get him back upon his bed. Then all the Prince's papers were collected; the room was cleared of every object which he might have used as a means of inflicting injury upon himself. The fire was put out. And Don Carlos was left alone in the cold and dark of the chamber which was henceforth to be his gaol.

The King, it was said, had listened impassively to his son and pronounced his cruel sentence without betraying any emotion. Then he had walked away without giving him a further glance. The windows were boarded up. Guards were posted at the door, with orders not to speak to the Prince or answer any of his ques-tions. Don Carlos never saw the sunlight again, nor the face of a friend—not even his father's face. The King not only refused to visit him, but also prohibited visits by anyone else. Isabella of Valois and the Infanta Juana begged to be permitted to see

C

Don Carlos, but Philip rejected all their pleas and commanded them never to mention his son to him again. Six months later Don Carlos was dead. Nothing was known at the time, little is known even now, of these last grim months of his existence.

The report of the Prince's death produced general consternation. People spoke of it in whispers. "The more discreet," Cabrera says, "looked at one another and kept their lips sealed; if silence was broken, some called the King prudent and some hard, for with him a smile and the knife were ever akin." Most people, however, criticized the King under their breaths, because they were affected by Don Carlos' youth and the severity of his punishment. And yet, who could claim to see into the King's mind? During his son's illness he had spent a whole night on his knees, praying for him. And later he wrote a letter of selfjustification to his sister, the Empress Maria of Austria, in which he said: "I wished to sacrifice my own flesh and blood to God, and to put His service, and the universal weal, before any human consideration."

Rumours about the Prince's end had scarcely died down when all Spain was shaken by the news that Queen Isabella had died. The King's sorrow at this new blow was so deep that he was seen to weep, perhaps for the first time in his life. His were not the only tears that were shed for Isabella of Valois, for few queens have won so much love.

People called her the "Queen of Peace", because her marriage with Philip had heralded peace with France. Charming and beautiful, she radiated kindliness; wherever she went, murmured blessings and praise followed her. Even the King was under the spell of her graceful ways. When she was ill he stayed at her bedside, when she was well he showered her with attentions and fulfilled her every wish. All his hours of leisure were spent in her company, and she used to describe herself, in her letters, as the "happiest woman in the world".

Isabella of Valois fell ill very soon after Don Carlos' death. She was racked by her compassion for him, and her always frail health gave way under the strain. For two whole days she wept, her child-like soul horrified by so much harshness. But with the same inflexibility with which he had refused her permission to visit the imprisoned Don Carlos, the King told her to stop weeping over his death.

During her last illness, the King sat by her bedside at nights, holding her hands and trying to raise her spirits, and then he would withdraw to pray for her. But in vain. An error of judgment on the part of the physicians who were attending her accelerated her end. She gave birth to a five months' child, a daughter, and then her death struggle began. She spoke to her husband, but no longer knew what she was saying. The King promised he would be a good father to her children—and went away to his own apartments to hide the feeling that contorted his face. Soon afterwards he was told that she was dead. He dismissed everybody from his presence and sat down, alone, to write to Paris, to Catherine de' Medici, his dead wife's mother. ". . . Nothing was left undone," he concluded, "to save her life, which was dearer to me than my own. Yet when the hour appointed by God approached, human remedies were of no avail. I beg Your Majesty to find consolation, as I find it, in the thought that she is in the Kingdom of Heaven and feels pity rather than envy for us who are left here below."

Isabella was twenty-three years of age when she died. Her coming had brought a little light and gaiety to the Spanish Court and to the soul of the King of Spain. With her death they, too, vanished. On the following day Philip II was back at his kingly duties, a little more sombre than before. With every succeeding day he was to become still more grave and more lonely, there at the centre of his far-flung realm. And the Spanish Court was enveloped once again in its bleak atmosphere of hushed words and muffled steps, with no dancing, no singing and no laughter.

5
Italy

FOR Miguel de Cervantes, the deaths of the heir to the throne and of the Queen were occasions to distinguish himself as a poet. When Don Carlos died, López de Hoyos was entrusted with the task of editing the *Account of the Death and Funeral Rites of His Royal Highness the Prince Don Carlos.* Among the contribu-tions by his students—funeral orations, elegies, stanzas and sonnets—those by Miguel were outstanding. When, at the death of Queen Isabella three months later, an elegy in the name of the whole college was to be sent to Cardinal Espinosa, President of the Council and Grand Inquisitor, Miguel was chosen to write it. He put the lament for the unfortunate princess into ingenuous verses and won the admiration of his fellow-students. His teacher, too, was lavish in his praise, and even the Cardinal himself may have shown his appreciation. It looked like a triumph for the young student and his master, a triumph which could well have been a turning-point in Miguel's still uncertain career. He was lauded by his teacher, spoiled by his family, envied by his friends, and credited with a brilliant future: on the face of it, his expecta-tions can never have run higher.

Nevertheless, we venture to suggest that precisely at this time he was experiencing his first grave disillusionment. It may have been due to the obstacles separating him from the woman he loved, or—more likely—some rash act on his own part. What-ever the cause, he seems to have had, as it were, a mental landslide, the fall into a chasm which awakens the dreamer. He discovered that he was alone, and saw himself as he really was: a poor young man with a doubtful future, who wrote occasional verse—the son of an impoverished hidalgo, of whom there were so many in the country, gentlemen who adorned their names with the high/sounding "Don" but went to bed hungry.

Poverty and wealth suddenly acquired for him their terrible true significance, and a sense of humiliation weighed him down. His self/respect told him that the only solution was to get away from it all—though he did not yet know where to go. Lofty sentiments led nowhere in Madrid; people earned success at Court through different attributes. This much Miguel had learnt from brief experience. There was the example of Mateo Vázquez, clad in his dark, drab clothes, with his grave manner and measured speech, who obtained his prominent position through influences behind the scene which had nothing to do with high/mindedness or talent.

Knowing that he must leave, Miguel was still uncertain as to how to go about it. Should he enlist like his brother? Or get one of his friends to recommend him to somebody? Or sally forth without any preparation, disregarding his parents' opposi/tion and tears?

He must have been battling with his doubts when Giulio Acquaviva Aragon, son of the Duke of Atri and special envoy of the Pope, came to Madrid on a delicate mission with King Philip II.

The Papal legate arrived at an unlucky moment, in a bad cause and on a worse pretext. When he left Rome some months earlier, it was officially stated that he was coming to convey the Pope's condolences over the death of Don Carlos to the King—who would not tolerate mention of his son. In reality, Acquaviva was sent by the Pope to discuss various pending matters con/nected with Spain's possessions in Italy—matters which the King did not wish to discuss. The death of the Queen which had occurred in the meantime made the coming of the envoy even more inopportune. He achieved nothing.

Giulio Acquaviva, who soon afterwards received a Cardinal's hat, was a favourite of the Pope and the descendant of one of those illustrious Italian families which had shone in the heyday of the Renaissance but had since begun to degenerate. He had before him a dazzling career at the Papal Court. Like his ancestors, he was pleased to surround himself with artists and writers to whom he could be a patron. True to his reputation, he did not leave Madrid without searching for promising young men to add to his retinue, which already included several poets. It is not surprising that the name of Miguel de Cervantes, just then in the first flush of his literary success, was brought to his notice. Whoever was the intermediary, whether Miguel's old teacher, one of his intimates, or Cardinal Espinosa to whom the elegy on the Queen's death had been dedicated and who might have dropped a chance remark, one day Miguel was able to tell his family that he was about to leave for Italy as a member of the great Roman nobleman's retinue.

*

We picture Miguel setting out on one of those bright mornings when the earth is decked in festive colours, a morning such as he was later to choose for the sallies of his Don Quixote. And we imagine his mind filled with a thousand fancies, as extravagant as the day-dreams of the Ingenious Knight himself.

What Miguel left behind we do not know. "The tears of his people", for one thing; he said so himself. Perhaps a trail of forlorn tenderness, of badly repaid sincerity, and the idealized memory of a woman.

We may be sure that he carried within himself a flame kindled by real and invented tales of chivalry, tales from books and tales from Spanish life, which merge into each other in people's minds. He promised himself wonderful experiences and a return to his country with a glorious name. Such a dream of triumphant home-coming is discernible throughout his life and work, as though it had been the lodestar guiding his course.

He did not, admittedly, burn with the white heat of the saints and mystics, nor with the indomitable urge, the blind faith, of the great Conquistadores. Spain's noonday hour had passed.

The country of knightly ideals and mystical questing no longer existed. What else had the Spain of St Ignatius been but a tale of chivalry incarnate? An austere house by an old town wall symbolized its spirit: the home of St Teresa of Avila. There had been seven children, of whom six brothers became soldiers of Spain, and the sister a soldier of God. Fighters or saints, they all had the same goal and pursued it with a like ardour. In them there was that element of madness without which nothing great is ever accomplished. Cervantes recognized this at a time when he himself had recovered from this madness and had come to curse the books of chivalry. It possessed St Ignatius of Loyola, during his night-long, knightly vigil on the sacred mountain of Montserrat, "at times on his feet, at times on his knees", as Pater Rivadeneyra reported, and as St Ignatius himself had learnt it from examples in those books of chivalry. Equally, it possessed Don Quixote during his vigil at the inn which his imagination had converted into a castle—that imagination in which fantasy and truth were fused, as they were fused in the minds of the Spaniards who saw in the desolate, mysterious sea lanes an open road to glory and riches.

Cervantes had his roots in this older period, but he was not of it. He was a man of the transition stage, harassed by feelings of insecurity and foreboding. If he was still excitingly aware of the last shimmer of heroic splendour, he was even more aware of the threatening shadows which were closing in on Spain and on his own life. His destiny and that of his country ran parallel. At the battle of Lepanto, his whole being thrilled with the victory which meant so much to the Christian and patriot in him; after the disaster of the Great Armada he wept, so keenly and painfully conscious was he of its true significance.

No, Cervantes no longer belonged to the period of the great upsurge, just as his country was no longer the Spain it had then been. He did not possess the old rigidity of character either. He was more human, more inclined to temporize and condone the weaknesses of others and his own, more capable of understanding and forgiving—more one of us. Gaiety and diversion could stop him on his way; he had a sense of humour; when the mood of exaltation had passed, leaving behind a flat feeling, he would hear the voice of Sancho Panza in his ear: "My lord Don Quixote, what madness is this? Look, there are no giants, no knights, nothing at all, no arms, and no shields, whole or in pieces. . . . Look, my lord Don Quixote!"

*

Cervantes, as we have already remarked, was one of those men whose imagination so transmutes every reality that they can no longer separate it from their dreams; whatever beauty a thing possesses vanishes, like a dream, when they come too close to it. While he was riding through France, he thought of Acquaviva's court as the place where all his ambitious hopes would come to fruition: he would hold his own with the greatest poets of the country, would be honoured and cosseted. Arrived at his destination, he found these hopes quickly evaporating. He was kept within narrow walls, surrounded not by poets but by a swarm of young underlings. These lads, though they belonged to powerful Italian families, were, like himself, the nobleman's servants and came running at their master's slightest nod, paying the right sort of respects at the best possible moment. If Monsignor Acquaviva had shown some interest in Miguel while he was in Spain, he now took no more notice of him than of any of the pages who served him, and no doubt served him better than young Cervantes. Perhaps they even subjected the Spaniard to humiliations, for in their pride of caste they could not fail to consider him an intruder.

In the serene evening hours, Miguel must have stood many times at a window to watch the last fiery tints of the sun setting on Rome, seeing in the drifting clouds wonders of his own imagining. Far off in the Campagna he would catch sight of companies marching, and their songs of war and a free life would make a brave sound in the quiet air, until they died away in the distance. Then the little court would appear more dismal, the walls of the splendid palace would seem to smother him. Miguel did not yet know his future road, but he knew that it was to lead him elsewhere. He decided, therefore, to approach his master and ask for his release. One day, soon after, he left the court of Acquaviva.

Like his Don Quixote, Cervantes went in search of adventure when he decided to join the soldiery. To be a soldier meant to hand over the reins to Providence, to cast yourself adrift. Once again Cervantes was uncertain of his course in life. He was never to be certain of it. He was only sure of what stood in his way, and always discarded it resolutely, as he did when he turned his back on Acquaviva's court. With his ready enthusiasm went an inner uncertainty which was at the root of all his actions, just as it speaks to us through all his writings. His intentions were neither firm nor consistent; his wishes veered with his every mood like a weather-vane in the wind. Underneath it all, however, his spirit was for ever watchful and tense, alert to follow the promptings of his own sensitive heart.

He became a soldier in one of the Spanish regiments—the Tercios—in Italy. Without too much regret, he gave up a position all young Spanish gentlemen coveted, and to gain which they would contrive recommendations, hatch intrigues, and even exploit family feuds. He may have felt some bitterness, he may have spent a few sleepless nights, but once he had reached his decision, taken his leave of Monsignor Acquaviva, and escaped into the vast open country under the vast sky, he felt alive and unburdened.

Indeed, his spiritual unrest was always to be more powerful than his day-to-day worries. In all his books and in many of their characters there is a nostalgia for a free life, for gay and venturesome roving. It dominated his own existence, ever driving him on and away, in search of the unattainable. With his moral integrity and sense of duty went a bohemian style of life, unordered and carefree, unconcerned about the future. For this reason he was fond of quoting the words of St Matthew: "Behold the fowls of the air; for they sow not, neither do they reap, nor gather into barns; yet our heavenly Father feedeth them." In truth, he

often had to wait for the Heavenly Father to provide his nourish-
ment. . . .

For the time being, the war chest took the place of Providence
for him. Only as a soldier was he safe from hunger and want,
able to roam through Italy and breathe the open air of which he
had been deprived in his glittering prison-house. The saying that
"he goes farthest who knows not where he goes" certainly applied
to Cervantes, even though he sometimes felt at the end of his
strength and complained about the hardships on his path. He
saw the great Italian cities, let himself be moved both by the
remnants of the past and by the beauty of the living present, and
enjoyed a happy-go-lucky existence. If he admired Florence and
Milan, he fell in love with Naples—more, maybe, with a woman
who lived there than with the city—and was deeply stirred by the
greatness of Rome. It may have been his first sight, while still in
Acquaviva's retinue, of the city walls, the towers and the soaring
cupola of St Peter's, which inspired his salutation:

> O great, O powerful, O sacred Rome,
> City and soul, I greet thee on my knees,
> A pilgrim new and humble. . . .

He wrote several poems during this period, possibly also a
fragment of a pastoral novel which much later went into the
making of his *Galatea*. For the rest, he dreamed and lived.

This was his mode of life, we assume, till the moment when the
first cannon-shot fired by the Turks in their attack on Cyprus
echoed through Italy, and reports of their atrocities on the island
roused the West.

6

The Turk

IN those times, it must be remembered, Turkey was a great world power. She occupied a wide coastal belt along the Black Sea, territory which belongs to present-day Russia, and her armies had carried their westward thrust as far as Vienna, at whose gates they had been halted only by a supreme effort. The whole Middle East up to the Indian frontier was under Turkish rule, as was the north coast of Africa including Tunis and Algiers, two ports which were strongholds of the Turkish pirates. Formidable as a military power on land, the Ottoman Empire was an even greater menace as a naval power. Under the iron discipline of Uluch Ali, successor to the corsair Barbarossa, the Turkish fleet had increased to such an extent that its ships freely cruised in the whole Mediterranean, and no port, however distant, was safe from piratical raids. It is a measure of the size of the Ottoman navy that at Lepanto not even the combined naval squadrons of Spain, Venice, Rome and Florence outnumbered it.

When the storm broke, its speed and vehemence took the West by surprise. The existing peace treaty between Turkey and Venice not only protected the trade of Venetian merchants, but also seemed sufficient to keep the Turks tranquil. Then as now, however, a peace treaty was observed only until the moment when one of the partners, finding it an obstacle to his plans, considered himself strong enough to achieve his aims by brute force. Sultan Selim II coveted Cyprus, then a Venetian possession; it had long been an object of Turkish ambitions and had been spared solely from fear of retribution. The Sultan was deriving confidence from the steady growth of his Empire, the current weakness of the

Republic of Venice, and the unceasing conflicts between the European nations. A pretext for action was readily found. At an earlier stage, Cyprus had paid tributes which served for the upkeep of the holy places of Islam, Mecca and Medina; now Turkey claimed a resumption of those payments as her right. The money was required for the building of a new great mosque at Istanbul, a cherished project of the Sultan's. Yet the really decisive factors of the situation were the fighting strength of the Turkish fleet in the Mediterranean, the short distance between Cyprus and the Turkish mainland, and the circumstance that a recent explosion in the arsenal had left Venice virtually defence-less and at the mercy of an aggressor.

Following the advice of his captains, and perhaps most of all his own inclination, Selim II sent a special envoy to Venice who was to inform the Seigniory of his master's demands. This the envoy did in a threatening manner, leaving no room for concilia-tion. Venice may have been prostrate, but she rose nobly to the challenge. The emissary found it wiser not to press his proposals. Had he not made his escape through a secret door and so evaded the furious indignation of the Venetians, he might well have shared the fate of Darius' emissaries to Athens, who were thrown into a well when they demanded the surrender of the city.

The incident suited the Sultan's purpose. Claiming that his ambassador had been ill-treated by the rulers of Venice, he sent his fleet against Cyprus.

In this quandary, Venice appealed for help to the Christian princes. The Pope and the King of Spain responded imme-diately; a squadron of Papal and Spanish galleys was assembled, and made ready to bring relief to the island. Among the soldiers who were to go with the expedition was Cervantes. At the same time, the Pope began negotiations for a European League in a "Crusade" against the Turk. From the outset, Spain was one of the League's strongest supporters, not merely because any increase of Turkish power implied a threat to Spanish interests in the Mediterranean, but also because Philip II was a champion of the Christian purpose behind the enterprise.

Representatives of the states concerned met in council, but, as usual, agreement was delayed by intrigues, intransigence, wilful blindness, national self-interest, and by the attitude of war lords who were less interested in defeating the Turk than in defeating one another. Precious months were lost. While on the Christian side there was a general jockeying for the command, the Turks took the initiative. They landed on Cyprus, ravaged the coast, and laid siege to the island's capital, Nicosia. The galleys under the command of Colonna, which should have intercepted the enemy, were delayed by rivalry between their captains and did not sail in time.

Soon alarming news began to spread. Turkish ships had boldly sailed up the Adriatic, laying waste the coasts on their way, had penetrated very close to the city of Venice itself, and had carried off several captured galleys. Shortly afterwards came the report of Nicosia's fall, with gruesome details of the Turkish atrocities which followed it. A cry for vengeance went up all over Italy; it was a harsh indictment of those who with their short-sighted wrangling had impeded the treaty of alliance. At long last Venice fell into line, under strong pressure from the Pope. On May 20, 1571, the treaty of the "perpetual" Holy League against the Infidel was ratified by Pope Pius V, King Philip II, and the Republic of Venice. On Philip's insistence, Don Juan of Austria was appointed Captain-General of all the allied forces.

Four months later, on September 20, when the young commander had arrived from Spain to assume his post, the Christian ships weighed anchor at Messina. By then it was too late to save the last fortress of Cyprus, Famagusta, from falling into Turkish hands—an event in which treachery had played an ugly part. Once again the victors committed those acts of unbelievable cruelty which characterized their method of warfare. And, at last, even nations not directly affected began to realize the true nature of the Turkish menace. When the Christian fleet sailed, the anxious wishes of the greater part of Europe went with it.

7

Don Juan and Lepanto

CERVANTES was in winter quarters at Naples, chafing under the rumours that ran rife while the League treaty was hanging fire. When it was finally concluded, the Spanish Tercios—with Cervantes as one of their soldiers—were shipped to Messina where the expeditionary force assembled.

In Messina he was a witness of the enthusiastic welcome given to Don Juan of Austria by an immense crowd gathered from all corners of Sicily. It must have kindled Miguel de Cervantes' patriotic ardour to see the young prince, fresh from Spain and in truth an incarnation of his country, ride through the exuberantly decorated streets of the city amid deafening cheers. The men who rode behind him bore illustrious names such as Cardona, Requeséns, Córdoba, Velasco, and were famous warriors, but at this hour all hope was centred on their youthful leader.

Don Juan of Austria was the illegitimate son of the Emperor Charles V. His mother, the Flemish dancer Barbara Blomberg, had never shown the slightest interest in him. As an infant he was brought to Spain, to the castle of Don Luis Quijada, the Emperor's chamberlain and one of the most influential men of his time. It was Quijada's wife, Doña Magdalena de Ulloa, who took charge of the little boy. Having no children of her own, she treated him like a son; and he, who never knew his mother, had a son's love for his "Aunt Magdalena". He was given the name Jeromín, and grew up in the freedom of the park of Villagarcía, dressed like any simple village lad, without an inkling of his true origin, yet developing a charm and grace all his own. There was always his kind Aunt Magdalena to share his joys and sorrows, to comfort and encourage him; her excel-lent qualities brought out much of the best there was in him. To the end of his days she was to be in his thoughts, while she never ceased to say her daily prayer for him. He would not leave Barcelona to sail for Messina—and the war against the Turk—without having first obtained her counsel and blessing.

In his retreat at the monastery of Yuste, after his abdication, Charles V sent for the boy one day; he was so taken with his gallant bearing and gentleness that he kept him for a while at his side, and later enjoined on his son and successor, Philip II, to recognize him as his brother. Early in October, 1559, Philip carried out his father's wish. At the Royal Palace of Valladolid, in presence of his whole Court, he embraced and kissed his half-brother and conferred upon him the name of his family, the House of Austria. Henceforth the young boy called Jeromín was known as Juan of Austria.

Don Juan gave early proof of his courage. At the time when the Turks beleaguered Malta and Spanish galleys were making ready to sail in support of the Knights of Malta, Don Juan of Austria was not yet twenty. One night he took a horse and rode at break-neck speed from Madrid to Barcelona, hoping to embark as an ordinary soldier. The ships had sailed by the time he reached the port after a reckless ride through night and storm, and his escapade earned him a sharp reprimand from Philip. From that moment, however, the King abandoned his intention to make his half-brother enter the Church, and tested him in various military campaigns instead. First, he appointed Don Juan Captain-General of the Mediterranean area, then he entrusted him with the command of troops sent against the insurgent Moriscos. If Don Juan distinguished himself by bravery in battle during that difficult campaign, he distinguished himself equally—or more—by his humane behaviour after victory. During the fighting in the wild mountain district of the Alpu-jarras he joined his soldiers in action because, as he said, "it would not be fitting for him to moulder in Granada while his men were dying in the hills". But he was never greater than on a certain bitter winter morning, when he stood at the roadside with his officers and saw wretched groups of Moriscos trudge through the snowstorm into their exile in the Northern provinces whence few were to return. In vain had he besought his brother, the King, to show mercy towards the vanquished; now he was seen weeping for them.

Such was the man whom Cervantes first saw during his trium-phant entry into Messina: a young man who was already a living legend, at once grave and candid, his features hardened by the experience of war, but his glance kind and gentle—a true Christian knight.

Don Juan of Austria and Miguel de Cervantes were both twenty-four at the time of the battle of Lepanto, in which their fate and fame came to be linked for ever.

*

The strain of the past few days has brought Cervantes to the point of collapse. He lies, sick and exhausted, on his pallet, his whole body throbbing with fever. Through his confused day-dreams he hears the waves battering the planks of the galley, the splash and creak of the oars, the monotonous beat of the boatswain's stick, and the rhythmical clanking of the galley-slaves' chains.

Images chase one another in his brain. He remembers the tales of the sack of Nicosia, which he had heard while he and his comrades were waiting to sail for Cyprus on one of Colonna's ships—the ships that sailed too late to bring help. He thinks of Corfu as he has seen it some days ago: villages and churches wrecked by fire, the bodies of butchered women and children among the ruins. And then the end of Famagusta, which sailors on the mole of Cephalonia had described: the Turks swarming through the breaches in the walls—the townspeople, men, women and children, gaunt and feeble after nearly a year's siege, staring with fear-filled eyes at the conquerors whose promise of life and liberty they dare not trust—then the first clash, panic, cries, a mad stampede—and the massacre. . . .

He thinks of Bragadino, the heroic defender of the fortress, subjected to inhuman humiliation and torture. The Turks had cut the throats of all his comrades before Bragadino's eyes; they had smashed his teeth, cut off his nose and ears; morning after morning they tied him to a tree and scourged him mercilessly. Every day he carried heavy baskets full of earth to the bastions which were being rebuilt by the enemy—the bastions he had defended as a free man until ammunition and food had given out. Each time he happened to cross the path of one of the Turkish commanders, the guards compelled him to kneel and kiss the ground, with the heavy load on his back weighing him down. There came a bright morning when the Turks flocked to the sea-shore as though to a fiesta. Four executioners led Bragadino aboard the galley of the Bey of Rhodes. Soon watchers saw him dangle from the ship's mast till the rope gave and he plunged into the water, only to be dragged out so that the game could start anew, not once but many times. And then his last hour in Famagusta Cathedral: the Ottoman chief, enthroned on the table of the main altar, jeering at his helpless prisoner till even he grew tired of it. At last the executioners carried out the death sentence. They flayed Bragadino alive, starting with his feet to prolong his agony. He intoned the *Miserere*, but when they came to his middle, his voice gave out. . . .

Cervantes tries to escape from the haunting vision. Again he listens to the waves, the oars, the clanking chains. Yet new images come to him unbidden. He sees a peaceful Spanish village, any village on the coast of Valencia or Andalusia or Catalonia, assaulted by Turkish pirates whose ships creep in under the cover of darkness. He sees fires breaking out, people fleeing in panic, doors battered in, rape and murder on the thresholds of small cottages. He hears the frantic clamour of bells, he imagines men hurrying to the shore with improvised, useless weapons, peering red-eyed after the ships which disappear in the dark. These ships carry off their prey: men who will serve in the enemy's fleet as galley-slaves, women who will be sold on the slave markets of Algiers or Istanbul. And hardly any of them will ever come back.

D

As if to banish these thoughts, Cervantes conjures up another picture: Messina, splendid with flags and tapestries, as he has seen it not many days ago. Again Don Juan of Austria passes under the triumphal arches spanning the streets, again he is engulfed by wave after wave of cheering. This time the crowds have come to speed him on his way, and their voices are rough with emotion. The whole army, from the general to the last soldier, has taken Holy Communion out in the open, under a radiant sky. Now the bells ring out, the cannons thunder their salute, the multitude on the jetty roars, and from the galleys sounds the strident answer of the trumpets. A thousand sails of every colour unfurl in the breeze. And the galleys stand out to sea.

*

A cannon-shot—the first—tore through the images which crowded Cervantes' feverish mind. After a moment's stillness, there rose the hoarse shout of the soldiers greeting the banner with the Cross, emblem of the League, which was hoisted on the mainmast of the flagship at Don Juan's command.

Miguel de Cervantes was a sick man, but it was unthinkable for him to stay under cover. It was his duty and his right to be in the fight, wherever the danger was greatest. He rose and went on deck to find his captain. But so pale and shaking with fever was Cervantes when he reported for duty that the captain ordered him back to the hold because, as he put it, "he was more fit for bed than for fighting". At this, Cervantes answered with words recorded by one of his comrades-in-arms, which have become famous: "I find it better to die fighting for God and the King than to go below deck and save my life."

The captain saw before him a thin youth, white-faced in the midday glare, who shivered so much that he could hardly stand as he spoke his brave words. However, the young man's spirit must have impressed the captain, for he changed his mind and posted Cervantes to a launch at the bows of the galley, *La Marquesa*, where he was to take command of a dozen soldiers.

It was October 7, 1571, a Sunday. By noon, the squadrons of the Christian fleet were deployed on battle lines in the Gulf of Lepanto. On the right wing were sixty-four galleys under the great Genoese Andrea Doria, at the centre Don Juan himself with an equally large group of galleys and supporting vessels, on the left wing another sixty-three galleys, mainly Venetian, under the command of Agostino Barbarigo, a patrician of Venice who was struck by an arrow early in the battle and did not live to see the victory. A Spaniard, the Marquis of Santa Cruz, for whom Cervantes expressed great admiration, commanded a reserve of thirty-five galleys which he was free to use as the situation demanded.

The Christian commanders were experienced fighters, and their Turkish counterparts were of the same mettle. The Turkish admiral cut a proud and conspicuous figure on the poop of his flagship, in his shining white-and-silver tunic and a turban adorned with gold and precious stones. Like Don Juan of Austria, he was young, valiant and ambitious. So great was his confidence in victory that he had his two small sons aboard, perhaps because he dreamed of having them at his side on his triumphant return to Istanbul.

The Ottoman admiral's ship fired a cannon-shot and hoisted the banner of the Sultan, as a sign that Don Juan's challenge had been accepted. Bugles and kettle-drums sounded the attack. When their signals reached the Christian fleet, a moment's calm settled on the wide area over which the armada was ranged. Don Juan, who had been standing on the prow of his galley, fell on his knees and prayed out loud to God for victory. On all the Christian ships, officers and men followed their commander's example, with the priests lifting up the Cross before the eyes of the worshippers.

With a shrill cacophony of war chants, howls and yells, the blare of trumpets and the rattle of scimitars on shields, such as always heralded their entering an affray, the Turkish ships advanced. And then the two great fleets joined battle.

Dense clouds of smoke from the artillery half-hid the medley of ships: ships ramming or being rammed, ships being boarded, and ships sinking. Soon the water was littered with shreds of canvas, splintered masts and human bodies. Sea and air seemed to fuse in chaos. In the words of one historian, the general destruction left nothing undamaged but human hatred.

In his small craft covering the galley's prow, Cervantes was in the thick of the fight. Twice he was hit in the chest by a bullet from an arquebus, but he paid no attention to his injuries. Light-headed with fever and the excitement of the moment, he went on firing, and even a third bullet could not stop him, though it crippled his left hand. He had his hand hurriedly tied up and stayed at his post. By late evening—an eyewitness said that the smoke had darkened the sun and turned day into night—the hotheads among the Christian soldiers began to cry victory. It was about this time Cervantes dropped in a faint. He may still have heard the great shout, as if from a single throat, which rose from the Christian ships when the remaining Ottoman galleys took to flight. On those which were taken, thirteen thousand captives were freed from the chains that fastened them to the rowing-benches.

Soon after the end of the battle, when night had fallen, a gale began to blow. The victorious squadrons were forced to turn back from their pursuit and seek the nearest safe port. All night long the wind and the rain, accompanied by thunder and lightning, lashed the wreckage and the mangled human bodies afloat in the Gulf of Lepanto.

Once again Cervantes lay prostrate on his bunk in the ship's belly. If he heard the rolling thunder and the pounding of the seas through the pain and fever, the savage echoes of the battle, the cries of the wounded and dying must have resounded louder still in his mind's ear. For in truth Cervantes was a man of peace. Many years after Lepanto, he tells us through the mouth of Don Quixote that only the cause of peace can justify and hallow wars. And the first occasion on which Cervantes' mind rose above the limits of his time and place, even above the limits of his national feelings, to dwell on humanity as a whole, may well have been this wild night. Perhaps he first pondered the curse that drives men into ever-renewed wars, and first dreamed of true peace and happiness for harassed mankind, while he was lying wounded in the hold of a galley which returned from the butchery of Lepanto.

8

Aftermath

THE news of the victory, sweeping through Italy and Spain, produced everywhere outbursts of joy and relief. *Te Deums* were sung, feasts and processions were staged, the name of Don Juan of Austria was extolled to the skies. When the Pope learnt of the outcome of Lepanto, he shed tears; then he said, paraphrasing the words of the Gospel: "There was a man chosen by God, whose name was Juan." The Spanish poet Herrera praised the battle in a stirring poem. In faraway Scotland, a King celebrated it in verse. Tintoretto and Veronese immortalized it in great paintings.

The Italian cities vied with each other in their receptions for the returning victors. The welcome that awaited Don Juan at Messina was overwhelming. On a sunny day in October, his ships entered harbour with all their flags and pennons flying, the captured Turkish galleys in tow, the banners of the defeated trailing in the water, while bugles and trumpets sounded aboard the ships and on land. The festive decorations were still gayer, the crowds still greater, their clamour still more jubilant than on Don Juan's departure. All night, huge bonfires were burning, and the singing never ceased. In a similar fashion, Naples celebrated the return of the Marquis of Santa Cruz with the Venetian galleys under his command. It was in Rome, however, that the pomp and splendour were greatest. The triumphal entry of Marco Antonio Colonna, the commander of the Papal galleys, was turned into an apotheosis recalling the days of ancient Rome, when the victorious general or emperor made his slow way to the Capitol at the head of his legions, followed by a pitiful horde of captives. Now nothing of the traditional ceremony was omitted, not even the mean and ugly exhibition of the two little sons of the Turkish commander-in-chief who had died in battle: they had to follow the procession, weeping, for the greater glory of the conqueror.

By all this, the importance of the victory came to be exaggerated. It was taken for granted that the total destruction of the Turkish fleet was only a matter of time—a short time. Even the sanest among the allied leaders were carried away by self-delusions. There was talk of liberating Cyprus, still in Turkish hands, of reconquering the African ports which were the hide-outs of the pirates; some, and by no means the most foolish people, dreamed of the conquest of the Peloponnese and even of Istanbul itself, or Constantinople as the Christians called it. Inevitably, Jerusalem too was mentioned, the highest goal of all.

All these hopes were far from being justified by reality. While the booty of Lepanto was shared out, friction arose among the allies. As time went on, and the impact of the common victory faded, their dissensions became more and more obtrusive. When the reorganization of the naval squadrons was tackled, it was found that many ships were in need of adjustments and repairs, that their crews had been sadly reduced, and that the number of sick and wounded men was very great indeed. Under the strain of mutual envy and distrust, the allies' enthusiasm for their cause waned. Old resentments revived. In short, optimism had by far outstripped the work which had to be done to give it substance.

On the Turkish side, things took another turn. At first, when news of the disaster reached Istanbul, it had been a great shock for the Turks. But the depression felt by the losers evaporated more quickly than the elation of the winners. It was driven out by a determined will to recovery; the outcry of the Turkish people at the loss of so many of their sons was silenced. The Sultan, who in a first access of rage had intended to order the execution of all Christian prisoners, was appeased, and issued a decree prohibiting any reference to the defeat. A period of feverish activity began at the shipyards of Istanbul, under the energetic direction of

Uluch Ali, the only Turkish commander who, with his ships, had escaped unscathed from Lepanto. One might even say he came out victorious, since he carried with him as his captive the wife of the commander of Malta.

Six months after Lepanto, a strong Turkish squadron was ready to sail from Istanbul and attack the Mediterranean ports with redoubled vigour; the Christian League meanwhile was bogged down in internal disputes.

For months Miguel de Cervantes was confined to a hospital bed in Messina, waiting for his wounds to heal. For many days more he had nothing to do but sit by the window and wait for the milder season when he would be able to take his first walks as a convalescent. He longed for the peace of the Sicilian country-side to make him forget the nightmare of violence which lay behind him.

But the time came at last when swallows soared and dipped under a blue sky, and the vineyards on the hill-slopes were gay with the first green shoots. Miguel's health was returning, his left hand disfigured but not absolutely useless. At this stage he may have looked at it in disgust and sorrow—in later years it was to become a source of pride. Then he began to go out; he would walk past the vineyards, the dark cypresses, the white houses, and the men working in the fields, till he found a quiet place by the sea where a soft, salty breeze was blowing. Perhaps it was there he began to write down snatches of verse, fragments of prose, on odd pieces of paper which he hid away as a man may bury his treasure until peace is come again.

Later, he made friends with Sicilian peasants and listened to their talk of homely things, of old customs, work, and the land. He must have felt a deep pleasure in those conversations, for in his mature writings he recounted them with the truthfulness that cannot be counterfeited.

Made cordially welcome in simple homesteads, but carrying the fresh impact of the terrible sea-battle in his mind, of which his mutilated left hand served as a constant reminder, he could not fail to dwell upon the desperate wastefulness of war.

His imagination was to merge memories of these halcyon days in Sicily with impressions of the Andalusian countryside, and to create out of it all the scene in *Don Quixote* in which the Knight, after sharing a scant meal with rough, primitive goatherds, speaks to them of the Golden Age of mankind. But he was also to create another, greater scene: Don Quixote sees a crude inn as an enchanted castle, with the starry sky for its roof and the wide world for its confines, and begins to speak like a seer. In his words there is something of the eternal longing of all those who are unhappy, poor and oppressed, of the prisoners in the dark dungeons of Algiers, of the slaves chained to galley-benches, of the countless human beings who in all times hunger for consolation and rest.

What is it Don Quixote tells the listening company—not rude goatherds, this time, but people of education and breeding, though with some fools and buffoons among them? He speaks of War and Peace, Arms and Letters. "Truly, the purpose of Letters is grand and noble, and worthy of great praise, yet less so than the purpose of Arms which, after all, have for their object peace, the greatest boon man can wish for in this life. The first good message that came to the world and humanity was the message of the angels that night—daybreak for us!—when they sang up on high: 'Glory to God in the highest and peace on earth to men of good will!' And the best of all teachers that ever were in Heaven or on earth taught His closest followers that, on entering a house, they should use the greeting: 'Peace be with this house.' On many occasions He told them: 'I give My peace unto you— I bequeath My peace to you—peace be with you.' Peace is the precious jewel coming to us from His hand, and without it there can be no good whatsoever on earth or in Heaven. . . ."

The young soldier of the Spanish Tercio may have spoken in similar terms on one of those magic nights in a Sicilian peasant's cottage, for even then he carried within him this dream of a world full of love.

9

A New Expedition

CERVANTES was not left long in the pleasantly languid mood which so often accompanies convalescence. Once again, rumours of war spread alarm along the Mediterranean coasts. Against all expectations, the Turks had already recovered from their defeat. The Spanish Tercios were in a state of alert.

Ruefully, Miguel contemplated his left hand. It had brought him neither distinction nor promotion, nothing but a few days' extra pay and, as highest reward, a personal congratulation from Don Juan himself. One memorable morning, the Prince had stopped by Miguel's bed in the hospital of Messina and praised his gallantry. Yet, the crippled hand still served to support an arquebus. Miguel could hope to repeat his feats of Lepanto, in a campaign which might lead to the total annihilation of the enemy, to a victorious entry into Istanbul and to the recovery of the Holy City of Jerusalem. It was not his way to stay behind when others burned with enthusiasm, and his own fervour was revived by the general exaltation. He embarked with the new expeditionary force, leaving his dreams apparently forgotten in the shadow of the lemon-trees of Sicily. Not really forgotten: rather, seeds lying dormant in a rich soil. . . .

This expedition against the Turks was a failure from the out-set. The exaggerated notions about the magnitude of the triumph of Lepanto recoiled on those who held them. As before, the formation of the squadrons was badly delayed by disagreements among the allies. When this obstacle was finally overcome, Don Juan was impatient to set sail. There were two main reasons for

48

his impatience: the reports about the Turks, and his ardent wish to win for himself a kingdom carved out from reconquered territory, the prospect of which the Pope had held out to him. Philip II, however, had little sympathy with the idea. On the eve of the departure, letters from Madrid ordered Don Juan to stay in Messina with the Spanish ships.

The young Prince felt desperate. He could not understand the King's motives. The season was already far advanced; if his galleys left port too late, they risked running into the heavy autumn gales. There was a saying in those days that the Mediterranean Sea had only two safe harbours—July and August. At any other season, a fleet might be wrecked without meeting an enemy. Don Juan bombarded Madrid with urgent letters, but never received an answer. Meanwhile the Turks were at liberty to renew their assaults on Christian ports. By the time Madrid decided to send orders for departure the most propitious moment had passed: before Don Juan's squadron was able to sail, it was already very late in the year.

Three months later, the ships limped back into port, battered by storms, without having engaged the Turks in battle or liberated any place occupied by them.

Cervantes describes an episode of this expedition in the so-called "Captive's Tale" interpolated in *Don Quixote*. It is a savage, brutal story. One of the Turkish captains was a son of Barbarossa, the great corsair, and a man of a singular ferocity. Once, when he thought that his galley-slaves were slack in their rowing, he pounced on the boatswain, hacked off the man's arm with his scimitar, grasped the severed limb by its hand, and trounced the slaves' backs with it. This Turkish galley was separated from the bulk of the Ottoman fleet while the Spanish squadron was in pursuit. Barbarossa's son, standing on the boatswain's platform, spurred the chained captives to greater exertions, with threats and blasphemies, but the Spanish galley *La Loba*—*The She Wolf*—under Captain Don Alvaro de Bazán drew rapidly near. When the slaves saw that their ship was being overtaken by a Christian galley, they all let go of their oars, and those in reach of the Turkish commander grabbed hold of him; he was passed on from rowing-bench to rowing-bench, and with their teeth the captives tore him to pieces. "Such was", Cervantes says, "the cruelty with which he had treated them, and the hatred they bore him."

Otherwise the Christian expedition achieved nothing. It seemed to have fallen under an evil spell. On one occasion, an imprudent manoeuvre brought the squadrons to the brink of disaster. On another, an error on the part of the pilots lost them an excellent opportunity—Cervantes considered it a unique opportunity—to destroy the naval power of the Turks. In the end Don Juan saw himself reluctantly compelled to order the fleet's return to port. The autumn gales had started; in their battle with adverse winds, several ships had foundered, losing the greater part of their crews and troops; and the danger of wholesale shipwreck threatened.

The worst blow was still to come. The squadrons were back in Messina, with men and ships in equally bad condition, when it was bruited about that Venice was negotiating a separate peace with the Turks, with France acting as intermediary. At first nobody wanted to believe the report, least of all Don Juan, whose inexperience in the ways of chancelleries was on a par with his daring. But in March, when his ships were being overhauled and made ready for the new season's campaign, he received confirmation of the bad news: Venice had signed the peace treaty. One of its conditions was that the Republic ceded to Turkey the island of Cyprus, in whose defence the Holy League had been formed.

Don Juan still refused to accept the truth, until he had seen it set down in black and white. After perusing the document he did not say a word, but walked to the poop of his flagship, followed by the officers of his retinue and a great crowd of people shouting insults against Venice. There and then Don Juan hauled down the standard of the League, and hoisted in its place the banner of Castile. With this final gesture of national pride, the chapter of Lepanto was closed. Or almost closed:

Don Juan was not the man to accept defeat, and the kingdom promised to him continued to haunt his mind. After the first shock and stupefaction, he returned to his preparations for a new venture.

10

Tunis

THE expedition in the following year was no more successful than the previous one. Once again its organization was faulty, its departure too long delayed. The troops became restive. Don Juan's halo of glory had lost some of its glitter, his dreams had lost much of their grandeur. He no longer thought of conquering Istanbul or liberating Jerusalem, but aimed at a nearer and easier target—Tunis. Charles V, his father, had once captured it from the Infidel, but now it was again held by the Turks and used as a place of refuge by their ships. Don Juan was anxious to win himself a crown, and Tunis seemed a ready means of fulfilling his ambition. Also, the Pope—no longer Pius V, but his succes-sor, Gregory XIII—favoured him and his undertaking. After approaching Philip II about it, the Pope gave Don Juan a formal promise that Tunis would be his as a sovereign kingdom.

Philip, however, had never made a definite promise. On the contrary, his instructions to Don Juan betrayed a very different intention: after the conquest of Tunis, Don Juan was to raze its fortifications to the ground and install Muley Hamet, a Moham-medan refugee in Italy, on the Tunisian throne. In spite of this, Don Juan chose to rely on the Pope's support and sailed for Tunis. Not for nothing has he been called the Last Knight Errant! And among the soldiers he took with him was that other dreamer, Miguel de Cervantes.

On October 24, 1573, both ships and troops were back in Palermo. Tunis had been taken without a fight. Miguel had been able to walk across the fields where Carthage had stood, and to evoke the shades of Queen Dido through Virgil's immortal verse. Don Juan had disregarded his brother's instructions. Instead of destroying the fortifications, he had repaired and enlarged them; he had strengthened the forts of La Goleta and Fuerte, and manned them with garrisons which he left behind. Within a year, the Turks were to crush these outposts whom no help could reach; they were to be wiped out almost to the last man in a heroic but unequal struggle.

Thus an enterprise which had promised well led to disastrous results. What had been quickly won was lost even more quickly. For Don Juan, the fear that his prestige had suffered added to the bitterness of defeat.

During the six months after the end of the expedition, Cervantes was stationed in Sardinia with the regiment commanded by Don Lope de Figueroa. The sharp edge of disappointment may have been blunted during the time he spent on the island, but a sense of discouragement took root—he tells us so himself.

In the meantime, Don Juan, with whose career the fate of Cervantes was so closely linked in those years, went to Gaeta to take a ship to Spain. Exasperated by the reports from Madrid, he found it imperative to have a personal talk with the King, his half-brother. Not only had he, despite the Pope's promise, been denied his Tunisian kingdom, but he had not even been granted the title of *Infante*—Royal Prince—which the King himself had promised to him.

Don Juan had long been aware that he had powerful enemies at Court, and he had a shrewd idea of their identity. The first unpleasant proof of their influence had come to his notice when his hopes were highest, just before he sailed for Italy and his triumph at Lepanto. At the very moment when he had been about to set out from Barcelona he had received a missive from the King. This royal letter has not been preserved, but Don Juan's correspondence of that time shows that the King—probably influenced by his secretary, Antonio Pérez—had written to reproach him in sharp terms for having let himself be addressed as "Your Highness" and so accepted honours reserved for Royal Princes, although he, the King, had never conceded them to him. Apparently Philip II had commanded Don Juan to reject a similar style of address in future; he had also sent dispatches to this effect to his Ministers in Italy.

The letter was designed to remind Don Juan of his illegitimate birth, and it hurt him. He sensed the hidden influences which had roused the King's ready distrust as soon as he himself was out of the way. In addition, his "Aunt Magdalena" had warned him to be on his guard, and had mentioned the names of men he had thought of as friends. He was not unduly surprised. "Not even the Saints are secure from vexation", he wrote in one of his letters. All the same, there had been a moment when he toyed with the idea of resigning his command and withdrawing from active life.

Now, when Don Juan had decided to clear the air by an inter-view with the King, a new incident interfered with his plans. In Genoa a feud between warring factions threatened to lead to a rising; from Madrid came orders that Don Juan was to go imme-diately to the danger spot and restore quiet. How profoundly this *contretemps* disturbed him is seen in his letters: again he had to shelve plans and preparations for a new campaign against the Turks, and he had to abandon his urgent journey to Spain. As it happened, Don Juan's stay in Liguria had to be extended; the re-equipment of his galleys lagged behind, since Madrid was withholding the necessary means. In letter after letter, Don Juan argued the need for another attack on the Turks. But Philip was in no hurry. Least of all was he in a hurry to further the ambi-tions of the impatient young prince, whose procedure in Tunis had confirmed his misgivings—misgivings cleverly nourished by the insinuations of the King's secretary, who hated Don Juan.

Philip II had a great interest in the defeat of the Turks, but an even greater interest in doing nothing which would assist Don Juan in his bid for power. Moreover, he always resented it if somebody tried to forestall his own decisions; he expected every-one to submit to his will. Thus all Don Juan received in answer from Madrid was excuses and procrastination. Spring passed, summer passed, and nothing happened to shake the King's calm, nothing to lessen Don Juan's impatience. Then came the autumn of 1574; it was exactly three years since the great victory of Lepanto.

Don Juan was still in Genoa, driven to despair by the slowness with which everything proceeded, when the news came that Uluch Ali was sailing towards the African coast with a strong fleet, and that he apparently intended to attack Tunis. Whereas the defection of Venice had weakened the forces of the League, the enemy had greatly added to his resources. At a time when weather and winds were particularly dangerous, Don Juan went on his last and most unfortunate expedition against the Turk. And Cervantes embarked with the troops.

The garrisons which Don Juan had left behind in the forts of Tunis succumbed after a savage, heroic struggle. A violent storm dispersed the squadron which tried in vain to bring them relief. Don Juan, the commander, and Cervantes, the soldier, saw ships sinking and men drowning. La Goleta was lost, Fuerte was lost, and Tunis, too, was lost. It was the greatest reverse Spain had suffered in many years. And at first sight, it looked as if Don Juan was responsible, because he had disobeyed his brother's instructions. A Papal letter, however, sent to Madrid about this time, went to the real root of the matter when it complained about the endless delays over every preparation and decision.

An exasperated Don Juan had to return to port without even trying to relieve Tunis. It was a step on the road which led to the disaster of the Great Armada off the English coast, and to Spain's gradual ruin. Squalls and hurricanes, Turkish tenacity, and above all the slow, suspicious policy of Madrid had done their worst. Of the splendour of Lepanto, all that was left was a battered naval squadron, a horde of hungry, listless soldiers, and a leader who, in spite of his splendid gifts, had been defeated without a fight and who carried with him the knowledge of having been abandoned to his fate, perhaps not without some justification.

Neither Don Juan nor Cervantes went on another expedition against the Infidel. For Don Juan it was a personal matter which

E

hurt him to the quick. Yet it was Cervantes who saw its deeper significance and recognized in the whole tragic interlude of Tunis the symptoms of his country's decline.

Many years afterwards, when Cervantes had been back in Spain long enough to be familiar with the seamy side of public life, he revived the memory of the heroes of La Goleta, whose fate he might so easily have shared. The tale of the ex-captive in *Don Quixote* gives an account of that luckless expedition and of the loss of life to which it led. In these passages there is an accent of bitterness and anger, otherwise absent in Cervantes' writing. Bitterness at the way in which the heroism of the men who defended their positions to the last was rendered futile by their superiors' indolence and irresponsibility, bitterness at the spirit of commercialism and soulless routine that was undermining the Spanish institutions. And anger against all those who, safely entrenched at home, trafficked in the lives of soldiers and robbed their deaths of any meaning.

Long after Cervantes had ceased to carry a musket and fight with the rank and file of Spanish soldiers, his heart went out to them; he fought for them with his pen, making people weep at their sufferings or thrill to their dauntless defence of a nation which had begun to disintegrate.

II

Naples

CERVANTES spent this winter, his last in Italy, in Naples. At first his mood was gloomy. As he went ashore—one of a band of weary and defeated soldiers, so different from the victors of Lepanto—he may have felt that the giants against whom they battled were turning into windmills before their eyes. It was as if a malicious sorcerer had cast a spell on everything, turning a bright dawn into darkness.

Yet Miguel had a resilient mind. In the darkest moments it always discovered a new ray of hope. This time he felt that one phase of his life was finished. If it left him with a sense of disap-pointment, he already had a glimpse of the next turn of the road. Hitherto it had led him away from Spain, now it would lead him back. In his powers of recuperation he was like his own Don Quixote: when Don Quixote emerges from his tilt with the windmills, flailed, bruised and mocked, he turns at once to a new skirmish with the flock of sheep which is, in his mind's eye, an army of giants; the more he is battered and ridiculed, the more brightly the flame of resolution burns in him, the more steadfastly he follows the dictates of his heart.

In the sparkling gaiety of Naples, Cervantes recovered his high spirits and his zest for life. There was much to distract him, and he found good company. His brother Rodrigo, like him a soldier of the Tercio, turned up at Naples out of the blue. There were local poets with whom he could exchange ideas, veterans of his regiment with whom he could drink heady wine in the taverns near the port. They would discuss news from everywhere, but above all news from Spain, Don Juan's journey and the

policy of the Madrid Court. And then Miguel would feel rest/
less and homesick, despite the fact that a woman in Naples—
we know nothing about her beyond the fact that she existed and
that he never quite forgot her—seems to have given him more
contentment, understanding and genuine tenderness than he
found in any of his other amorous adventures.

Many of the ships putting in at the port brought advices that
revived in his mind the possibilities of advancement which Spain
held for him. As far as his own family was concerned, there was
little to encourage him; his parents were worse off than ever. It
was different with some of his friends who had made their way at
Court. Possibly he heard more of Mateo Vázquez's brilliant
career. The plan to go to Madrid took shape in his mind, and
when he broached it to his brother, he received his eager en/
couragement.

The first step, however, was to get the right letters of recom/
mendation. Miguel decided to approach the Duke of Sesa,
Viceroy of Sicily. On several earlier occasions he had sought the
great nobleman's support, and it seems likely that these interviews
had led to longer conversations. Certainly there is every indica/
tion that the Duke had a personal liking for Cervantes. The link
may have been the Duke's interest in literature, or his appreciation
of Miguel's conduct at Lepanto. In any case, the weight of the
letters of recommendation the Duke provided for Miguel, and
even more the tone of the Duke's own subsequent letters, when
he intervened in favour of Miguel's ransom during his captivity
in Algiers, speak of a somewhat closer relationship than the
official contact would explain.

The Duke of Sesa apparently approved of Miguel's intention
to go to Madrid. No doubt it was he who advised Miguel to
wait for Don Juan's return to Naples. Don Juan would not
only receive him—the Duke himself would see to this—but
would also arm him with the most effective recommendation
of all.

*

In mid-June, Don Juan of Austria came to Naples. Before long, he granted Cervantes an interview.

In the short time of his absence, Don Juan had greatly changed. He was no longer the man of Lepanto, that fiery youth spurring on his soldiers in the thick of battle, nor the admired general striding through the streets of Messina. Those days were over. Around Don Juan the cheering had died away, perhaps for good. His face had grown more serene, his movements slower, his whole expression graver. A faint shadow of fatigue veiled his eyes, and his voice was soft and quiet.

Don Juan had just returned from Spain. There he had seen much, and guessed even more. He had accepted the fact that there was little or no future for him in Spain. The state of the country itself worried him, its atmosphere of ignoble deceit and base treachery seemed to cling like a pall. It had been brought home to him that the memory of Lepanto had not only faded, but indeed was buried in oblivion. Soon he was to go to Flanders; perhaps he had a dim presentiment of his coming end there.

Cervantes was deeply moved by his meeting with Don Juan, whom he had always loved and admired and in whose qualities as a leader he had great faith. After serving under him in victory and defeat, Miguel felt an even greater sympathy for Don Juan now, for he knew that his eclipse had been caused by the jealousies of the Court. What bound him to the prince was not so much his noted bravery, of which Miguel himself had seen so many proofs, as his generosity. There was the incident at Lepanto, when a soldier presented Don Juan with the head of the Turkish commander on a pike-staff, hoping to curry favour; Don Juan had not even looked at the gory trophy, but had given orders to cast it into the sea. Then there was Don Juan's treatment of the Turkish commander's two little sons. The elder of the boys died of sorrow in captivity; their sister in Istanbul implored Don Juan to restore at least her younger brother to her, and offered to pay any ransom he demanded. Don Juan immediately sent the boy to her, but rejected any ransom even under the guise of a free gift, because "it was not the custom of one of his great ancestry to accept gifts from those in need of favour, but rather to give bounties and grant favours".

Cervantes was never to forget his general. The ghost of Don Juan haunts the pages of *Don Quixote*. There is a direct reminiscence in the figure of the "Knight of the Lions": Don Juan of Austria had taken with him from Tunis a lion cub, which figures in most portraits we have of him, and used in those days to sign himself, jokingly, *Caballero del León*, "Knight of the Lion". Above all, was not Don Juan the last of the Knight Errants?

In this last encounter between the two, the talk may have touched upon Spain, the war, the future, the reasons for the most recent defeat. If so, Don Juan must have spoken with the frankness he always showed towards good soldiers, while Cervantes may have surprised his chief by his shrewd insight and his courageous spirit. When Cervantes finally made his plea—he wanted a captaincy and later a posting to one of the regiments in Italy—Don Juan at once granted the favour for which he was asked. He wrote and signed letters which were to support Cervantes' application in Madrid.

From this point, their ways parted. Miguel, who expected to go home and finally get promotion as a reward for his services, was captured by the Turks. Don Juan of Austria, still in pursuit of his glittering dreams, achieved a few last victories in Flanders before his dark and sudden end.

*

Late in September, a homeward-bound Spanish flotilla sailed from Naples, and with it the galley *Sol*—the *Sun*—which had Miguel and Rodrigo de Cervantes on board. In one of his "Exemplary Novels", Miguel has told us how their journey ended.

The *Sol* had entered the Gulf of Lions, still in sight of the French coast, although it seemed to the Spaniards that the night air carried the scents of their own country to them. The wind

freshened, all sails were set. In the bright moonlight, the small
harbour of Les Saintes Maries was visible in the distance. Suddenly the watch raised the alarm: Turkish galleys!

The Spanish captain's galley was out of touch with the rest of
the flotilla; there were four Turkish ships, each in size and armament at least a match for the *Sol*. But he was a hard-bitten sailor
and kept his head. He decided to attempt a break-through.
With a favourable wind to fill his sails, and his artillery ready for
action, he hoped to hold off the enemy long enough to be able
to reach the French port. But when he set course for the coast,
the wind died down unexpectedly. The Spanish galley was
becalmed, and at the mercy of a greatly superior Turkish force.

The Turks did not attack at once but waited till dawn. Then
they sent a skiff to the *Sol*, to demand immediate surrender. The
captain brusquely refused. When someone in the skiff shouted
that their commander, Dali Mami—a famous Albanian renegade
and corsair—would hang the Spaniard from the yard-arm unless
he surrendered at once, the captain of the *Sol* shouted back: "Off
with you, or my cannons shall sink you!" Thereupon the battle
started.

It lasted from daybreak until dusk—as it had at Lepanto.
The Spaniards defended themselves with stubborn fury. Once
more Miguel de Cervantes was in the thick of it, firing away for
all he was worth. As evening fell the end came. The *Sol* was
burning fore and aft, the flames could no longer be kept under
by the few survivors; the ship's sails were in shreds, her cannon
silenced. "Freedom, Sancho, is the only thing for which a man
can and must give his life." More than half of the men on board
had given their lives, but all had been in vain.

Miguel's strength was spent; the musket slid from his nerveless
hands. In the evening shadows, dyed red by the glow from the
fires on his ship, a Turkish galley loomed up. Miguel awoke
from the nightmare of the fight only to find himself encompassed
by another, grimmer nightmare. The edifice of his hopes had
crashed, the world in which he had thought to fulfil them was
lost to him. He knew what was coming—he would share the

ghastly fate of so many others, about which he had heard tales to make him shudder: a galley-slave's chains, torture, humiliation, an agonizing captivity in Istanbul or Algiers, and the slow agony of dying far from home, a thousand times worse than quick death.

He felt as helpless and defenceless as a child. The fight was over, the sea was calm. But he was still alive; and though the blood ran down his face, blurring his sight, he was not even seriously wounded. Nevertheless, the sinister bulk of the Turkish galley blotted out everything, the sea, the sky, his very thoughts. He could only stand and stare, as fierce, gloating faces surrounded him and his ears were filled with the sound of harsh voices. Brutal hands searched him and bound him. Then he knew nothing more.

12

Algiers and Captivity

IT was a painful awakening. For many hours Cervantes had lain unconscious and abandoned, while his captors were drawing lots for their shares of the booty. He had fallen to the Turkish commander, to Dali Mami himself. Now he was the property of his master, a piece of merchandise.

Bit by bit, Miguel came to recognize his plight. When he moved, chains clanked. When he betrayed his stupor and bewilderment, foreign sailors jeered at him in words he could only guess. Then he caught sight of the other Spanish captives: his brother was among them.

The sea was rough now. As the galley rolled and the wind whistled through the rigging, Miguel was reminded of the many shipwrecks along these coasts. The other prisoners kept a sombre silence. All were in chains, but Miguel was more tightly and securely shackled than any other. This was the sole benefit he had derived from Don Juan's letters of recommendation. On seeing the greedy satisfaction of the corsairs when they found letters with Don Juan's signature among the papers they took off him, Miguel must have reflected bitterly on the uncertainty and treachery of human affairs. Yesterday, those letters had seemed to promise him a captaincy and his return to Italy as an officer in one of the new Tercios; today, they made him the most important of the captives, the one who would fetch the highest ransom and had to be most carefully fettered and guarded. His apparent good fortune had been turned into a great misfortune.

At last an African city emerged on the coastline, with white

63

houses, palm-trees swaying against the background of a deep
blue sky, gardens, and undulating hills. It was Algiers, the
town whose very name struck terror into the hearts of people
living on the Mediterranean coasts. These chalk-white houses
and peaceful palm-trees concealed a cruel despotism, were the
haunt of robbers and killers. "A shame for humanity", Cervantes
was to call it. Later he confessed that his eyes had filled with tears
at the first glimpse of Algiers. Had there not been a time when
he dreamed of entering it as a soldier of the victorious army of
liberation, greeted by the joyful shouts of thousands of Christians
released from their underground dungeons? Now he had come
to swell their pitiful ranks. Yet even Miguel's imagination did
not forewarn him of all the cause for tears Algiers would provide.

The ships had moored. Their masters shouted commands for
the final manoeuvres. The galley-slaves rose from their benches
and dropped the oars overboard; this was the established custom,
to prevent them from attempting flight in the turmoil of the
disembarkation.

The crowd on the mole was visibly growing in numbers.
News of the return of the admiral's ships with a new prize had
quickly spread through the town. Each time the corsairs came
back from one of their cruises they were given a great welcome,
but particularly when they had made an important capture.
"When this happens," said Pater Haedo in his chronicle, "all
Algiers is happy. For the merchants are able to buy many slaves
and goods which the corsairs have brought, and the town officials
sell clothing and food from their stores to those who have returned
from the expedition, since many want to dress in new garments,
and there is feasting, drinking and triumph everywhere."

It was like a public holiday, above all in places of entertainment, because the whole town shared, to a greater or lesser
degree, in the profits from the captured loot. Thus, people of
every race gathered in the port when homecoming ships cast
anchor. There were Jews, Turks, Moors, Greeks, and men
without a country. There were beggars from the slums, display-
ing their running sores, and strumpets who looked forward to a

profitable, noisy night in the company of drunken sailors flush with money; there were slaves, gaunt and ashen, many with mutilated noses or ears, their status proclaimed by the foot-irons on their ankles; and there were hordes of street-arabs, expert at the sport of prisoner-baiting.

The first to go ashore were the commander and his captains, to the sound of the high, clear notes of flageolets, and acclaimed by the waiting multitude. Then came the ships' crews, and finally the captives, guarded by soldiers. They were received with gibes and abuse from the adults, rude songs from the children. They were marched along in groups, one of which included Miguel de Cervantes. There, surrounded by a mob howling insults, he began to show himself for the man he was, walking quietly and composedly, without a sign of either dejection or arrogance. As long as there had still been a chance to ward off disaster, he had fought determinedly, but now that further resistance was useless, he faced the inevitable with cool courage.

Among the six hundred pages which Diego de Haedo devotes to his chronicle of Algiers—a statement of horrors that belong to the darkest chapters of human history, all the more moving because of its simplicity of language—there is one passage of special interest to our story. It is where he speaks of "a captive called Miguel de Cervantes, a hidalgo from Alcalá de Henares", whom he, the chronicler, knew only in his capacity as captive and hidalgo, and who impressed him by the valour he showed in the most difficult situations.

That short passage has to be read in its context to reveal the full extent of Cervantes' merit. Thousands of Spaniards had passed through the city of Algiers as prisoners, and when Miguel arrived there, many Spanish nobles were being held captive. There was Don Antonio de Toledo, a brother of the Duke of Alba; Francisco de Valencia, a Knight of St John; Don Juan de Lanuza, son of the Chief Justice of Aragon; the clerics Doctor Becerra and Doctor de Sossa, and many more. But in a situation beset with perils, where it was necessary to behave with firm determination, none took pride of place before Cervantes.

He had always distinguished himself: in his childish games, at his studies, as a soldier. His record at Lepanto was excellent, but there he had been one among many heroes; now, with no examples of soldierly heroism to inspire him, and upheld only by his own standards of conduct, he showed himself the bravest of the prisoners.

Even while he was being marched through the winding streets of the African town, he attracted attention by the exceptional weight of his chains. It was not, however, these alone that marked him out, but his whole bearing; and maybe the gaping crowds sensed something of the qualities which were later to make the slavery of his fellow-prisoners less unbearable and to buoy them up when they were most in need of encouragement.

A steep, narrow alley led them to the upper part of the town, to the gate of Dali Mami's *bagnio* in which many hundreds of Spaniards were languishing. Cervantes, together with a handful of his comrades, passed through the gate; the rest had been taken away by other masters to the various *bagnios* of Algiers, and Miguel's brother had been carried off by the Bey of Algiers, Ramadan Pasha himself.

The newcomers crossed the prison-yard under the silent gaze of older captives huddling in the corners. While his comrades were left in the yard, the guards led Miguel into a dank, fetid dungeon with hardly any light. There was a thick stone slab at the far end and two heavy chains with rings hung from the wall. Exhausted, Miguel sank on to the stone and suffered the guards to lock gyves on his ankles, chains about his wrists. Then he was left alone, chained to the wall like a wild beast, as sad at heart as poor Don Quixote locked up in the cage on an ox-cart.

*

We do not know exactly for how long the young captive was kept in the dungeon, but we know that it was long enough to bring him near to death. Far from life, light and human voices, he passed his days in the damp, bare corner of his prison-hole, listless and immobile. The alleys outside were quiet. In the

mornings and evenings he could hear muezzins calling the faithful to prayer from the balconies of minarets, but he missed the
sound of bells which marked the passing hours in all Christian
towns. The murmur of fountains filling the air after dark may
have carried his mind back to the starlit nights of Seville, but
this must have made his awakening all the harder.

While at the *bagnio*, Cervantes was visited by Spanish friars
who had come to Algiers to arrange ransoms and give the
prisoners consolation and advice. For fleeting moments their
words unfroze his heart, as if he were hearing the distant call of a
beloved voice. But it brought him no help, it only served to make
his anguish more acute and increase his longing for freedom.
Words were not enough; what he needed was a breath of fresh
air, the sight of the sky, and above all, the feeling that he was able
to do something. As things were, he was in danger of either
sinking into a fatal lethargy, or of his mind giving way through
brooding on the liberty which seemed unattainable.

At last even Miguel's guards noticed that their captive had
grown so weak that he was scarcely able to stir. It alarmed them;
they dreaded their master's fury should the prisoner, of whose
ransom he had extravagant hopes, fall ill. They reported Miguel's
ailing state. Immediately there came orders to relax the strict
regimen of his confinement, and a little later he was permitted
to move about in the town of Algiers. With this began his active
struggle for liberty, in which he was to show not only great
courage and dignity, but the most unselfish generosity as well.

When Miguel came to explore Algiers in all its vileness, and
saw how many people went under in misery and degradation,
he had moments of helpless despair. As Pater Haedo remarked,
it was one thing to hear about it, and another to see and suffer it.
Yet Miguel never gave in to desperation. The more he saw, the
firmer became his resolve to find a way of escape. All around him
he found instances of sacrifice and self-denial, as well as of baseness and cowardice. What impressed him most deeply, however,
was the spectacle of the anonymous mass of captives, twenty-five
thousand of them, who filled the *bagnios* and slaved in the house-

holds of rich Algerians. They had to suffer cruel punishment, and this for no apparent reason. They toiled in quarries, or worked on fortifications in the port, below the walls of Ead-el-Ouad, their naked backs exposed to the scorching African sun and covered with weals from the whips of their overseers, who would lash them at the slightest sign of flagging. Others manned the rowing-benches of the corsairs' galleys. Cervantes would see them coming ashore after an expedition—those who came back, for the sea claimed many of them!—just as Pater Haedo saw them, "so sick, thin, emaciated, worn-out and disfigured, that they would hardly stand on their feet and were well-nigh un-recognizable".

Most of them were men for whom there was no redress, no ransom. They were fishermen and peasants from the coasts of Valencia, Catalonia and Andalusia, who had been carried off while peacefully working in their market gardens, tending their nets on the shore, or resting from their labours in their homes at night. They were simple men with no thought for anything but their family and plot of land, who zealously attended every reli-gious service which took place in the *bagnios*, and began to weep when they heard a song from their native province. A great many of them had their noses or ears mutilated, in punishment for a slight misdemeanour. There was, for instance, a young man from Ibiza who had been thus treated merely for plucking a twig from a shrub, for which he was denounced by the owner of the garden. A simple accusation was enough to cost Juan Angelo of Majorca his ears. Others were mutilated for no better reason than that their gaolers had been drunk and wanted their fun.

Among countless passive, cowed men, Cervantes found some whose patience sprang from moral courage and so set an example to others. This was the case with Doctor Sossa, who resigned himself to an underground dungeon, with nothing more than a hole in the roof for light and air; three times he was taken for dead and dragged out by the guards. Another man of the same stamp was the Mercedarian friar Jorge del Olivar, whose charity was so great that he offered himself as hostage in place of two prisoners.

Cervantes, however, had little use for patience and resignation. None of the friends he chose were given to meekness: they were Sergeant Navarrete, who had lost his ears through an attempt to escape, but was already busily planning another attempt; young Captain Francisco de Meneses, and Beltran del Salto y de Castillo, both taken prisoner at La Goleta; Ensign Ríos; the knightly Osorio—all men of the same stamp. Almost from the start, Cervantes dominated them with his strength of personality, which was coupled with so much kindliness and human warmth. They sought him out, and not long after he had been granted comparative freedom of action, he found himself the centre of a small group. He began to plan their joint flight.

Escape was ever in the forefront of Miguel's mind throughout his long years of captivity in Algiers. And every attempt that was frustrated merely added to his determination to succeed. He put it in these words: "While there, I never lost my hope of regaining my liberty. And even when a scheme I had conceived, prepared, and put into practice, led to results far short of my intentions, I did not give in but set my imagination to work to find another hope, however scant and faint, that could sustain me." Each new plan was more ambitious than the last, each time he thought less of himself and more of the others. Each time he was more Don Quixote.

"Four times", says Pater Haedo, "did he come near to losing his life, either by being impaled, or 'hooked', or burnt alive." These were the three forms of capital punishment then used in Algiers. Cervantes knew about them; he witnessed executions. The most common and most horrible was death by "hooking". The condemned man, naked and with his hands tied behind his back, was placed on the top of a wall the middle part of which was studded with needle-sharp protruding hooks; he was then hurled over the edge, to be impaled on one of the spikes, and left hanging—maybe by an arm or a leg, maybe hooked in the flesh of the body—until he died.

Shortly before Cervantes came to Algiers this sentence was carried out on an Italian renegade who had been caught while attempting to flee in disguise. We know for certain that Cervantes was present at the martyrdom of Fray Miguel de Aranda, a friar who was dragged through the streets by a rope round his neck, mercilessly flogged, thrown into the flames, and stoned to death before the fire had finished with him. The pitiful remains, and the stones that had killed him, were left lying on the beach for a long time.

Cervantes was well aware of all this, but nothing deterred him, neither the threats of the Bey of Algiers, nor the tortures which followed any attempt at flight or the mere suspicion that such an attempt was planned. Unless we are able to visualize this man's strength of spirit during those five years in Algiers, as well as the misfortune that dogged him and the ingratitude with which he was repaid, we shall understand neither him nor his Don Quixote.

His first escape plan was simple, and it was laid for a small group of eight comrades, among them his brother Rodrigo. His second plan was intended for fifteen or twenty prisoners—it was thwarted by the double-dealing of one of the associates. Another scheme involved more than seventy prisoners, the secret hire of a ship, and the active support of several Spanish merchants living in Algiers; this too failed, through the treachery of one of his own countrymen. Finally, Cervantes envisaged the organizing of a general rising of the captives, which was to lead to the cap-ture of Algiers itself. We know about it through the letter from Miguel to Mateo Vázquez and, more explicitly, through a remark in Pater Haedo's chronicle. To this, his most ambitous idea, Cervantes was moved by a mixture of patriotism, desire for glory, and human compassion. If it was quixotry, it was at least a great dream.

I3

The First Flight

THE prisoners in Algiers were allowed to celebrate Christmas according to their taste, custom and creed. The priests, of whom there were a number among them, said Mass in all the prison/ houses on Holy Night, after which the prisoners acted little plays, gave recitals, and sang songs. Against a fixed payment, all Algerians had access to these celebrations. No doubt the main reason why they were permitted was that the owners of the *bagnios* found them a useful source of income. They involved a certain risk for the Christians. On one occasion, the mob of spectators was roused to fanatical fury, assaulted the priest at the altar, dragged him through the streets till he was dead—and continued to do the same with his body.

Soon after his first Christmas in captivity—in which he appears to have taken little part, unlike in subsequent years—Cervantes called his friends together, among them his brother Rodrigo, and outlined a plan of escape. He had found out all he could about previous escapes, examined their problems and difficulties, and roughly assessed the chances of success. The truth of the matter is that all his planning was governed more by audacity than by cool reasoning, and in this instance he had not probed deeply enough.

He had quickly ruled out escape by sea, since the obstacles seemed insuperable. An attempt by land meant marching to Oran—then a Spanish possession—across sixty leagues of moun/ tainous territory covered with dense, matted scrub. Furthermore, one was likely to encounter roving patrols all the way to the frontier. In the waste lands, nomad tribes had their camps; these tribesmen lived by marauding, and by tracking down escaped prisoners, for whom their owners would always pay a reward of some sort. Also, there were lions in the hills, which sometimes roamed near to Algiers itself, terrorizing the townspeople.

Cervantes refused to consider any of these as grave obstacles. The real difficulty was to find an experienced, trustworthy guide who would take them to Oran. Within a surprisingly short time Cervantes managed to establish contact with a Moor who promised to lead them by mountain paths to Oran. At last the day dawned which Cervantes and his friends had fixed for their flight. For food, they had biscuits made of a paste of flour, egg and honey, which was particularly sustaining, and edible herbs in case of emergency. They also carried extra pairs of shoes. And with this scant equipment in their packs, they took to the road along the seashore.

It was a spring night, soft and warm. They could hear the waves splashing on the nearby beach, while the all-pervading murmur of the fountains in Algiers' many gardens grew steadily fainter. Beyond the cultivated green belt, past the first range of hills, the path ran up steeply through deserted ground, winding between rocks and thorn-thickets. They were at least eight men —there may have been ten, but we lack exact information— marching close together, in complete silence. Whenever they heard hoof-beats in the distance, they cowered among the shrubs till the sound died away. Thus they continued the whole night, under a starlit sky. At sunrise they found themselves in a maze of arid, inhospitable hills. Their feet were torn, swollen and bleed-ing, making progress increasingly difficult. Now their guide showed signs of restlessness; he would look about him in all directions, double back in his tracks, and then go on again for a short distance. Before long he explained that he was not certain that they were on the right route, and that he wanted to retrace his steps until he found his bearings again. In the meantime they should rest in a copse by a little stream, where they would have shade and water. They were so weary and footsore, the spot was so cool and peaceful, that they saw no reason to distrust the Moor's motives, but let him turn back. He went, and never returned.

One, two and more hours passed. Finally, when the sun had set behind the hills and night was closing in, they gave up hope of seeing their guide again. They were now in a serious dilemma. To press on towards Oran meant almost *certain* death; they did not know the way and would become a prey for wild beasts, or be waylaid by patrols or native bandits. To go back to Algiers meant no more than *probable* death; if they were not intercepted, they might even be able to cover up their flight or explain it away. They decided to turn back and, starting on their way at once, reached Algiers while it was still night.

The first attempt had failed.

[The exact circumstances of that return journey, and the wiles they used to elude any serious punishment, are unknown. Cervantes only mentioned that he was more rigorously confined than before, and had to suffer new privation and ill-treatment. The arrival of the sinister Hassan Pasha, the newly appointed Bey of Algiers, was still a few days off: the retiring Bey was rather less harsh, and at this time fully occupied with his preparations for handing over the command to his successor. Perhaps the prisoners owed it to this combination of circumstances that they had to pay a comparatively cheap price for their escapade.

Cervantes passed through another period of darkness and despondency.

14

In Spain

IN the first days of 1576, the ensign Gabriel de Castañeda was able to sail to Spain; we do not know whether he was freed by ransom or managed to escape. Before he left Algiers, Cervantes entrusted to him a letter to his parents.

After the failure of his first attempted flight, he had found it more difficult to bear his captivity. His comrade, Juan Valcárcel, said in a memorial that during this period he had often heard Cervantes complain of maltreatment by his master. We have a document which shows that he had to ask for a loan "because the Moor who kept him prisoner gave him neither food nor clothes".

In the letter he had given to the ensign de Castañeda, Cervantes informed his family about his and his brother's plight; in the certainty that they would do everything in their power to find ransoms for them, he had suggested how they should start their negotiations for the money. Castañeda seems to have reached Spain in the summer. On his arrival in Madrid he went at once to his friend's family, to deliver the letter and explain the position of the two brothers by word of mouth.

Miguel's relatives had heard nothing since the news of the capture of the *Sol* and feared the worst. To learn that the brothers were captives must have brought them both joy and sorrow.

As usual the Cervantes home was short of cash, but family loyalty and a deep love—above all for Miguel—asserted them selves at this juncture. Not one member held back. The parents pawned their meagre belongings, the sisters sacrificed their dowries, they approached friends and acquaintances. Every

available sum of money, down to the smallest, was set aside, but
in the end it amounted to very little. It was Miguel's bad luck
that his master demanded an exceptionally high ransom, having
been misled about his prisoner's importance by the letters of
recommendation that had been found on him. If the Cervantes
family was to raise the money for the release of the two brothers,
they had to look elsewhere than to their private means.

Following the hints in Miguel's letter, they began to seek
influential people who could pull strings. If they wore themselves
out with tearful applications, they wore other people's patience
out as well. As part of their campaign Doña Leonor dressed up
in widow's weeds and went, accompanied by her two daughters,
on a painful round which led her from one antechamber to the
next.

At this time Spain's affairs of state were going from bad to
worse. With the Turkish threat in the East not yet averted, a
new crisis was developing in the North, in Flanders, where the
subversive movement was gaining impetus, secretly supported by
France and England. So far all counter-measures had failed. In
this critical situation, no one had a thought to spare for the
twenty-five thousand Spaniards in Algerian captivity. The
outcome of Doña Leonor's naïve trickery and sincere tears was
a foregone conclusion.

Don Juan of Austria had serious worries of his own. With
every step, he found himself more deeply entangled in Court
intrigues, and graver perils loomed ahead. Yet, like Cervantes,
Don Juan never stopped dreaming; like Cervantes, he fashioned
his most grandiose dreams when his situation was worst.

The episode of Tunis had closed for Don Juan the way to an
empire in the East. Now his imagination carried him in a different direction, to the North, where he discovered a brilliant
opportunity for conquest. Somewhere in the fogs of the North
was a small island, racked by internal conflict; there, in a bleak
English castle, a young Queen was imprisoned and dreamed of
the hero who would free her.

The story of Mary, Queen of Scots, sounded in the ears of Don

Juan of Austria like an echo of old legends. Here was an adven‑ ture worthy of one of the Knights of the Round Table: here was an adventure fit for one of his own breed. He, Don Juan, was a fighter and a lover. When he had come to Naples, in the first flush of youth, to assume command of his fleet, people had noted that he went in silk and velvet, though carrying a sword, and that a heart was engraved on the ring he wore on his finger. At the festival in his honour he had enchanted all by his skill as a dancer and by his courtly grace; the most beautiful noble ladies of Naples had competed for the distinction of dancing with the youthful general. If the rough Venetian sailors had snickered then, they had soon learnt at Lepanto how wrong they were.

More than one young gallant had given his life for Mary, Queen of Scots. The danger of the enterprise was an added lure, enhancing the glory that beckoned. Don Juan would not only come to the rescue of a queen whose beauty was famed at the Courts of Europe, he would also have a claim to share the island throne with her.

Don Juan's project was something more than a figment of his imagination. Pope Gregory XIII had sent for him to discuss plans for the Queen's liberation; he had given Don Juan definite promises and guarantees. While Don Juan was in Italy, English, Irish and Scottish Catholics had called on him to offer their support and allegiance, as though to their future sovereign. Moreover, he was informed that the Queen had accepted his proposals with enthusiasm; he had heard that she had agreed to wed him on being shown his portrait—this could not fail to please Don Juan—and that she saw in him her last hope. All this served as fuel for the fire within him. Yet once again the dark shadow of the Spanish Court fell across his path.

At the Court of Madrid, Don Juan's latest aspirations were known and carefully watched. His chief adversary was the King's secretary, Antonio Pérez. Possibly Pérez was actuated by an old resentment against Don Juan, from the days when he himself was an underling in the household of Ruy Gómez, Prince of Eboli, and had to watch Don Juan's courtly graces and budding fame win him easy triumphs in the state rooms of the Princess. Though Pérez was now the Princess of Eboli's lover, and the power behind the Throne, it may be that he had not forgotten his days of humiliation. Certainly he considered the King's affection for his half-brother the greatest flaw—perhaps the only flaw—in his own position as royal favourite.

Don Juan's recklessness on the one hand, and the King's suspicious nature on the other, gave Antonio Pérez a welcome opening when the idea of the English enterprise was broached. As a first step, he was clever enough to make the King feel that Don Juan's intention was an offence against his, the King's, authority. Then Pérez tactfully suggested that it would be expedient to have Don Juan adopt a friar's habit, as a cure for all his vagaries. At this juncture a Papal envoy came to Madrid on a mission to secure the King's agreement and Spain's active support for the English venture. Philip II listened to everything and everybody, but committed himself to nothing. "We shall see", was all he would say. In reality, he had his own plan ready; he meant to send Don Juan to Flanders.

Flanders was the King's gravest worry. The Duke of Alba's "iron hand" policy had been followed by three years of temporizing under Requeséns, but neither method had achieved lasting results. The Prince of Orange had raised the battle-cry against Spain, and rebellion spread through Flanders like wildfire.

In these circumstances Philip considered Don Juan of Austria the best possible choice for a Governor-General of the Flemish provinces. He was popular there, because of his Flemish origin, because of his renown as a general, and not least because of his youth. Moreover, in recent negotiations in Northern Italy he had shown considerable talent as a diplomat. Thus, if Philip appointed Don Juan Governor-General of Flanders, it would be not only a gesture of affection and esteem, and a sign that the King favoured his half-brother's ambitions (or at least seemed to favour them), but also a step towards a final solution of the vexed Flemish problem.

Antonio Pérez was too adroit to oppose the King's decision. He pretended to welcome it, and kept his counsel. In any case, Flanders was not a bad expedient; though it was no monastery in which to cloister Don Juan, it might turn out to be something worse for him. After all, Requeséns had lost his life and his reputation there. In the meantime, however, Pérez did his best to circumvent a meeting between Don Juan and the King. He was well aware of the young Prince's gift for winning people over and disarming their suspicions. Two of Pérez's own henchmen, Quiroga and De Soto, as well as the dour Escobedo, had fallen for Don Juan's charm and become his ardent supporters, after entering his retinue as spies or informers. And the King's weak- ness for Don Juan was undeniable, a factor which Pérez had to take into account. He managed to persuade Philip that Don Juan should go to Flanders at once and not spend time on a journey to Madrid, for which he had requested the King's authorization. The letters the King sent to Don Juan were all Pérez could desire.

Don Juan was anything but pleased with the news of his appointment. He did not fancy Flanders as a permanent place of residence, and the civil war raging there, with its tangle of hatred, savagery, intrigues and treachery, had little attraction for him. He was wholly occupied with thoughts of the conquest of England, of which the Pope had spoken to him a second time. He had to see the King at all costs; to tell him frankly that he was not eager to be made Governor of Flanders, and why; to explain about the English enterprise and the Pope's wishes; to expound all the advantages of such a plan. In this mood Don Juan received another letter from his brother, the King, which told him peremptorily and for the last time—Antonio Pérez had done his work well—that he should "by no means, and for no reason whatsoever" attempt to visit the Court at Madrid before proceed- ing to Flanders.

This time, however, Don Juan was determined to go to Spain in defiance of all orders and at any risk. But first he sent Escobedo, with letters informing the King of his immediate arrival, and with instructions to prepare the ground for the matters which Don Juan meant to discuss in person.

Escobedo irritated the King with his long list of complaints on behalf of his master. He mentioned all the difficulties the administration of Flanders would entail, and stated the conditions under which Don Juan would go there. Also, he unfolded the plans for the English enterprise, plans of which Philip was well informed. At this stage the invasion of England from the Flemish coast with the help of English Catholics was envisaged; it was to be followed by the liberation of Mary Stuart, her marriage with Don Juan, and Don Juan's proclamation as King of the British Isles, after Queen Elizabeth had been dethroned. Elizabeth's policy was a constant threat to Spain, Escobedo argued; England was behind the unrest in the Low Countries; once England was brought to heel, Flanders would be pacified.

Philip II had never liked Escobedo. The former servant of Ruy Gómez, Prince of Eboli, and present secretary to Don Juan, was a rough, obstinate and not very intelligent man. The King listened to his disquisition in complete silence, and dismissed him with a "We shall see what is best", much as he had dismissed the Papal envoy. When Don Juan landed in Barcelona, he was handed a letter from the King which expressed displeasure with his unauthorized journey. It was left to Antonio Pérez to receive Don Juan in Madrid, while Philip deliberately prolonged his sojourn in the Escorial so as not to be present at his half-brother's arrival.

Pérez staged a great reception and housed the Prince in a well-equipped summer house he possessed in Madrid, thereby lulling him into a false sense of security. He assigned his own bedchamber to his guest, with an inscription fastened to the door: "Speak softly, Don Juan is asleep." He even offered to intercede with the angry King, and his offer was gratefully accepted by Don Juan. Pérez did in fact speak with the King, who thereupon not only deigned to come to Madrid but also to receive his half-brother in audience.

Don Juan wanted to kneel at the King's feet and ask his

pardon, but the King would not let him. Instead, he embraced Don Juan with warm affection. Afterwards they discussed the problems of the Flemish appointment and, quite as Pérez had forecast, their mutual distrust melted away—at least for the moment.

King Philip was kinder to Don Juan than he had ever been. Patiently, and apparently with seeming approval, he listened to the explanations about the planned conquest of England, the Pope's wishes and promises, and the optimism of the English Catholics. Then came the King's turn. He talked of Flanders, the grave situation there, the importance of the post he had destined for Don Juan, and the high appreciation this choice implied. It was necessary first to pacify Flanders. This done, the King promised his consent and active support for the English project—"with no intention of keeping his promise", as Antonio Pérez said later. Only then did Don Juan accept his assignment wholeheartedly, for he thought he saw the glitter of the crown of England behind the thunder-cloud that was Flanders. And now he was suddenly eager to go to the Low Countries, in secret, as he had promised the King. He was going to cross France incognito and appear in Flanders unexpectedly. After a few more days in Madrid, in his friends' company and fêted by Antonio Pérez, Don Juan had completed his arrangements with his Aunt Magdalena's help. One night he left for Flanders with the faithful Escobedo. He went disguised as a Moorish slave, "his fair hair dyed black, his white skin darkened, and his thirst for adventure satisfied".

No wonder Cervantes' parents had to give up hope of Don Juan's help.

Among the many letters they wrote were missives addressed to Don Juan in Flanders; either he did not receive them, or they were overlooked at a time when the young general was overwhelmed with new duties and problems. Soon Don Juan himself was to be in dire need of help; an early death was awaiting him—just as it awaited Mary, Queen of Scots, whom he had hoped to rescue and win.

On their humbler level, the Cervantes family did their best, and more, to rescue the two brothers. The meagre sum they had been able to accumulate was far below the target, but the three women, still dressed in mourning, took it to Friar Jorge del Olivar in the monastery of the Mercedarians. He had been chosen by his Order to negotiate the next ransoms of the captives. On their knees, the women begged him to take the money and do his utmost for their Miguel. Their first thoughts were for Miguel, because the men who returned from Algiers had frightened them by their tales of his audacity and the accompanying hazards. Later they would buy Rodrigo's liberty.

When the friar started on his onerous journey to Algiers, he left the Cervantes poorer than ever, but not without hope.

15

New Plans

In Algiers, Miguel de Cervantes had not been inactive. Communications with Spain were slow and difficult, his rescue by ransom was after all uncertain, and his days were filled with harassing doubts. Despite his confidence in his parents, whose efforts on his behalf he believed would sooner or later be successful, he felt unable to wait indefinitely. His first attempt at flight, and the punishment in its wake, were scarcely forgotten when he was again busy scheming.

The plan was basically simple, but difficult to execute. To the east of the city of Algiers, the Caïd—or City Governor—Hassan had a country house. Its large, leafy garden was in charge of a Spanish prisoner named Juan, a young man from Navarra. How Miguel came to make friends with this gardener has not been reported. It may be that he had been struck with the possibilities for escape which the garden offered: it was densely overgrown, covered a vast area, lay in open country, lonely and isolated at night, though only a league from the town, and—above all—it stretched down to the seashore. It may also be that the gardener had described special features of the estate to some friends and that Miguel had heard about them. What interested him most was the existence of a large cave, unknown to most people and hidden by thickets at the bottom of the garden. Around it Cervantes worked out his new plan. Those who were to take part in this escape, among them the gardener, were to hide in the cave; a ship navigated by an expert sailor was to enter one of the inlets on this stretch of coast. Warned of the ship's imminent arrival, the fugitives would leave their hide-out and wait on the beach, so that their embarkation could proceed without a minute's loss. Then they would set sail for Spain.

This scheme was in an embryo stage when the mission of the Mercedarian Order came to Algiers, headed by Jorge del Olivar, the brave, self-denying friar who had been entrusted with ransom money and messages by Miguel's mother and sisters. Perhaps through the priest Don Antonio de Sossa, who greatly admired Cervantes and knew him well, the friar was able to find Miguel in the warren of Algiers. The two met, and for a moment it was as if Spain were in reach of the captive. But when the friar spoke, Miguel's hopes were shattered. The money which had cost the family so much came nowhere near the ransom the grasping Dali Mami demanded. The Mercedarian tried hard to convince Miguel's masters that they had assessed his value on false grounds. In vain—Dali Mami was absent from Algiers on one of his privateering raids, but he had left stringent, unequivocal orders about this particular prisoner.

When Miguel realized that there was no hope for him, he decided on his course of action. The money was not enough to ransom him, but it was enough to buy his brother Rodrigo's liberty. He spoke to the Mercedarian. Soon the ransom for Rodrigo was paid over. In his brother's safe return to Spain Miguel saw a great advantage for the second stage of his scheme —a method of securing a ship. Among his close associates, committed to take part in the escape, were two Knights of St John, Don Antonio de Toledo and Don Francisco de Valencia. At his request, they wrote letters to the Spanish Viceroys in Valencia and the Balearic Islands, in which they recommended Rodrigo de Cervantes and begged for the loan of an armed frigate, to be sent to Algiers as soon as possible. Rodrigo was given these letters, together with instructions about the steps he was to take in Valencia. The ship was to be chartered already on his arrival in Majorca. Miguel also arranged with his brother how he was to let them know in good time of the ship's approach.

The negotiations for the ransoms were completed, the friars and ransomed captives ready to board ship, when the long-expected new Bey of Algiers finally arrived. Hassan Pasha was a Venetian renegade whose reputation for cruelty and greed had spread far and wide. This was an additional reason why the Mercedarians pressed on with their negotiations. They feared Hassan Pasha would find that the ransoms paid for certain people of high standing were too small, and would demand more, upsetting all existing agreements. Their fears were justified. Hassan Pasha at once suspended the embarkation. On the pretext that they had insulted the Moors, he gave the order that Canon Villanueva and a gentleman by name of Zamora should be handed over to him; he swore he would have them burnt alive, as the friar Miguel de Aranda had been burnt.

The Mercedarians secretly smuggled the two threatened men out of Algiers, as a result of which all the remaining Christians were exposed to Hassan Pasha's fury. One day the captives heard that friar Jorge del Olivar had gone to the Bey and offered himself as a hostage in place of the two fugitives. Since he was prominent in the powerful Order of Mercedarians, Hassan Pasha had a valuable pawn in him and could feel certain that the Order would leave nothing undone to pay his ransom. Therefore the Bey accepted the offer. Friar Jorge del Olivar was put in chains and taken to the *bagnio*, while the two ex-captives continued on their way home.

Rodrigo de Cervantes, too, had sailed for Spain, carrying Miguel's precious letters. With him went another ransomed Spaniard, Viana, a fearless man and skilled sailor who knew the Barbary coast well. Viana had promised to act as captain on the ship which was to be sent by the Spanish authorities in answer to the request of Miguel's friends.

Four months later, an armed frigate under Viana's command set out from Majorca to bring rescue to the group of prisoners.

16

Second Flight

ON about September 20, 1577, Miguel heard the news that the frigate had sailed. He said goodbye to a few friends, finished his final preparations, and, happy in his secret knowledge, walked through the streets of Algiers to visit the dungeon where Doctor Sossa was kept a prisoner. Cervantes had informed Sossa of everything that was going on; now he tried for the last time to make him join their group and flee with him, but the priest was too shattered by illness and suffering to take the risk. The two friends parted, deeply moved; that same night Cervantes escaped from his master's house.

When the leader—for so Cervantes may be called—entered the cave in Hassan's garden, he was greeted with joy by the others, some of whom had been hiding there for as much as six months. The cave was damp; when they wanted a breath of fresh air, or to move about, they had to wait until night, when they emerged singly and cautiously. Some had fallen ill, others were downcast by the long wait, and all were worrying about the ever-present danger to which their existence in the cave exposed them. Yet, incredible as it sounds, Cervantes had all this time been able to supply them with the necessities of life with the help of the gardener and of a Spanish renegade nicknamed "El Dorador", the Gilder.

Most of the men in the cave were "very important personages", some of them noblemen, but now the most important among them was Cervantes. Once back in Spain, they might come to forget what he did for them, they might snub and humiliate him; but there in Hassan's garden they were all dependent on him. When he joined them in the cave, he inspired them with a sense of security. But he, for his part, went out every night into the garden and from a hillock gazed seawards, trying to see the first faint point of light which would announce their hour of liberation. Eight days passed before the light was seen.

With extreme caution the frigate skirted the shore. Under cover of the dark night, some of the sailors landed, while the fugitives slipped away from their cave and proceeded to the beach. There was no sound but the shrill chirping of the crickets, the croaking of frogs in the marshy places, and the faintly lapping waters.

The fugitives had their backs to the nearby town, their eyes on the sea, waiting for a call from the ship. Suddenly they heard shouts and the patter of running feet, which gradually died away in the direction of Algiers.

It was the merest chance, nothing that could have been foreseen, nothing directly connected with their attempted escape. A few Moors had been walking on the beach, perhaps to fish in the quiet of the night, and had stumbled across the sailors from the frigate. This was enough to undo all Cervantes had prepared for so long, and with such admirable patience. Once again, the whole edifice of his hopes crashed in a single instant.

It seems that the sailors rowed back to their ship even while the Moors were still running about in confusion and before the Algerian sentries were alerted; whereupon the frigate set sail at once, not waiting to take aboard any of the fugitives who were so near. This they might have done, and still got away before the Moors came back with an armed escort, but they did not— "because the mariners were wanting in spirit", said Cervantes. Pater Haedo said the same in other words, when he reported that the sailors were so frightened by the shouts of the Moors that they rushed off to their ship which stood out to the open sea.

When the fugitives saw the frigate disappearing from sight, they ran back to their shelter. Cervantes, no doubt, tried to comfort them, but even he must have felt powerless and discouraged; and his misgivings must have grown when he thought of El

Dorador. The main reason why Cervantes had employed the
man to carry the supplies to the cave was the fact that in his
position as a renegade he was able to move about freely. Even
so, Cervantes had never completely trusted him. Now that El
Dorador had ceased to be under Cervantes' direct influence, but
was alone with his own cowardice, he trusted him even less. Or
so we may assume. In the event, El Dorador betrayed them
almost at once. Presumably he came to hear of the incidents of
that night, without knowing what exactly had occurred, and
was so afraid that the whole plot would in any case be uncovered
that he hastened to expose it himself. This act may well have
been in line with his evil disposition.

On September 30, the Day of St Jerome, the renegade went
to the castle and asked to be received in audience by the Bey,
saying that he had important secret information to convey to him.
Before Hassan Pasha he abjured the Christian faith once more
and proceeded to reveal the whole plot, including the hiding-
place of the fugitives, their names and qualifications. He did not
omit to stress that Cervantes was the instigator.

Hassan Pasha was a man in his thirties, by origin a patrician
of the Merchant Republic of Venice. His ferocious cruelty used
to frighten even his nearest associates. His prison-house was filled
with captives who had lost nose and ears. The five years he
ruled over Algiers constitute the worst chapter in this tale of
horrors. Cervantes said—and Pater Haedo bore him out—that
scarcely a day passed without Hassan Pasha venting his brutality
on some unfortunate prisoner.

Haedo tells us, for instance, how Hassan Pasha dealt in
person with two Spaniards who had been caught in an attempt
to escape. First the Bey asked why they had done it, and they
answered that "they longed to be free". Then, "in a great rage,
he ordered them to lie on the ground; and with his own hands
he began to beat the Castilian's belly, first with the short spear
he always carried and then, when the spear splintered, with a
cudgel—not ashamed to act as a vile hangman though he occupied a King's place—until the Spaniard died, to the last invoking

G

the sweet name of Jesus Christ. When the first one was dead, he flogged the man from Ibiza so heavily on his belly and under-belly that he was taken out for dead, to be buried like the other; however, he lived two more days." Hassan Pasha gave orders to have the ears of a man called Diego Ruiz, who was suspected of planning to escape, cut off and stuck to his forehead; then the man was led through the streets of Algiers by way of an example, and to amuse the children.

Hassan Bey had himself been the captive of Uluch Ali; after abjuring his faith, he had gained great influence over the admiral, who had in the end procured him the appointment as Bey of Algiers, one of the most lucrative posts in the Ottoman Empire. His savagery was only matched by the cupidity with which he exploited his position. For such a man, the secret El Dorador had betrayed was a great asset. As soon as a captive escaped from his *bagnio*—the private prison-house of his owner—he came under the jurisdiction of the Bey. In this case, El Dorador at-tempted to add significance to his denunciation by insinuating that other prominent people, perhaps Friar Jorge del Olivar himself, were implicated. This last piece of information was particularly to the Bey's taste, and he promised the traitor a good reward. The commander of the bodyguard was ordered to go at once to the garden of the Caïd with a detachment of eight soldiers on horse and twenty-four on foot, most of them armed with muskets and cutlasses, some with spears. El Dorador was to act as their guide to the cave, and also to point out the ringleader.

In the garden, the soldiers arrested Juan, the young man from Navarra. When Cervantes heard the noise of men and horses, he knew at once what had happened. He told his comrades to put all the blame on him, and went out to face the soldiers. Turning to their leader, he said that "none of those Christians in there had anything to do with this affair, that he was the insti-gator of everything and had induced them to flee". This firmness so surprised the officer that he sent one of his horsemen to Hassan Pasha with a report. The soldier soon returned, with orders to imprison all the offenders, but to bring Cervantes before the Bey at once. Cervantes was shackled and dragged along the four leagues of the road to the castle, walking on foot, but surrounded by horsemen.

Through the crooked, steep, sordid alleys of the town the Spanish prisoner was followed by a swarm of little boys, who, as Pater Haedo says, confidently looked forward to the spectacle of his torture and execution in the great market place, the Zoco. Perhaps there were people who glanced as Miguel's tense face and turned their eyes away in pity. Miguel forced himself to maintain his accustomed calm. He may have been strengthened by the thought of a greater Calvary in Holy Jerusalem.

At last Cervantes stood in the palace of the new ruler of Algiers, face to face with the despot, ready to accuse himself as the sole originator of the plot.

We may imagine Miguel's feelings, but we have no inkling of what actually happened while he stood there. The Bey's subsequent leniency has never been explained. Did a gleam from Cervantes' luminous mind penetrate the tyrant's dark soul, impelling him to impose no punishment on the captive but merely to threaten him? Earlier biographers of Cervantes have suggested that Hassan Pasha was impressed by the personality of the man before him. In this case, he cannot have been quite so base as he appeared—at least not so base as were certain others who later, back in Spain, no longer deigned to know their comrade.

The second act of the drama was played a few hours later, not far from Algiers. The crew aboard the frigate had waited till dark, in ignorance of all that had happened meanwhile, and had stood by, out of sight of the coast. Then they took their ship to the shore to pick up the fugitives, whom they still assumed to be hiding in the cave. The Turks, however, were informed of the ship's proximity and picketed the beach. After allowing the sailors to disembark, they fell upon them, and took them prisoner without meeting any resistance.

Miguel did not know what fate the Bey had in store for him. He had been locked up in a cell, awaiting sentence. When, after a few days soldiers came to remove his fetters, he was ordered to accompany them. This only confirmed his worst fears. Outside, he found the other captives waiting, with the same dread clearly stamped on their faces.

At that moment it must have appeared to Miguel as though an evil genius was playing with his life and his feelings, causing him to alternate between the extremes of despair and hope. He was taken not to his own execution, but to that of another victim, Juan, the gardener. Juan's master was so incensed at the part he had played in the affair that he asked Hassan Pasha to let him in person inflict exemplary punishment on his servant. The other prisoners involved in the attempted escape were taken to the garden of the Caïd, to witness the execution.

It was a horrifying spectacle indeed. For hours which seemed centuries, they had to watch the torture of the young man who had been their helper. Juan was strung up on a tree by his feet; the Caïd alternately pulled the rope and lowered it until his victim's head almost touched the ground. The wretched man put up a desperate fight, gyrating in violent contortions on the end of the rope, but was finally choked by his own blood.

The captives were then marched back through the streets of Algiers; without speaking, almost without daring to look at one another, they crept into their prison cells. But, with that long agony perpetually re-enacted in their minds, they found no sleep.

*

Days passed; Miguel was once more chained to the wall in a bleak dungeon. In the big prison-yard outside he could hear the voices of the Bey's prisoners. There were two thousand of them in the *bagnio* to which Miguel had been transferred. He was in the Bey's power, because the Bey wished to have him safely put away in his own prison-house. It was the worst *bagnio* of Algiers. Speaking of this period of his captivity, Cervantes says: "And although hunger and nakedness could harass us at times, at most times, nothing harassed us so much as to hear and see at every step the cruel things, never seen or heard of before, which Hassan Bey inflicted upon the Christians. Every day he would hang this man, impale the other, cut off the ears of a third, and on such slight grounds—or on no grounds at all—that the Turks themselves acknowledged it as an outcome of his innate assassin's temperament."

Yet, although the sight of a comrade horribly done to death through his, Miguel's, fault had moved him to pity and rage, he treated the Bey's threat not as something to be feared, but as a challenge. In his mind, desperation was transformed into an obsession with the thought of escape to freedom.

The Bey had bought Miguel de Cervantes from his master for the sum of 500 escudos, so as to be able to keep him safe in his private *bagnio*. "If I have this man secure," he said on one occasion, "I have all Algiers secure." But in this secure prison, Cervantes began to search for a new way of escape. For a time, during the Christmas days, he may have lost himself a little in the songs and the music, in attempts to bring a spark of gaiety to his comrades; and no doubt he joined them in prayer before the improvised prison altar. Before long, however, plagued with homesickness and longing, he evolved a new scheme.

He knew that in Oran, the Spanish possession he had hoped to reach in his first attempt at flight, the ruling Governor was Don Martín de Córdoba, a famous war leader and great gentleman. He also knew that Don Martín had himself been a prisoner in Algiers twenty years ago, and had met his misfortune with exceptional bravery. People in Algiers still spoke with bated breath of his attempt to rouse the resident Christians—at all times a strong group—to rebellion against the Turks. His plan to capture the town had failed through the treachery of one of the conspirators. Many captives paid for this failure with their lives, among them the renowned corsair Canete, the details of whose torture people recalled with a shudder. Don Martín de Córdoba himself was gaoled in a tower far from Algiers and ransomed, after long negotiations, for a very high sum.

In Oran there were men who had served with Cervantes at

Lepanto or in Tunis; they would be willing to help him and speak up for him with the Governor. In Oran, then, Miguel saw a gleam of hope. He wrote letters to Don Martín de Córdoba, asking him to send a few resolute, trustworthy men to Algiers, to help him and a group of other Spaniards to escape. Again, Miguel had found friends willing to risk flight. He had also—somehow, we do not know by what means—discovered a Moor who undertook to carry his letters to Oran and bring back an answer.

The Moor started on his journey, with the letters well hidden, but aroused the suspicion of the guards at the very gate of the town. He was detained, interrogated and searched; the letters were found. The Moor was brought before Hassan Bey. Although the papers were signed by Cervantes, it was thought that other important prisoners were involved. Hassan Pasha, meaning to make the Moor talk, ordered him to be impaled. The Moor died at the hands of his torturers, without giving away anything, not even the name of the man who had sent him.

For the second time, Cervantes had to confront Hassan Pasha. Although the attempted escape had not proceeded so far as the last one, he had committed the same offence twice and had every reason to fear the consequences. The Bey sentenced him to two thousand strokes on the belly. It was, in practice, a death sentence; a fraction of it was enough to finish the strongest man. Miguel was tied hand and foot, and once again thrown into his cell. The cruel game was repeated. He waited days on end for the punishment to be meted out, but it never came.

With the passing of the immediate danger, however, came new disturbing reflections: what more could he attempt? Hope had grown dim. Looking back, he would find a hundred reasons to be proud of his actions, but even more reasons to fear for his life. In what did the greatness of his actions really consist? What was it he had achieved at the cost of so much risk and effort? One day he had come across a poor gardener from Navarra, a captive who was, if not content, at least resigned to work in his garden and hope for a ransom, with no other thought to disturb his quiet days. Then Cervantes had spoken to him; the young man's imagination had been fired by his words, lured on by the bait of a prompt return to his native soil. Shortly afterwards he had died in the presence of his comrades, strung up by his feet from a palmtree.

And there had been a simple Moor who lived in Algiers with his wife and children. Perhaps he was quite contented with his existence. One day Cervantes crossed his path and gave him letters to take to Oran. A few days later the Moor died in torment. How could Cervantes have failed to ponder the implications with something like superstitious dread?

These events throw a penetrating light on Don Quixote's misfortunes and failures. Cervantes' Algerian experiences and the enterprises of his Knight from La Mancha follow precisely the same pattern: a worthy resolve to serve the cause of goodness meets an immovable obstacle, good turns into evil, the wellintentioned, generous effort into harm to its author and calamity for those for whose benefit it was undertaken. In the case of Cervantes, as in the case of Don Quixote, the noble impulse remains unimpaired, in defiance of its consequences and with supreme disregard of the costs. With every disastrous setback, after every disillusionment, the battle is renewed. What alone counts for Cervantes, and for his Don Quixote, is the need to follow the inner call. If the results fail to coincide with the intentions, "God in His Heaven judges the heart".

17

Sorrow in Flanders

WHERE was Don Juan? Cervantes asked the same question every spring, always with a faint stirring of hope. After the hard months of his last spell in a dungeon, he was again allowed out in the streets of Algiers. Sometimes, when he was lost in dreams, the urchins of the town mocked him with their song in faulty Spanish:

> *Don Juan non venir,*
> *cristiano aquí morir. . . .*

> Don Juan not near,
> Christian die here. . . .

Cervantes permitted himself to relax a little. For a time at least he betrayed no sign of activity, however active his mind may have been. No doubt his succession of failures had made him more circumspect, less cocksure, and he was biding his time.

It was at this time that the young King of Portugal, Dom Sebastian, made a sudden landing on the coast of Africa. It was a mad, fantastic venture. When the startling news reached Algiers, the streets soon became crowded with agitated people who ran about helter-skelter, shouting in their excitement. No one dared to insult the Spaniards. A fresh breeze of hope seemed to sweep through the town of the captives. Cervantes and other "dangerous" prisoners found themselves anxiously guarded, since their masters feared that they might stage a rising under cover of the general confusion.

But the fears of the Moors and the hopes of the Christians

subsided as quickly as they had risen. The children in the streets resumed their singing of the provocative doggerel:

> Don Juan not near,
> Christian die here!

For, Dom Sebastian and nearly all his army, the flower of Portuguese chivalry, had perished on the plain of Alcazarquivir. The gloating of the Algerians gave the Christians a shrewd idea of the disaster that had overtaken the reckless expedition. Nothing was known about the young King's end—nothing was ever to be known with certainty. For Cervantes, however, the incident not only came as a shock but served as a stimulus. Although the enterprise had ended in tragedy, the panic of the Algerians had proved to him how easily Algiers could be seized.

By a ransomed prisoner, Cervantes sent to his former friend Mateo Vázquez a letter addressed to no less a person than King Philip II. It was in verse, couched in lofty, elaborate language. The poet spoke of his pitiful situation, of his experiences in Italy and Africa, and then touched in guarded words upon the real purpose of his letter, the suggestion that a naval squadron should be sent to Algiers to liberate the captive Spaniards.

Cervantes confidently expected an answer which would confirm that an expedition against Algiers had set out. To meet this eventuality he was ready with a plan that he confided to a few intimates: they were to seize power in the city by inciting the twenty thousand prisoners and the many discontented among the population to revolt. Above all, Cervantes put his trust in the abject fear which would overcome the Moors at the first hint of an expedition. As he put it in his verse-letter:

> The mere thought of your coming will strike fear
> Into the enemy, and I forecast
> His ruin and perdition now and here.

Also, he trusted in the terror which the very name of Don Juan —whom he expected to lead the expedition—would produce.

This time, Cervantes thought that the silence following his

letter augured well. Rumours reached Algiers that Philip was occupied with large-scale preparations for a war. What more natural than that Cervantes should believe that one night the Spanish galleys would appear out of the dark and take the town by surprise? Many a time he must have settled to sleep in the hope that he would be awakened by cannon-fire heralding Don Juan's arrival. He would picture himself jumping up, giving the sign for the captives' revolt, and then marching to the shore at the head of his men, to welcome the Spanish general and surrender the city into his hands. Instead, he would awake to the monotonous call of the muezzins sounding through silent streets.

It was not easy for Cervantes to face the reality of the situation. As always, he needed a dream, a faith and a hope, if he was not to yield to despair, and so he went on dreaming, believing and hoping.

The real Spain, however, was not as Cervantes remembered her, nor as he would have wished her to be. When he left home, he had been no more than an adolescent, his head full of exalted visions, and he still viewed his country with the eyes of an adolescent.

In Spain—the real Spain, not the mirage of the prisoner's dreams—events had taken a prosaic and unheroic turn. Few people, and those not always the best, thought in terms of grandiose deeds. Nobody planned the conquest of Tunis or Algiers. Lepanto was forgotten. The victor of Lepanto, Don Juan himself, was scarcely less neglected than the obscure soldier, Miguel de Cervantes, who happened to have lost the use of his left hand in that same battle.

No sooner had Don Juan left Madrid than Antonio Pérez resumed his machinations. Don Juan was securely caught in this web of intrigues. He had only just reached the Low Countries and was still in Luxemburg, outside the boundaries of Flanders, when he was informed of the gravity of the problems with which he was faced. The Spanish soldiers in Flanders were rebelling against their commanders because for many months they had received no pay. They had sacked the city of Antwerp, killing a great number of its inhabitants. This news boded ill for Don Juan's mission.

Soon after assuming command of the army, he won several victories on the battlefield, but the enormous difficulties with which he had to grapple bewildered and exasperated him. He asked for help from Spain, but help never came. He was unable to pay his soldiers, and his troops were in a dangerously restive mood. So far their devotion to him had held them together, but the situation was becoming untenable. Don Juan had his suspicions, though he still failed to understand the exact nature of the game in which he was being used as a pawn. Day after day he wrote to the King. Yet before those letters, written in cipher, came into the King's hands, they had to be deciphered by Antonio Pérez. In his transcripts, Pérez turned every plea of the Prince's into a brusque demand; where Don Juan complained, Pérez substituted words which sounded like a threat. Not unnaturally, the King's suspicions were roused anew, as his secretary had intended. In Flanders, the hero of Lepanto had fallen into a hornet's nest.

Don Juan of Austria had never really liked Flanders. "It is too sad for me", he wrote in one of his letters to Aunt Magdalena. He had gone there only because he had been promised that it would lead to better things, but now he began to fear that the promises would never be fulfilled. He found himself farther away from his shining goal than ever before. With the coming of spring, Don Juan tried to forget about his surroundings. From the mud and the bleak moors of Flanders, his thoughts turned to the South, the Italian seas, the scenes of his triumphs. For, his dream of a kingdom in the North having proved a mirage, the image of the imprisoned Queen had faded. But he could not escape for long from harsh reality. The bitter struggle in Flanders bewildered and discouraged him. What could he achieve here? Clamour as he might, he received no answer from Spain. "I am a voice crying in the wilderness", he exclaimed. The air was thick with suspicion and distrust. He was never sure of anyone who professed to be his friend. "I feel desperate," he wrote, "for I am sold among these people . . . I have fallen into a hellish pit and find no way out. . . ." Only in his letters to his Aunt Magdalena could he express his whole bitterness at the lack of support, the discontent among his troops, the hatred and treachery which dogged his steps.

In letter upon letter he had begged for assistance, but the replies from Madrid dwelt exclusively on inessentials and evaded the important issues. Finally Don Juan decided to send his secretary, Escobedo, to the Court. Since their arrival in Flanders, Escobedo had become his intimate friend, adviser and confidant. He held him in high esteem for his fidelity—one of Escobedo's few good qualities—and for his bluntness, just as Escobedo's former master, the Prince of Eboli, had done. Don Juan had accustomed himself to speak to his secretary without restraint. He now told him how he suspected a love affair between Antonio Pérez and the Princess of Eboli. Escobedo had great respect for the widow and felt sincere friendship for Pérez. What he now heard pained him. It also angered him. Moreover, he blamed Pérez for their difficulties in Flanders. Being a stubborn and blunt man, Escobedo left Flanders with the firm intention of discovering the truth of the matter and, if necessary, discussing it openly with King Philip.

By the time Escobedo arrived in Madrid, the relations between Pérez and the Princess were a byword in the city. The first thing he did was to seek an audience with the King and explain the purpose of his mission. As on the former occasion, he annoyed the King with his endless complaints on behalf of Don Juan, and with a recital of the insuperable difficulties they faced in Flanders. Philip II replied with his usual exasperating vagueness: "The question will be studied", scarcely bothering to hide his profound contempt for the Ebolis' former servant.

Next, Escobedo called upon the Princess and told her in so many words what the gossips of Madrid said about her. He showed all the respect of which he was capable—which was not much—and all the calm his state of burning indignation per mitted. The Princess, it is reported, rose with a drawn face and merely remarked: "Squires have no say in the doings of great lords." With this she swept out of the room. Escobedo's fate was sealed. The Princess immediately informed Pérez of the incident, and Pérez hatched a plan to eliminate not only Escobedo but, through him, Don Juan as well.

It was a monstrous plot that Pérez invented. According to him, Don Juan intended first to conquer England and then, once enthroned there, to drive Philip out of Spain. The real instigator, Pérez informed Philip, was Escobedo, who spoke of the plan with great arrogance and complete disregard of the King.

That Philip was prepared to credit this tissue of lies sounds incredible, but he did. Any talk of conspiracy was apt to impress him, and his dread of it may explain the severity of his countermeasures. The days went by, and Escobedo tried in vain to obtain another audience of the King. While Don Juan grew impatient in faraway Flanders, Pérez evolved his campaign with the help of the Princess. He was able to convince Philip that the plot existed and that Escobedo might even dare to make an attempt on the King's life. Finally Philip dropped a hint to the effect that it might be best to wipe out Escobedo. This was all Pérez needed. The remark, though anything but definite, implied the King's authorization of the steps necessary for Escobedo's removal.

Then followed a whole series of attempts on Escobedo's life. They were killing him piecemeal, as though with a blunt knife, to paraphrase a saying of Plutarch's. Three times they tried to poison him in Antonio Pérez's house, even while his host made a show of loyal friendship for Escobedo. Whether the would-be assassins were too clumsy, or their victim too tough, they failed. Finally they smuggled one of Pérez's henchmen into the kitchen of Escobedo's own house. The slave-woman who looked after her master's meals was an old servant who had held her job for many years; when her attention strayed for a moment, Pérez's emissary dropped poison into a dish. It was discovered in time.

The old crone was subjected to torture, until she could no longer stand the pain and confessed herself guilty. Although she afterwards protested her innocence, she was hanged in the Plaza Mayor of Madrid.

There is some evidence to show that the King had meanwhile dropped his intention to have Escobedo killed, perhaps because he began to suspect Pérez's information. Also, he received a letter from Don Juan which urged Escobedo's return to Flanders and, ironically, recommended him for "certain favours which he well deserved". The King might in the end have acceded to Don Juan's request, had not the whole affair taken an unexpected turn which led to its abrupt conclusion.

Escobedo went once more to the Princess's palace. Apparently he used a private entrance and walked without further ado into the inner apartments. There he saw with his own eyes—it may have been his set purpose to surprise the lovers—that the gossips had been well informed. Escobedo thereupon told the Princess and Pérez in no uncertain terms what he thought of their shameless conduct. Pérez slunk out of the room. The Princess, however, gave vent to her violent temper and retorted haughtily, with words which contained insults to Philip. No doubt she soon repented of having gone so far, for she was seen hurrying to her lover's house.

Three days later, on a dark March night, Escobedo was found in one of Madrid's back-streets, stabbed by Antonio Pérez's hirelings. While Don Juan was still counting on Escobedo's return to Flanders, and hoping that he would bring not only material help but also explanations which could clear the air, the messenger with the news of Escobedo's murder was already on his way.

Such was the state of affairs in Spain—different from anything Cervantes in his captivity imagined. Vázquez and Pérez were the King's powerful favourites. Escobedo's murderers were rewarded with commissions as ensigns and posted to the Tercios in Italy. It was entirely out of keeping that Cervantes should write letters echoing the novels of chivalry, in the belief that the

Court would pay any attention to them. Again, as so often before and after, he was in for a harsh awakening.

*

In October, 1578, Don Juan of Austria fell ill. Lately he had contemplated retreating to the peace and tranquillity of the monastery of Montserrat, where he had spent three days in prayer and meditation on his first journey to Catalonia. "If God rescues me from this hell, I shall join the hermits of Montserrat in their place of retirement", he wrote. It was a last illusion, and showed how deeply he was affected by the ingratitude and treachery by which he was surrounded. On hearing of the crime against Escobedo, he went down with a malignant fever. At the time there was talk of poison. It would have been consistent with the character of his adversaries; also, two attempts had already been made to poison him. The actual cause of his death, however, was not foul play, as far as we can judge. It was not his body that was poisoned, but his mind and soul. Don Juan's last letters are full of outcries from an oppressed heart: "The work that is done here is such as no man's health can stand and no one can survive for long. . . ." "It has broken my heart to be in this hell and to find no way out. . . ."

Escobedo's death impelled Don Juan to write a last letter to his half-brother, the King, which is highly characteristic. It is full of the profound indignation of a man who finds his most faithful servant and companion a victim of base cowardice; of distress on realizing who was the probable instigator of the crime and what were the secret motives behind it. He sensed that his secretary had died for his, Don Juan's, sake. But what caused him the deepest anguish was the haunting fear that the crime would go unpunished—because of those secret motives.

Don Juan of Austria died on a pallet in the attic-room of a Flemish farmhouse. Outside, a misty afternoon sun shone from the pale autumn sky of Flanders, the country to which he had been so loath to go. A few men, the captains under his command, were standing by in silence. One of them, Francisco de Orentes, afterwards wrote to Philip II: "He died in the garret of a house in the country, as poor as a simple soldier, therein following our Lord Jesus Christ."

The body of Don Juan of Austria rests in a solitary enclosure of the Escorial. His tomb bears his marble effigy, the great sword lying on his breast to keep him company.

18

Disillusionment and Hope

ANOTHER winter came to Algiers, the last leaves drifted from the trees, and with them Cervantes' hopes. The children's ditty —"Christian die here"—took on a new, ominous ring.

Shortly before Christmas, Cervantes and a number of other prisoners were taken to the courtyard of the fortress, the Alcazaba, to witness the execution of a captive who had been caught while attempting to flee. He was a young man called Vizcaino. Try' ing to reach Oran, he had lost his way among the hills and was recaptured; the local wild beasts might have been more merciful executioners. Naked, his arms tied to his back, he was laid out on the ground. Hassan Bey himself came to help his hangmen; with a great whip he lashed the young Spaniard's naked back till his arms were tired. Thereupon the victim was turned over, when the Bey and his henchmen lashed his belly till death released Vizcaino from a long and hideous agony.

A year before, at Christmas'time, on the same spot, by the same method, and in the presence of Christian prisoners, Pedro Soler from Majorca had been done to death. Who was to be next? Where would it end?

Cervantes spent his fourth Christmas in Algiers in a state of dejection similar to that which had followed the torture and death of Juan, the gardener. These four years had aged him in body and soul. They had been a constant struggle for freedom, yet freedom seemed as far away as on the first day, particularly now that a strict watch was being kept on him.

Don Quixote says: "The sorcerers may destroy the outcome, but not the effort." Once again, Cervantes got the better of his despondency. This was his creed. "As the light shines more brightly when it is dark," he tells us, "so hope must be firmer under trial; to despair then is the act of a coward, and there is nothing so pusillanimous as the surrender of a hard-tried man— however great his trials—to desperation."

He thought often of Spain, but his country seemed to him as good as dead. No message, no voice from home had reached him since he had sent his letter to Mateo Vázquez. The ex-captives who had bought their freedom were so happy to have escaped that they forgot the comrades who were left behind in Algiers. Jorge del Olivar, the friar who had offered himself as a hostage, was still a prisoner. The men for whom he had sacri-ficed his liberty were safely back in Spain, while he waited, sick and dejected, for the ransom—or for death—to set him free.

When the watch on Cervantes was relaxed, his most recent bid for freedom conveniently forgotten, he began again to study possibilities of flight. It was to be his last attempt.

*

There lived in Algiers a Spanish renegade, the son of a dis-tinguished Granada family, whose name had originally been Girón but who now called himself Abderraman. This man seems to have felt certain doubts about the new faith he had embraced, and to have voiced them to a friend. Cervantes came to hear of this, and it planted the germ of a new idea in his mind. His past misfortunes had taught him to restrain his impetuous nature to some degree, therefore he waited till he had made sure of the renegade's trustworthiness before he decided to meet him. It was in keeping with his deeply sincere religious faith that he should try to make contact with the renegade; on more than one occasion he had been able to lead back to their true faith young men who had felt attracted by Islam. Nevertheless his driving motive was the ceaseless urge to escape from slavery.

Once it was clear that Girón was sympathetic, Cervantes started negotiations with a Valencian merchant named Exarque with whom he was acquainted and who did a considerable trade between Algiers and Spain. It was known that he not only bought and sold merchandise but also negotiated ransoms for prisoners, and it was said of him that he was a "merry, good-tempered man, the friend of Moors and Christians", since he did business with both sides. As the most important trader of his class, he owned a house in Valencia and another in Algiers. To Abderraman-Girón, Cervantes had spoken of Spain and of his returning to the faith of his fathers. To the Levantine trader he spoke of the advantages to him and his trading house, were he to assist in an enterprise involving many captives of high stand-ing, people who would reward him generously for everything he might do. That is to say, by using just the right psychological approach in either case, Cervantes was able to win both over to his plan. To persuade the shrewd, hard-headed merchant to risk life and property in the perilous adventure was a truly astonishing feat. Partly to impress Exarque and partly for the sake of his own peace of mind, Cervantes might stress that it was a noble task in the service of God, but it is unlikely that either was deceived as to the real motives: Exarque sought profit, Cervantes sought his freedom. On the concrete issue, they came to an agreement.

It was the most ambitious and most dangerous of all Cervantes' schemes. Exarque agreed to advance the money necessary to buy an armed frigate. Cervantes was to hand this sum to Girón, who would make the purchase in his own name, pretending that he meant to become a privateer; as a renegade and a man well-known in Algiers, he could do this without being suspected. The frigate would sail under Girón's command. Her secret cargo would be a number of Spanish captives, among them Cervantes, and she would change course to Spain as soon as it was safe to do so. The transaction was carried out in the utmost secrecy; only Cervantes knew of Exarque's share in it. It was Cervantes, too, who selected and briefed the captives who were to join in the venture. Over sixty of them were waiting for the signal to leave, the frigate was at anchor in the port, the day of departure was fixed—two more days to go. Alonso Aragonés says in his memoir that they were "all excited, all joyous and happy to see that the business was going so well". Then the blow fell.

There was in Algiers a certain Blanco de Paz, a Spaniard from Montemolín, who claimed to be a priest. Nobody knew why he was in Africa or how he had come to be there. He acted, or at least posed, as a commissioner of the Holy Office, the Inquisition. This title, combined with a violent character and a talent for intrigue, made him universally feared.

Juan Blanco de Paz was a strange figure in the Christian under-world of Algiers, a strong but destructive personality. When the Trinitarian friar Juan Gil asked to see his credentials as officer of the Inquisition—possibly at Cervantes' request—Blanco de Paz failed to produce any. Some have doubted whether he really was an ordained priest. If he was, he must have been one of the breed of aggressive clerics who are at loggerheads with the whole world. Twice, when another priest dared to berate him, Blanco de Paz hit his challenger in the face. His vanity and arrogance were such that he deeply resented the popularity Cervantes enjoyed in Algiers. In particular he found it intolerable that the Trinitarian-Redemptorist and Mercedarian friars liked to have Cervantes with them at their table, and that all important Spanish prisoners treated him with deference. For some time before the mass escape was planned, he and Cervantes had been cutting each other dead, an indication that there had been a clash between them. It may also explain why Blanco de Paz alone among the prominent Spaniards in Algiers was not in the escape secret. He heard of it by accident, two days before it was to take place, but early enough to do mischief. It was an unforgivable insult to a man of his ilk that he had not been considered worthy of sharing this vital secret, and now he thirsted for revenge.

We know from the existing documents that Blanco de Paz did not go so far as to betray the plan to the Bey himself, but that he mentioned it to a renegade from Florence, called Caibán, in the obvious hope that this man would tell the Bey without disclosing

the name of his informant. Caibán did report to the Bey immediately, and on being pressed also gave the name of Blanco de
Paz. Hassan Bey then sent for him, and extricated a full account
of all Blanco de Paz knew. He was told that it would cost him
dear if he let out anything about the interview. It suited the
Bey's purpose to wait till all the preparations for the flight were
complete and then, at the last moment, to arrest all those involved.

In some way, however, it leaked out that Hassan Bey was in
the know; soon the Christians in Algiers heard of it. The men
who knew themselves implicated were panic-stricken and did not
know where to hide. No one doubted that at least half of their
number would be tortured to death. Even Cervantes was
alarmed. Twice before he had been indicted for the same offence,
and twice he had escaped with his life as though by miracle. He
could scarcely hope for a third miracle of this kind.

Cervantes therefore slipped away from his master's house and
went into hiding with a friend, the ensign Diego Castellano.
When the Bey found himself foiled, his fury was boundless—as
boundless as the terror of the Christians. The town-criers raised
the hue and cry for Cervantes. Anyone who sheltered him was
threatened with execution. Exarque began to tremble for his
fortune, if not for his life. Cervantes alone knew him as an accom-
plice: the trader felt convinced that, once captured, Cervantes
would confess everything on the rack, and he was mortally afraid.

However, Cervantes had already decided to give himself up
voluntarily to Hassan Bey. He thought that he owed it to his
comrades. It was the most heroic decision of his life. Later he
wrote: "I resolved to surrender myself, because I did not want a
Christian who hid me to come to grief, and also because I feared
that, unless I appeared, the Bey would find some other man whom
he could torture and from whom he would learn the truth."

First, Cervantes went to see Exarque. The trader was so terri-
fied at the thought that Cervantes might give him away that he
offered to arrange for his immediate flight. He would take him
to a ship which was to sail from Algiers this very night, and would
pay his ransom as well. Few people would have failed to be

tempted by such an offer. Miguel turned it down. As he said, it was not in him to leave his friends in the lurch in order to save his own life, and so to bring dishonour upon his name. Nor could he possibly permit the friend who had risked his head by hiding him to be exposed to the greatest danger should the truth come out, while he, Miguel de Cervantes, was happily away on his journey to Spain. He needed no time to think it over. In his exalted mood, it would have been as useless to argue with him as to argue with Don Quixote when he spurred on his rickety steed to ride against the giants.

Cervantes went to great trouble to calm the merchant. He thanked him for his offer and for his kind interest—which was, of course, self-interest—but said he was unable to accept it. Nevertheless, he assured Exarque that there was no reason for him to tremble. "I answered him that no torment, no, not even death, could compel me to implicate anyone but myself. And I said the same to all the others who were involved in the affair. I begged them to be unafraid, because I would take the whole guilt upon my own shoulders, although I was certain that this would be my death." Thus Cervantes in his written statement on the matter. Exarque, who knew him, needed no further assurance: come what may, his life and property were safe.

From the house of the trader, Cervantes went to another of his friends, Morato Ráez from Murcia, nicknamed Maltrapillo (roughly corresponding to Rags-and-Jags), who was a renegade in great favour with the Bey. Cervantes revealed to this man his guilty secret and his decision to own up to Hassan Pasha. Maltrapillo no doubt tried to dissuade Cervantes, knowing the Bey as he did, but in the end he gave in and promised to do his best to intercede for him with the Bey. He kept his promise. As soon as Maltrapillo returned from his audience with the Bey, Cervantes went to the castle to give himself up.

Here again we do not know precisely what happened when Cervantes stood face to face with Hassan Bey. We can only imagine that every word he spoke radiated the constancy and calm resolution of one who knew he was about to die. Afterwards the Bey himself expressed his admiration for the manly spirit and fine tact of the Spaniard. In Algiers, the memory of the incident died hard, for the Bey had never before shown such tolerance, nor an accused man such fortitude.

At all events, Cervantes kept his word to Exarque and his fellow-conspirators. He did not mention a single name, but insisted that the preparations for the flight had been made by himself, with the help of four Spanish captives who were already on their way home. He was subjected to the pressure of threats and promises. They put a rope round his neck and tied his hands to his back, as though about to hang him on the spot. He refused to be intimidated. And the incredible happened once again: he was not tortured, he was not hanged, and he was not even made to suffer insults.

Years later, Cervantes alluded to this stage of his captivity and Hassan Pasha's cruelty in a story. Speaking of himself in the third person, he said: "The only man who came well out of it was a Spanish soldier named de Saavedra. Though this man had done things which the people remembered for years, always with the aim of getting free, the Bey never flogged him, nor gave orders for him to be flogged; nor did he say a harsh word to him. We all feared that he would be impaled for the least of his many actions, and he feared it himself more than once."

The mysterious intervention of a woman has been conjectured on no evidence at all, but there is no need for such romantic inventions. We may safely assume that the most powerful protectors Cervantes could marshal were his own sangfroid, and the clever way in which he defended himself before the despotic Hassan Pasha.

Cervantes' last attempt to escape cost him five months in chains, but rather as a precaution, it would seem, than as a punishment. The mirage of freedom was gone.

19

Despair and Relief

THE months of close imprisonment quenched Cervantes' ardour and taught him resignation. Although he gradually lost his fear of imminent torture and death at the hands of his captors, he saw but one alternative: that of being transferred to Istanbul. Hassan Pasha's term as regent of Algiers was drawing to its close. In the castle, preparations were made for his journey to the Ottoman capital. He intended to take his treasure and his captives with him—and Cervantes was one of his captives.

To be taken to Istanbul meant bidding good-bye to all hope of freedom. And it was useless even to contemplate another plan for escape while he was still in Algiers. There was not enough time left, and in any case he was too closely guarded. The exorbitant ransom Hassan Pasha demanded was virtually unobtainable. Thus all doors seemed closed. Don Juan of Austria was dead. Miguel's letters to Mateo Vázquez had not elicited a single reply. To make matters worse, the plague had broken out in Algiers and claimed hundreds of victims among the prisoners.

This last year of Cervantes' captivity was his worst. But it was also the year when freedom, apparently out of reach, was granted to him—smoothly, quietly, without any effort on his part.

In May, while Cervantes was still in his dungeon, a new mission of Trinitarian friars landed in Algiers. Its leaders were Father Juan Gil and Brother Antonio de la Bella. The ship that brought them arrived on Trinity Sunday. At once, new hope inspired the captives. Word went round that huge ransom moneys would be paid out this time. It was an illusion. Out of 25,000 captives, only 130 were ransomed by the mission. Yet on that Sunday, every man languishing in an Algerian prison saw himself already on his way home. Cervantes could not help sharing in the joyous excitement. At his first meeting with Father Juan Gil he was profoundly moved.

The Redemptorist—to call him by the name of his Brother-hood so fitting to the occasion—had heard reports about Cervantes in Madrid, and stories about his latest achievement after his arrival in Algiers. Miguel's personality did the rest. The friar immediately took to this prisoner. Answering his questions, he spoke to him about Spain and Spanish affairs, about his parents and friends, before he came to the problem of Miguel's ransom. He informed him that he had 300 *escudos* at his disposal to buy his release, a sum scraped together from various sources.

Three hundred *escudos*? But Hassan Pasha had bought Miguel from his former master for 500 *escudos* and expected to make as much again in profit! In a moment his world collapsed about Miguel's ears. In vain the good friar tried to comfort the captive with the assurance that he would do everything in his power to secure his freedom. Cervantes knew that it was practically im-possible to raise the difference between those 300 *escudos* and the price Hassan Bey demanded. And it was altogether impossible to imagine Hassan Bey reducing his demand. The sands were running out. Already the Pasha's treasures were loaded on board the ships which were to take him and his chattels to Istanbul.

When Father Gil began his negotiations, he soon discovered that Cervantes had every reason to despair. But he was an obstinate man who would not easily give in. He had taken a personal liking to the captive, and had sworn to himself that he would use every means to have him free by the time he himself left Algiers. Meanwhile, less difficult ransom transactions were completed. In August, the first transport of redeemed prisoners sailed for Spain. They numbered 108, and were in the care of Brother Antonio de la Bella.

The joy of those who depart is always selfish and somewhat cruel. It wounds those who have to stay behind. Cervantes felt utterly deserted as he watched the ship sail away, and then looked at Hassan Pasha's galley riding at anchor. True, Father Juan Gil was still in Algiers, still negotiating. He had spoken yet again to Hassan Pasha, but there was no change in the situation. The day when this galley would carry him and his fellow-sufferers to Istanbul and its slave market was drawing near, inexorably.

By the end of August, all the departing Bey's goods and treasures, his women, his household and his slaves, were on board the galley. Cervantes had not heard anything more from the Redemptorist. One morning he and other captives were taken to the ship, in chains and with gyves on their ankles. They stood herded together on one side of the deck, dumbly waiting. It was then Father Juan Gil suddenly came to tell Cervantes that his ransom had been paid.

Miguel might have truthfully said, like his Don Quixote: "If there are sorcerers who maltreat me, there are also sorcerers who defend me."

They removed his chain and fetters, and he felt himself once again master of his destiny. The image of Spain as the incarnation of all he longed for, of all he hoped from the future, rose before his eyes.

First, however, he had to arrange everything so that his homecoming should be free from any possible slur upon his integrity. This meant, in the first place, that he had to clear away all the malicious insinuations Blanco de Paz had spread about him, under cover of his cleric's habit and his alleged office—insinuations which, if not disproved, might become obstacles in his path. For Blanco de Paz had not relaxed in his efforts to ruin Cervantes. To spike his guns, Cervantes now found twelve men among the prominent Spaniards in Algiers who were willing to testify to his conduct during captivity. This they did in writing, in the presence of Father Juan Gil and the Apostolic Notary in Algiers, Pedro de Rivera. This document, which has come down to us, is an invaluable account, in lapidary words, of Cervantes' whole odyssey.

Cervantes intended the document to serve a double purpose. First, it would refute and shame his adversary—which it did with complete success. Secondly, it would put on record all he had done since his capture, in addition to his service in the army, of which other records existed; this would help him when he applied in Madrid for the favours which, in his opinion, were due to him. But on this second point he was a victim of his own imagination which conjured up splendid castles where there was at best a roadside inn frequented by muleteers, wenches and rogues.

Thus we see Cervantes in his incurable optimism—or blind-ness—collect signatures to establish his just claim in the eyes of the powers-that-be of Madrid.

He imagined he would only have to arrive there, invoke the name of Don Juan of Austria, show his crippled hand, produce his credentials which he guarded like a treasure, and collect the well-deserved reward. And then he would give himself time to rest and shake off the immense weariness those five terrible years in Algiers had induced in him.

In short, Cervantes still preserved a remnant of faith in the world of the books of chivalry, where the weak find protectors, the strong a field for their prowess, the oppressed justice, and the righteous peace. The bitter awakening was not far off. Then he would ask his own heart, as Don Quixote asked the magic oracle of the "Enchanted Head": "Tell me, you that reply, is it true what I saw, or was it a dream?"

For the present, the sun shone, the sky was blue, and Miguel de Cervantes was happy. He had his cherished document, his verses, his fragments of prose and of plays—and his illusions. In the port of Algiers a white ship waited for him, its sails filling with an impatient breeze.

PART TWO

20

Homecoming

AFTER a slow journey, Master Antón Francés' ship at last reached the Levant coast of Spain near the port of Denia. Cervantes has left us a description which, though part of a tale, sums up his memories of this return to his country:

"Shortly after daybreak they found themselves no more than a league from the town. Rowing, tacking and gaily shouting, they drew into the harbour, where all at once a dense crowd of townsmen had assembled. . . . One by one, as if in a procession, they went ashore and kissed the ground many times, with tears of joy . . ."

The ex-captives stayed for some days in Denia, while Valencia, the capital of the region, was preparing a reception for them. Then they took to the road and walked like pilgrims through all the small villages along the coast. On a clear autumn evening at the beginning of November, 1580, they made their solemn entry into the capital city. Doors, windows and balconies were crammed with people who wanted to see the group pass through the streets. The air was full of the sound of kettle-drums, flageolets and church bells. The men marched to the cathedral bareheaded, with the scapular of the Trinitarian Order round their necks, and still wearing the garb of their captivity, the blue Moorish *chilaba*. Behind them ran small boys who with shrill voices offered a broadsheet entitled *Account of the Ransomed Captives* on sale to the crowds. It had been printed by the Trinitarians, and the proceeds were to go to the ex-captives.

As always when Spanish prisoners had been ransomed and so restored to the Church, the cathedral was lit by thousands of candles. While the priest preached his sermon on the tragedy of being held captive among infidels, the freed men gave thanks to the Almighty on their knees.

At last Cervantes' brain began to clear. He had received his share of the alms the friars had collected, he was equipped with the Order's *cédula*—a sort of identity paper or pass—and with it went the permit to go wherever he liked. Surprisingly, he stayed two months in Valencia.

It was a good place in which to make the transition and throw off the effects of the nightmare that was Algiers. Even if the language of the people around him was not his own Castilian, it had a homely sound; it was the speech of Spain. The city was bright, gay and clean, the winter sunshine mild, the air soft, with a faint scent from the orchards and the tang of the sea. The waves lapped on a sandy beach as in Algiers, but here they provoked no painful longing for the home country, they revived simple, half-forgotten pleasures. The songs he heard in the streets of Valencia after dark had a certain African flavour, but princi- pally they reminded him of the songs of his boyhood in Seville. And in the night, when the city grew silent, he could go to sleep relaxed and free from fear.

There were other, more concrete reasons why Cervantes pro- longed his stay in Valencia. The Court was not in residence in Madrid just then, and it was at the Court he hoped to find em- ployment. Until the men on whom his future depended were back in Madrid, there was nothing he could do there but wait, and seek shelter with his family. It was perhaps easier for Cer- vantes to spend this time of waiting among strangers. Whereas he was sure of his family's affection, he also knew that they had scarcely anything else to share with him.

He had business to settle in Valencia as well. Three of his friends in Algiers, the Valencian merchants Exarque, Torres and Fortuny, had advanced the balance of the money needed for his ransom—this was the secret of that miraculous last-minute turn of events. He had, in all probability, to come to some arrange- ment with them about the money. In any case he had his own preparations to make. Through another ex-captive, the Valencian Juan Estéfano, who had to go to Madrid, he sent a letter to his parents with the good news of his homecoming. At the same time he asked them to procure a testimonial, and have it ready so that he could use it on his arrival in Madrid, together with the document he had brought with him from Algiers. Finally—hardest of all—he had no choice but to beg them to send him some financial help since he had come back penniless.

During these two months in Valencia, Cervantes gathered his first detailed information about the state of Spanish affairs.

The great political problem of the day was the succession to the crown of Portugal. Shortly after King Sebastian's death in the battle of Alcazarquivir, his aged uncle, Cardinal Enrique, had died. Since there was no direct heir, several claimants to the vacant throne came forward. In the first place there was Antonio, the Prior of Crato, an ambitious and dissolute young man who could claim to be a descendant of King Manoel and was supported by a large part of the nation. But there were other factions as well, and the country was on the brink of anarchy. King Philip II was one of the claimants with a legitimate title to the succession—he was the son of King Manoel's eldest daughter—and he was, of course, the most powerful among them. He briefed his foreign envoys, sent a sharp note to the Pope, who wished to incorporate the kingdom in his own possessions, and instructed his ambassador in Portugal, Don Cristóbal de Moura, to put his just cause before the Portuguese nobles.

For Philip this was a unique opportunity to realize an old Spanish dream, the unification of the peninsula under the crown of Spain, and to acquire for his realm the country then held to be the richest of Europe. He was convinced that God had chosen him to achieve this great aim. Nobody could accuse him of duplicity, since he had done his best to dissuade young Dom Sebastian from his hare-brained crusade in Africa. For this very reason, the course of events seemed to Philip the work of Divine Providence: it was willed that Portugal should be united with Spain. Don Cristóbal de Moura argued on similar lines with the grandees of Portugal; the diplomatic campaign was launched.

Not all, however, accepted this reasoning or thought the King's claim legitimate. Philip therefore summoned the Duke of Alba —Alba was in retirement and in disgrace, but at this juncture the King conveniently forgot the reasons for it, even though he did not forgive them—and appointed him commander of the army which he sent against Portugal. Philip himself went to Badajoz, close enough to the centre of action to make his official entry into Lisbon at the most opportune moment.

*

On the eve of Christmas, Cervantes came back to Madrid after ten years' absence. He found his family in dire poverty. Their efforts to raise funds for the ransom of the two brothers had finally ruined them past remedy. Miguel's sister Andrea had lost her husband, the Florentine Ovando, and lived in an apartment by herself, together with her daughter, Constanza de Ovando. His brother Rodrigo, now an ensign in the regiment of Don Lope de Figueroa, was serving with the army in Portugal. Only his parents and his sister Magdalena were in their old home to welcome Miguel. Magdalena had lost all interest in affairs of the heart and devoted herself to religious duties and prayer. Both his parents were old and ailing; even his mother, once so lively, had lost her verve, although the return of her favourite son, the pride and hope of the family, may have raised her spirits. He, after all, had faith in himself. Yet as Cervantes went round to see old friends and make new contacts, he began to experience a vague uneasiness in spite of his high hopes, in spite of the peace Madrid gave him after the torment of Algiers.

People spoke of nothing but the story of Escobedo, Pérez and the Princess of Eboli. The mystery in which it was still shrouded added to the fascination. Above all, it was the personality of the proud, reckless, unfortunate Princess which provided the gossips with endless material.

Ana, Princess of Eboli, was the daughter of a Viceroy of Peru, Diego Hurtado de Mendoza. When she was no more than sixteen, she was married to Ruy Gómez de Silva, later Prince of Eboli. It was whispered that he owed his immense influence at Court mainly to the fact that his young wife became the King's mistress. In her youth, Ana had been considered one of the loveliest women of Madrid. Even now, in 1580, when she was a widow in her forties, mother of ten children, one-eyed and with the empty eye-socket covered by a piece of black taffeta, she was remarkably attractive. Even more than for her beauty, she was famed for her intelligence and sparkling wit. While her elderly husband was still alive, the élite of the Court had flocked to the receptions in the Ebolis' town palace, there to dance, to discuss literature and politics, to chatter and intrigue—and to give fresh food for gossip. At that time Antonio Pérez and Escobedo had both been servants in the princely household.

The Princess, no doubt, wished to play at Philip's side the same rôle that certain famous Frenchwomen played in the lives of French monarchs. It is practically certain that she was the King's mistress for a time. Yet the attitude of Philip II of Spain towards women and sentiment differed notably from that of a Francis I. Whenever he had a love affair, he conducted it with the utmost discretion and broke it off immediately there was the faintest hint of scandal, the least indication of possible harm to his royal dignity or personal independence. The Princess, on the other hand, was a woman of strong passions. Having been greatly spoilt as a child and young girl, she took it for granted when adult that she could dominate, command and rule by the sheer power of her spirited tongue and her beauty. In the austere, almost monastic style of life affected in sixteenth-century Spain she was never quite at home. Her glittering talents would have burgeoned in the greater licence of the French or Italian Courts; in her own country she was a misfit, and soon the target of every pernicious rumour. While the strictures of good Madrid housewives only spurred her on to still greater defiance and insolence, the King's disdainful attitude exasperated her beyond measure. It may well be that this sense of being slighted by the King drove her into the arms of Antonio Pérez, her former servant who had come to be the first man in Spain next to the King. Not only did he serve her as an instrument of vengeance, but his bold ambition matched and complemented her own. Before long, a new wave of rumours spread, until nothing was too vile for people to say about her. Her reaction was to give free rein to her importunate pride, and to play the dangerous game of provoking one and all, which in the end ruined her. Thus the most brilliant woman of her era became a restless intriguer who, in the last resort, did not shrink from crime.

The vehemence of her feelings is most clearly expressed in a letter in which she asked the King to act as her avenger upon her chief enemy, Mateo Vázquez, for, "if the sovereign failed to do it, she herself was willing to make an end of that man, even if it meant that she would have to stab him dead in the presence of His Majesty."

Although he dared not come out into the open, Mateo Vázquez had espoused the cause of Escobedo's relatives, who were tireless in their efforts to unmask the man responsible for their kinsman's murder. Vázquez, the King's second secretary, sought not so much to see that justice was done, but to destroy his rival, the first secretary, whom the King preferred to him, and whose superior intelligence and political skill had often led to Vázquez's humiliation. This time, private interest happened to coincide with the interests of justice. Unless he wanted to risk the possibility that Pérez might recover from his setback and destroy his enemies, he had to destroy Pérez himself. Therefore Vázquez was very thorough in his investigations; he approached all those whom Pérez had ever offended, and there were many of them, including people in powerful positions such as the Duke of Alba. While Pérez was still at the height of his influence, nobody had dared to stand up to him, but now, when they saw the King wavering in his attitude to his first secretary, they all suddenly found courage.

Philip at first assumed that the campaign concerned nothing

I

more than Escobedo's death, to which he himself held the key—
as he thought. For this reason he did not let the denunciations
go any further. Gradually, however, more and different evidence
against Pérez piled up on the King's desk. Though it went
against the grain, Philip had to admit that his secretary had
abused his confidence. Even then he showed no change in attitude towards Pérez, but continued to work with him on the state
papers. One day he even gave Pérez a list of accusations which
Mateo Vázquez had submitted on behalf of all the others. Pérez
defended himself with his usual dexterity. He belittled his
accusers and insinuated that their action was dictated by mere
envy, because the King was gracious enough to show him favour.
The King gave no answer, and Pérez continued in his post.

Nevertheless it was true that the King was wavering, and more
than wavering. Every day that passed showed more clearly that
his gravest doubts were justified. Soon he knew every detail of
the scene in the Princess's apartments. The inconceivable had
happened: he had been betrayed by the man in whom he had
placed his trust. Hitherto Philip had disliked the Princess because
of her provocative insolence. Now his dislike turned to furious
hatred. On one occasion, when letters she had written to her
lover—letters which, according to her accusers, contained ugly
insults against the King—were put before him, Philip gave the
order to destroy them unread.

Finally the King was forced to come to a decision. It was impossible to let things drift on. As always when faced with an
important decision—that concerning Don Carlos was a case in
point—he withdrew to the Escorial. He went there to confess,
take Holy Communion, and confide in God, as he said, "so
that He should enlighten me and guide me in this business, and
so that during the Easter days I should arrive at the best resolve
in the service of God and for the peace of my conscience". By
the time Easter was over, Philip had made up his mind. He had
decided on the fate of Antonio Pérez and the Princess of Eboli.

In Portugal, the situation had developed just as the King had
anticipated, and he would soon have to go there himself. He

wrote to Cardinal Granvelle, his representative with the Pope, and bade him to come to Madrid at once. He considered it best to entrust Granvelle, who had won his confidence by his handling of the Flemish problem, with the government of Spain during his absence, and thereby remove Antonio Pérez from his post in a roundabout fashion. On August 20, 1580, Granvelle arrived in Madrid. Nobody was aware of the purpose of his visit.

The Princess alone seems to have had an inkling of what the King had in mind, for that same evening she hurried to her lover's house, only to find the door locked. After remaining in the vicinity for some time, she returned to her palace. She was never to see Pérez again. Before midnight struck, Antonio Pérez and the Princess of Eboli were detained by order of the King. The secretary was confined in the house of Don Alvaro García de Toledo, the Alcalde of Madrid, where he had been arrested. The Princess, however, was imprisoned in the tower of Pinto Castle, three leagues from Madrid.

The news caused an enormous sensation in the capital. But most people knew no more than that something had happened to rouse the King's intense displeasure, and so all kinds of wild rumours spread. It was said that the Princess's palace had been the centre of a conspiracy against the Throne; that she and Pérez had plotted to marry a son of hers to a Braganza, another pretender to the Portuguese crown; that Pérez had boasted of having stolen the King's mistress from him. The words which the Princess had used to denigrate the King in Escobedo's presence were repeated with glee. Some predicted that Pérez would be executed without further ado, others that he would be banished from the country, and still others that he would be clever enough to ingratiate himself anew with the King. Nobody saw through Philip's real intentions. Pérez himself was not without hopes. After all, the King had summoned him to the royal palace again, even after his detention and while he was nominally confined in the Alcalde's house.

Philip was in Badajoz, and about to cross into Portugal to take possession of the kingdom as soon as peace was restored,

Granvelle was the regent of Spain—a warning circumstance, which Pérez would have done well to note—and the first secre- tary was handling the state papers together with him. On the surface everything appeared normal. Antonio Pérez may have thought that the conquest of Portugal would make the King forget, or ignore, all that had happened; that the King would find him indispensable; that the affection born of so many years of close collaboration would sway him. Should all those hopes prove abortive, there was still the fact that he, Pérez, shared so many grave secrets with the King.

As we have seen, however, when his duty—or what he con- ceived to be his duty—was involved, Philip was capable of setting even his paternal feelings aside. There was all the more reason to expect him to ignore the bonds between him and a trusted collaborator, when more than duty, when his honour as a sovereign and a man was involved. It was strange that Pérez should have stayed on, blindly self-confident to the last, only to find himself the defendant in a dramatic lawsuit and trial.

It has never been fully established what was the real substance of that "shady affair", as it has been called. The documents relating to the legal investigation and trial were destroyed. When the Chief Justice of Aragon—Pérez finally managed to seek asylum in the Kingdom of Aragon, where legal procedure was independent of the King's Court—asked Philip II of what crimes the defendant was accused, the reply was: "I say that the crimes of Antonio Pérez are the gravest anyone could commit against his King and Master." When the Chief Justice insisted that those crimes should be specified, Philip answered: "I cannot say more, without touching upon secrets which must never be revealed, because they concern a person whose reputation is more important than the sentence against that man." These cryptic statements, the fury with which the King persecuted the guilty pair, and the character of the accusations which have come down to us, are the only indications we have as to the contents of the destroyed legal documents.

Doubtless they referred, among other things, to the murder of

Escobedo. Facts about the preparations for it, the identity of the assassins and their rewards, had been ferreted out. There was evidence to prove that Don Juan of Austria's secretary had not been sacrificed in the higher interest of the State but in the personal interest of Pérez and the Princess of Eboli. Another point that was raised was Pérez's bad faith in dealing with Don Juan; this was amply proved when the ciphered letters were compared with the transcripts Pérez had produced. Perhaps Don Juan's death was investigated, though all we know about this is that certain suspicions were bruited about. In any case, the general conclusion was inescapable: the King's favourite had been perfidious, and the King of Spain, so jealous of his royal prerogatives, had been his credulous tool.

*

Cervantes came back to his native Madrid in the middle of all this. We may assume that there were two aspects which most impressed him. Firstly, the revelations about the fate of Don Juan; only then did Cervantes understand how desperately sad the young general's end had been. And secondly, there was the depressing inference that the prudent, cautious Philip II had been living in an atmosphere of deceit and treachery.

The moral degradation of the protagonists, which was uncovered by the *affaire* Pérez, made a nauseating impression. Cervantes may have told himself "Guarda e passa", look and pass by, as Virgil told Dante in the Inferno when they saw the wretched beings damned for having lived only for themselves. In that morass of selfish passions, there was only one figure to move the poet to pure pity: that of the poor old slave-woman, Escobedo's cook, who had been caught between the cog-wheels of the intrigue and was hanged in the main square of Madrid, innocent of any crime.

21
Portugal

It did not take Cervantes long to discover that in Madrid his out-look was exceedingly poor. The antechambers of the mighty were filled with other veterans, who showed their scars and begged to be rewarded for their services in wars—which were forgotten. There was a pervading atmosphere of poverty and neglect. He felt that his place was not among those pitiful hangers-on.

The man who first suggested to Cervantes that his future lay in Portugal may have been Juan Rufo, another hero of Lepanto, who at that time was working on his epic poem of the battle. As soon as Portugal was mentioned, Cervantes was all en-thusiasm. Every ambitious Spaniard had his eyes on that land. Under the new government the entire public services were being overhauled and manned with new personnel. There was a great shortage of gifted and honest men who were not only loyal ser-vants of the King, but also acceptable to the Portuguese, and sympathetic towards the country. Cervantes felt that he was exceptionally well equipped for the task, and he thought he would find strong support among the King's entourage.

There was, for one, Mateo Vázquez. Cervantes preferred to gloss over the fact that Vázquez had ignored his letters from Algiers: after all, the King's secretary was snowed under with letters and applications. But even should Vázquez fail him, there was still Don Antonio de Toledo, the Duke of Alba's brother, and Cervantes' friend in the bad days of Algiers. He was now with the Court in Portugal. Surely he would remember their common danger in the cave of Hassan's garden, and how Cervantes had risked his life to protect his comrades?

Cervantes did not yet realize how easily a man's head is turned by homage, adulation, and a position of power. But time was to teach him this lesson, for later he made his Don Quixote say: "Take care, Sancho, high office changes people's habits; it may well be that, once a Governor, you will no longer know the mother who bore you."

Full of confidence, Cervantes waited for the last of the papers which would help him to establish his claim to a post. Meanwhile he was a frequent guest in literary and theatrical circles, where he found people who still remembered him. In those days there was a fashion for recitals of unpublished works; indeed, more works were made known in that way than by print. Cervantes made the most of the situation, declaiming the poems he had written in Algiers, possibly also fragments of dramas, and listening in his turn to rising young poets reciting their works. This contact with Madrid's intellectual life revived his longing to be a writer. He began to study the new literary trends, and to read the most popular books.

Pastoral novels were much in vogue. The genre had been imported from Italy, through tanslations from Sannazaro, and had ousted the novels of chivalry, in particular among the intellectuals who eagerly adopted the new aesthetic ideal. The last great success was Gil Polo's *Diana*, a work that had been even more acclaimed than the *Diana* of the Portuguese writer Montemayor, published a few years earlier; both were imitations of Sannazaro's *Arcadia*, which Cervantes must have read while he was in Italy. He now felt that he had to make up for the lost years, to draw abreast of the times. And a pastoral novel, *La Galatea*, began to take shape in his mind. It was, no doubt, a concession to current taste; but it also derived from his deep-rooted belief in an ideal life, which disillusionment had not yet destroyed.

During these months in Madrid, Cervantes occasionally went to see his favourite sister, Andrea. She was a staunch realist. Though Miguel may have tried to dazzle her with his prospects, in which he believed so firmly, she would not allow herself to be carried away by his oratory. "Miguel may achieve something of what he wants to do—or he may not...", she would say. And maybe she would introduce the name of Doña Catalina de Salazar, a gentlewoman from Esquivias, who seems to have been a distant family connection. The quiet, pale young woman had once met Miguel in Andrea's house and had listened to him entranced. She was rich and came from an excellent family— surely Miguel had not forgotten her? We can picture him smiling at his sister's sly hint. Later, when his self-confidence had taken a severe jolt, he was to fall back on the suggestion; but at this moment, the mere thought of sharing his existence with that colourless girl, whose narrow world did not extend beyond her family, her land and her rambling old house, went against the grain. It was not long before he was on his way to Portugal, together with a friend, Rodrigo de Chaves.

In Portugal, the Duke of Alba's troops were finishing the task which Don Cristóbal de Moura's skilful diplomacy had initiated. The adherents of the Prior of Crato were everywhere defeated, except in the Azores. King Philip II was on his way to Tomar, where he had summoned the Cortes because an epidemic was raging in Lisbon, the capital.

Cervantes' actions on his arrival at the Court are a matter for conjecture. It has been assumed by some that he rejoined Lope de Figueroa's regiment and took part in the expedition against the Azores. Yet this assumption rests entirely on a few vague words of Cervantes, which can be interpreted, with greater justification, as a disingenuous turn of phrase he used to render more effective an application he was drafting. It seems most improbable that he would have taken such pains to establish his qualifications in a series of documents, and to mobilize strong protectors at Court, if all he wanted was to re-enlist as a simple soldier. In any case, he had never felt strongly drawn to an army career, even though he had done more than his duty in the ranks; and whatever devotion he might have felt at the beginning had since cooled off. It was natural that he should now seek to obtain

an appointment, preferably at the Court, which would relieve
him from financial worry, give him the opportunity to distinguish
himself, and in due course leave him free to devote himself to a
literary career.

In this purpose he neither quite failed nor succeeded. He was
entrusted with a secret mission, whether through the good services
of Mateo Vázquez or of Don Antonio de Toledo, we do not
know. It was no sinecure, and not a task to arouse his enthusiasm, but he accepted it, perhaps on the strength of a half-
promise of better employment after his return.

In reality Cervantes was side-tracked. The outcome was that he
was sent away from the Court, where only mediocrity was considered safe and where he had turned up at an inopportune
moment to remind certain people of an old friendship which
could only be a source of embarrassment to them. His mission
was not without importance, and not without danger. He was
to sail to Oran and go from there to Mostaganem with papers
and confidential instructions for the Alcalde of the fortress. This
meant returning to North Africa, whence he had not long ago
escaped with so much difficulty, and cruising in coastal waters
where the Turkish corsairs were a constant peril. The risk he
would run was obvious; but Cervantes never shrank from danger.
As soon as he was briefed for his mission and had the papers for
Mostaganem he went to Cadiz, the port where he was to embark
for Oran. The Naval Paymaster at Cadiz, Lope Giner, paid
him—on a written order signed in Tomar—fifty *escudos*. This
was half of the sum allotted for travel expenses. The second fifty
was payable on Cervantes' return. He appears to have accomplished his mission, and was fortunate enough to be back in time
to see Philip II's entry into Lisbon on July 31, 1581.

*

The Portuguese capital extended a gala welcome to its new
King, whatever discontent its inhabitants may have felt underneath the festive clothes. Philip made his entry with solemn

pomp, bearing sceptre and crown, but as a conqueror rather than as a sovereign. At the same time he made a few gestures calcu-lated to please his new subjects: instead of his accustomed black garb, he wore shimmering brocade, and he had his beard trimmed in the Portuguese fashion. Back in Spain his subjects rarely caught a glimpse of him, but in Lisbon he showed himself all the time, on the promenade, at festivals, at receptions—it was a painful duty, but he saw it through. If Paris was worth a Mass to Henry IV, the rich kingdom of Portugal was worth a sacrifice of personal habits to Philip II.

His triumph in Lisbon found the King stricken in body and mind. On his way to Portugal he had fallen gravely ill and though he had recovered, the same illness had taken the life of his fourth wife, Anne. Within a short space of time he lost two of his children by her; in the middle of the celebrations in Lisbon he heard from Madrid that Prince Diego, his heir-presumptive, had died. And he himself had already developed the first symptoms of the grim disease which was to leave him in constant pain until the day of his death. Bald-headed, his beard snow-white, his features haggard and lined, he rode through the streets and tried to thank people for their homage with a smile that his sombre face wore strangely. He was a sad and lonely man. With the exception of his two daughters by Isabella of Valois— the only beings to whom he sometimes opened his heart—all those dear to him were dead; those he had trusted had betrayed him; he no longer believed in anybody. And yet, to his two daughters he wrote regularly, as soon as he was back in his apartments, letters full of a melancholy tenderness and an intimate feeling which no one would have expected in one so stern and ruthless.

Philip's empire was everywhere showing cracks. Flanders was aflame, Italy a hive of unrest, France was hostile, and an even graver threat came from distant England. In spite of all, in this glorious hour Philip was conscious of his own and his nation's greatness. "Decadence, too, has its plenitude", a foreign his-torian has commented, adding, "This was a supreme moment for Spain, such as had hardly ever come to another nation." The most ambitious conqueror can ask no more.

The conquest, however, was not quite complete. The Azores were still upholding the pretender, Antonio. England had pledged her discreet support to his faction, and France had even come out into the open: it was reported that a naval squadron had left French ports to come to the assistance of the besieged islands. Philip concentrated his fleet in Lisbon and put in command of it the Marquis of Santa Cruz, "thunderbolt of war, father to his soldiers, fortunate and undefeated captain", as Cervantes described him. Though lame, ailing and advanced in years, the Marquis unhesitatingly responded to the royal summons. On June 29, 1582, the King reviewed ships and troops before the squadron sailed for the Azores.

*

Cervantes had seen his brother Rodrigo and many old comrades depart for new battles, and it had stirred up memories of his own exploits. But he stayed on in Lisbon, letting things take their course. This time inactivity was wholly delightful, not only because life in the Portuguese capital was easy and pleasant, but also because there was nothing to disturb his peace of mind. He was convinced that sooner or later he would be given the post of which there had been talk—or a promise, as he saw it—before he left on his mission to Algeria. He had satisfactorily accomplished this task and had been paid the balance of fifty *escudos* due to him, so that he was not short of money either. It was festival time in Lisbon, and Cervantes opened his heart to all the beauty around him. He felt buoyant and happy. "Lisbon is a great city." . . . The banks of the Tagus "are an earthly paradise". . . . The beauty of Portuguese women called forth his "admiration and love", the Portuguese language was "the sweetest he had ever heard". . . . "I can say no more than that, if the Elysian Fields are to be found anywhere on this earth, it is here. . . ." Never before had he been so brimming over with gaiety.

The carefree existence of which he had dreamed so often became a reality during this bright interlude, the happiest time of his life. His mood spilled over into the pages of the book he was writing. He lived an idyllic existence on two planes, that of his poetic imagination, and that of real life—for he was in love. Was she a certain Portuguese lady, in later years a nun in the Trinitarian Convent of Madrid, as has been conjectured? Or was she the elusive Ana Franca? It does not matter. Whoever the woman may have been, it is evident that through her Cervantes was able to recapture the enchanted mood of Naples. "For feasting— Milan, for loving—Portugal", he said later, as though still savouring the honey of a sweet memory.

In quieter hours he worked with astonishing speed at his novel which, so he thought, would make him famous, and in which he sought to enshrine the gossamer beauty of those days in Lisbon. So Galatea came to life, "a shepherdess born on the shore of the Tagus, unrivalled in beauty and virtue"—in fact, Dulcinea's sister.

This first work of Cervantes is not a great book, but it had kindness and purity, a candid tenderness, and a wealth of illusion, all of which mirror the poet's feelings at this time. It betrays far more of his psychology than of his genius. The action takes place in an imaginary republic governed by the laws of love and friendship, above all of friendship. The landscape is modelled on the charming valley of the Tagus, with features deriving from Italy, Corsica and Sardinia, and from Miguel's childhood in Alcalá de Henares. It is an Arcadian world. All property is communal, every grief and every joy is universally shared. The men are always ready to give their lives for a friend. When Salerio sees his best friend being led to his death, he promptly draws his sword and falls upon the executioners. People live and die for friendship as much as they live and die for love. If one friend gives a promise to another, it has the ring of passionate sincerity.

In his last work, the *Persiles*, Cervantes returned to this ideal. Thus his early manhood and his old age, *La Galatea* and *Persiles*, are linked by a yearning for harmony and friendship. It was a lifelong yearning. In short, the spiritual climate of *La Galatea* was not so much the product of literary considerations as of an inward necessity. Diego Benavides, one of the twelve Spaniards in Algiers who contributed an account of Cervantes' conduct to the composite memorandum, provides a case in point: he came to Algiers equipped with a friend's letter of introduction to Cer-vantes to whom he was a complete stranger. At once Cervantes behaved towards him as "father and mother". True to his conception of friendship, he took Benavides home, gave him shelter and food, offered money and clothing. If *La Galatea* is imbued with the highest ideals of friendship, courtesy towards women, love for all creation, and a joyful response to life, this is truly somewhat more than a sentimental fiction which happened to be in fashion.

Nevertheless, *La Galatea* is not a well-written novel. Its pace is unbearably slow, its dialogue unnatural and prolix. The shep-herds all seem to have graduated from Alcalá de Henares, if not from the great university of Salamanca, for they have read Plato or at least León Hebreo. The style is diffuse, cumbersome, adorned with those dreadful "colours of rhetoric" for which Cervantes had unfortunately been praised by his old tutor in Madrid, López de Hoyos. That was exactly what the current literary taste demanded, though the day was to come when Cer-vantes himself would ridicule it. Only here and there, in descrip-tions, in the underlying sentiment, in a few essentially dramatic scenes, and in some wise, elegantly phrased thoughts, the poet's hidden power breaks through the artificial shell.

The novel tells of love and hate, joy and tears; but the tears are gentle, and the hate is softened by pity. Happiness brims over, grief finds relief in song. At dusk, shepherds and shepherdesses meet in the sheepfold to talk about love, the beloved's indifference, the lover's jealousy. By moonlight they make merry in the pasture and sing to the sound of shepherd's flute and three-stringed fiddle, while the old people tell legends of bygone days.

This peaceful idyll did not, however, quite satisfy Cervantes.

There were other sentiments he felt the need to express, even if it meant spoiling a beautiful passage.

In an episode based on Sannazaro and on reminiscences of ancient pagan rites surviving in Sardinia, he first described an annual pilgrimage to the grave of a young shepherd. The older men recall his virtues, his constancy in love and his faithfulness in friendship, which brings tears to the eyes of the younger ones. Then night falls and "a soothing silence spreads over the whole sacred valley". The tired shepherds rest. Suddenly a great flame shoots up out of the darkness and quiet above the tomb. As they gaze with wonderment and awe into the dazzling flame, they see a lovely apparition. It is the Muse Calliope—and the poetry of the scene evaporates, for she launches into a long, tedious speech. Finally she chants to the music of her lyre a song of praise, a song with pedantic detail but without charm, which enumerates every Spanish poet in Spain, Flanders, Italy and America. She eulogizes each in turn, irrespective of his merit; the least dis‑tinguished is compared to Homer, Dante or Virgil, and the greatest of the young poets, Lope de Vega, is given no higher praise than others who are long since forgotten. In his enraptured state, Cervantes wished to include one and all in his hall of fame. His heart, not his critical mind, dictated this clumsy peroration to his Muse.

22

Failure

BEFORE long he was back in Madrid. The annexation of Portugal was a fact, the new administration was installed, all the posts were filled; and there had been no place for Cervantes. The last ducats had slipped through his fingers, as money was to slip through his fingers all his life. Penniless and unemployed, he had to take refuge with his parents once again. The Portuguese dream had dissolved.

We may assume that he had been encouraged to return to Madrid by another vague promise of a job waiting for him there. If so, disappointment came quickly, even before he had finished his novel and while he was pinning his faith on a new hope, that of making good as a dramatist.

Cervantes found himself a failure in peace-time, as he had been, in sober truth, a failure in his army career. Once again he was haunted by the suspicion he had felt long ago, when he had left Acquaviva's little court: "I am not cut out for the Court." This time the implications were far more serious. For he had to admit to himself that in this world of sordid intrigues and soaring ambitions his code of friendship and loyalty went for nothing. Men who had battened on his courage when in mortal peril in Algiers, and who now were wealthy and prosperous, had no wish to revive those memories but coolly left him in the lurch. If he called on them, he was fobbed off with one of those vague promises. To make life easier for himself he would have to humble himself day in, day out, before a number of influential gentlemen. But this he could never do. At long last the mortifying knowledge dawned on him that his real testing time would be here and now in Madrid: his bitter struggle against misery and want which had just begun was to be a greater trial than those five years in Algiers.

Even in his home he felt a failure. His parents, far from being in a position to help him, were themselves in need of help. His mother looked at him sadly, as a mother may look at the son of whom she had once had the highest expectations but who seems with every passing day less likely to fulfil them.

For Cervantes this was one of the turning-points in his life. The foundations of his most cherished beliefs were being under-mined and he felt himself an outcast in a harsh and alien world.

He was to transpose this devastating experience into the scene in *Don Quixote* in which the good Knight, emerging from the cave of Montesinos with all its wonders, has a brief glimpse of reality as others see it and is for the first time mocked by his squire, Sancho. Don Quixote is assailed by doubt; he feels as if his whole beautiful world were threatening to collapse. But the moment passes. Don Quixote—and Cervantes—will never re-nounce their illusions. Quiet, Sancho! Don Quixote needs to dream and go on dreaming, otherwise he ceases to exist. To save one's soul, one has to inhabit two worlds, set illusion against reality, believe stubbornly in one's dream, make this dream live and endure. Thus a princess is fashioned out of a country wench, a castle out of a cottage, a palace out of the cave of Montesinos, heaven out of earth—and the dream is sustained.

Cervantes went on dreaming, but doubt had seeped into his mind. Never again was he to lose his profound melancholy, never again was he to be certain of his steps.

*

In the depth of their poverty, the Cervantes family clung to their rank in the social hierarchy, and the high-sounding title "Don" was never missing when one of their names appeared in a document. On a September day in 1583, Don Miguel de Cervantes pawned to the Genoese broker Napoleon Lomelin five pieces of yellow-and-red taffeta hangings for the sum of thirty ducats. He did it in the name of his sister Magdalena, but the taffeta seems to have been part of the gift his other sister, Andrea, had received from Signor Locadelo years before. Much of Andrea's dowry had gone into the ransom for Miguel, now the rest went to help him in his desperate financial straits, although Andrea herself lived in poverty. Yet, helpful as she always was, Andrea had few illusions about her brother's prospects. As a practical woman, she seized upon the most opportune moment to revert to her little plan for a suitable match, which had earned her Miguel's smile on the eve of his departure for Portugal.

He may have met Doña Catalina again in Madrid, through his sister, or he may have gone to see her in Esquivias, her estate. We do not know. We know that she was very young at that time, scarcely nineteen, and we like to imagine that she was lovely.

To judge by such details of her actions and behaviour as have come down to us, Doña Catalina de Salazar was Miguel's opposite in character. There was much of the knight-errant and the vagrant in him; she was wholly engrossed in her home and her family traditions. And yet she fell in love with him. Andrea's fascinating tales about her brother had had the desired effect, they had played upon the young girl's feelings. Miguel sensed her affection as soon as he spoke to her. What was he to do? The ink had scarcely dried on the pages of his *Galatea*, and he was still dreaming of life on a higher plane, of the language of the heart, of an ideal woman: Dulcinea. But what about the real world, as opposed to that of his imagination? He was nearing forty, crushed by disappointments, with an uncertain, unpromising future before him. And this girl was wealthy. She owned land, and the old chests in the manor might well be filled with doubloons. Above all, she loved him. Cervantes may have begun his courting out of self-interest, but her devotion touched him and he soon grew fond of her. Her family's opposition added a dash of spice. He made up his mind to marry her.

Doña Catalina saw him as a mature man of noble bearing,

K

whose tired features added to his attraction in her eyes. He had been in foreign countries, spoke with marvellous fluency, and was surrounded by the aura of a heroic legend. No doubt, Andrea had forgotten neither to embroider her brother's adventures nor to dwell on the success his plays had recently had on the stage in Madrid. Altogether it was quite enough to make the little girl from the provinces believe that she had met her ideal mate. Her sceptical relatives discovered that she was determined to follow this man, whom they saw in a very different light, and that their warnings only served to strengthen her resolve.

Before their marriage, however, Miguel had to sever relations with his last love, the mysterious Ana Franca (or Ana de Rojas, or Ana Franca de Rojas). As with other women who played a rôle in Cervantes' life, biographers and commentators have tried in vain to solve the riddle of her identity and to guess at the story behind the meagre facts at their disposal. Some suggest she had been his mistress in Lisbon, others, that he met her in theatrical circles in Madrid and had only a brief affair with her; some, that she was a great lady; others, that she was a little-known actress. Only two things are certain: that she had a daughter by Miguel, whose name figures as the child's father in all the documents, and that shortly after he broke with her she married a man called Alonso Rodríguez.

The secret of their relationship was well kept; Miguel's illegitimate child grew up in the household of Ana Franca and Alonso Rodríguez. Doña Catalina may have had an inkling of her bridegroom's recent entanglement, but she certainly was unaware of his daughter's existence, of which she first learnt many years later. Thus she went into her marriage with an untroubled mind.

Catalina de Salazar y Palacios and Miguel de Cervantes were married on December 12, 1584, in the little church of Esquivias. No relatives were present, neither his nor hers, a clear indication of the state of tension between the two families. It speaks highly of Doña Catalina's strength of will that she, a spoilt only daughter who had had a strict upbringing and whose young life had been spent entirely between the parental home and the confessional, married a man eighteen years her senior, in the teeth of her family's opposition. And if she did not bring him what he hoped for, it was because it was not within her power. All she had to offer she gave him.

On leaving the church, the couple had to face groups of villagers who had come to see the adventurer carrying off the young heiress. The majority of the onlookers were bound to believe that he was a good-for-nothing who had arrived out of the blue to turn an inexperienced girl's head and get hold of her fortune. Among them, very likely, was an old woman who had known Catalina since she was an infant in arms, and who, dabbing her eyes, mumbled: "Poor little girl!"

And this old woman, if indeed she existed, had good reason for her fears.

Before long Doña Catalina's desire for an austere home life clashed with Miguel's impulsive moods. He had no more intention of shutting himself up with her in the manor of Esquivias, of spending his time looking after the new vines in the vineyards, than she had of sharing his bohemian existence and following him wherever his dreams might lead him, in imagination or in reality. They had both been living in a fool's paradise.

With the same obstinacy with which she had opposed the wishes of her family before her marriage, Catalina now opposed her husband's wishes. She felt called upon to defend the family estate—her father had died some months before her marriage—and her settled way of life against his waywardness, his "lunacy". This was sufficient to rouse his inherent dislike of anything that smacked of imposition. Another illusion gone: instead of peace, he had warfare in his home, reproaches, sour looks and freezing silences from his wife. The manor house saw him less and less. The intervals between his visits to Esquivias grew longer, and each visit became shorter than the last, until it amounted—very quickly—to a separation.

Life had cheated them both.

23

The Stage

CERVANTES threw himself heart and soul into work for the stage. He was writing one drama after the other, as though he hoped thereby to drown his sense of frustration. In the year of his marriage, his first plays had been performed, with sufficient success to bring him several commissions for the next season and to launch him on ambitious theatrical experiments. If, in a moment of despondency, he had thought of building his future on Doña Catalina's property, he had ceased to entertain the idea even before he was disappointed in his marriage. He saw himself as a successful playwright, well able to stand upon his own legs. But he aimed high: he intended to restore dignity to the Spanish theatre. With a tragedy such as his *Numantia*, with *Jerusalem* and with the *Naval Battle*, his drama of Lepanto, he would sway the masses as Aeschylus and Euripides had done in ancient Greece, by extolling the virtues of his nation. Thus he would rescue the Spanish stage from the triviality and vulgarity which threatened to engulf it.

His *Galatea* had appeared in print in 1584. In the spring of 1585, several plays of his were produced in Madrid. So wholeheartedly did he concentrate on play-writing at this time that he churned out drama upon drama in quick succession. He still wrote poetry, but mainly occasional verse and eulogies. It was his nature to be generous with praise, but those effusions were also intended to attract the attention of people who counted. His was an uphill struggle, and he knew that he still had a long way to go.

In the intervals between work, he frequented the many literary circles where he had friends. He did not lack good companions who treated him with affection and esteem, rather more, perhaps, because of his personality than because of his literary achieve/ ments, even though *La Galatea* had earned him a certain renown and, in consequence, some envy. Yet Cervantes was not at ease in this set. Whatever they discussed—poetry, love stories, cur/ rent rumours—was always treated with levity. Every slander was gloatingly repeated. But there was poison in the anecdotes that caused so much malicious amusement.

The King was back in Madrid, therefore the Pérez/Eboli affair was again the main topic. The Princess of Eboli was imprisoned in the bleak, dank tower of Pinto Castle, but she was said to be haughtier than ever. She refused food, she refused to listen to advice, she even refused to hear Mass. All she did was to denounce the injustice she had suffered and to revile the King; all she thought of was her revenge on Mateo Vázquez. When the King's own Father Confessor came to Pinto to talk her into a better frame of mind, she told him "not to give her messages from the King, because she did not wish to hear them".

Meanwhile Pérez was strutting about in Madrid, still acting as the King's secretary, and still drawing his salary. His so/ called confinement in Alvaro García's house was a farce. He had his own apartment of twelve rooms, with two outside doors which were not guarded, so that he came and went as he pleased. But he was too sure of himself, and this was to be his downfall. With every day that passed, the judges working on the legal case against him found more evidence on which to convict him of double/dealing.

Cervantes was dismayed by the tone of the comments he heard. Nobody worried about the origins of the law/suit, or the villainy that had come to light, let alone the lessons to be drawn from it all. The only thing that counted was the entertainment value of this or that episode. He, for his part, wanted to get to under/ stand the causes of the trouble. But the nearer he came to under/ standing them, the more disheartened he felt. The attitude of this frivolous, unprincipled crowd angered him. He was at heart a

serious man with a strict sense of values, his mind conditioned by
those tense years in Algiers. He was made to feel an exile in his
own country, and at times even to look ridiculous. The new
intellectual and moral climate was breeding authors fit to prosper
in it. Nearly all of the new poets were men without a trace of
enthusiasm, whose studiously ambiguous and over-elaborate
works were a reflection of the time.

Cervantes himself was changing. At the literary gatherings a
different Miguel de Cervantes was beginning to make his appearance, a gloomy, short-tempered man whose writings were tinged
with an acid irony. There is nothing improbable in the assumption of some of his contemporaries that he was the author of a
scurrilous *letrilla*. Such a rhymed lampoon tallies with our picture of a new, sardonic Cervantes superimposed upon his true
candid self.

The worst blow he received in this period of his life was his
eclipse as a dramatist. Not only had he expected that his new,
promising literary career would be his salvation, he had also had
faith in his work. As so often when he thought to have success
within his grasp, it eluded him as though snatched away by some
maleficent spirit. This time, the mocking spirit took shape in the
person of a young man called Lope de Vega.

Lope had started as a brilliant lyrical poet and was now, at
twenty-one, turning to the stage. He had just returned from the
expedition against the Azores, in which he had taken part less
as a soldier than for the sake of the emotional experience. Now
he paraded his laurels through the streets of Madrid, accompanied
by a boisterous gang of young aristocrats whose impudent revels
and brawls set tongues wagging. It was astounding how skil-
fully Lope managed to divide his time between his writing,
making love to widows, married women and young girls, and
getting himself into trouble. As a young boy he had run away
from home "to see the world", and had tramped through half
Spain before he returned. Not unlike Cervantes in his youth, he
craved adventure and new experience. His greed for life and his
greed for fame were equally measureless. Not content with his

exploit in the Azores, he sailed five years later with the Great Armada against England, as usual followed by his boon com/ panions, the "greatest scatterbrains of Madrid". Patriotism, however, had little share in his actions. Lope de Vega was a child of the new era.

Handsome, with a natural elegance of manner, he went through life as a spoilt darling of fortune, with a characteristic mixture of pride, bravado and childish vanity. He was the nephew of a famous Inquisitor and liked to sport an aristocratic name. Physically and mentally he possessed every desirable accomplishment. He played musical instruments, was a good dancer, an excellent swordsman. And if his early poems had put the foremost elder poets in the shade, his plays immediately set a new fashion and pushed all other playwrights into the background.

As soon as he had encountered Lope, Cervantes acknowledged his title to fame. This needed no special insight. Lope de Vega was one of those privileged beings who have only to appear on the scene, in whatever guise, to convince the world of their mani/ fest gifts. That Cervantes should swell the chorus of praise everybody accepted as only natural and just, Lope himself included. Nevertheless a mutual aversion soon sprang up between the two.

Various reasons are put forward for their enmity. It has been blamed on Cervantes' attitude to Lope de Vega's youthful love affair with Elena Osorio. Elena was one of the most beautiful women in Madrid, and Lope, by his own reckoning, wrote some two thousand verses extolling her charms. She was a married woman separated from her husband, an actor. Her father, Jerónimo Velázquez, was a well/known actor/manager, her mother an actress; they had produced some of Cervantes' dramas, and he was a frequent guest in their house, apparently even an intimate friend. It has been suggested that Cervantes was some/ how involved in the Velázquez' original violent quarrel with their daughter's lover, young Lope. Certainly the wicked little verse about the affair which went the round of Madrid was attributed to Cervantes. It may also be that Ana Franca—on the assumption that she herself was an actress—added to the friction between the two men; in the narrow theatrical world of Madrid, Ana and Elena were bound to meet, and there may have been rivalry between them. In the end, Cervantes found himself re-placed by Lope in the Velázquez' favour. Impressed by the overwhelming success of Lope's comedies, they dropped their attitude of resentment against him—and dropped Cervantes. Soon not only they alone, but all directors of Madrid theatres ceased to be interested in plays by Cervantes. After all, they had to please their public, and their public clamoured for comedies by Lope, and those alone.

It was, however, no single factor which raised the permanent barrier between the two poets; it arose from their fundamentally different circumstances. Seen through Lope's eyes at that time, Cervantes was an ageing writer, querulous and sarcastic, who had written mediocre and sometimes even bad verse, a few plays which could not begin to compare with Lope's own, and one novel which was damned with faint praise. For the rest, he was a man with no known occupation, one of the thousands of ex-soldiers in Spain, making great play of the hand he had lost in a forgotten battle, complaining—again like thousands of others—about the neglect from which he suffered. In short, more or less a failure. The successful Lope, fully taken up with his own tumultuous life, had neither time nor inclination to bother with this Cervantes.

Cervantes, for his part, recoiled from Lope. He was never able to forget their early encounters; they left him with a bad after-taste. From now on, whenever their paths crossed, they kept their distance, at most bridging the gap with studied insults. Lope would hurl his dreaded poisoned darts, Cervantes would attack him covertly—and all the more cruelly—at the least oppor-tunity. Towards the end of his life he was to pay high tribute to Lope. Otherwise it is true to say that Cervantes acted towards Lope with a spitefulness and persistence, often unprovoked and un-justifiable, which make it difficult always to accept his good faith.

Thus the two greatest geniuses of their country and—next to Shakespeare—of their age, met, clashed, and went their opposite ways. Whereas Lope tended to ignore Cervantes, Cervantes remained constantly aware of Lope. Lope's fame reached its zenith very quickly, the fame of Cervantes grew with the centuries. Lope was prosperous, celebrated and envied. Cervantes, poor, inglorious and dogged by misfortune. What kept Lope aloof from Cervantes was his indifference to anything outside his personal orbit, and the fact that he was himself blinded by the success he achieved from the very start. What kept Cervantes aloof from Lope was pride, the consciousness of his own worth, and a sense of hurt dignity.

From now on, Cervantes was to go downhill, sometimes by slow degrees, sometimes almost rolling down. He was to lead a vagabond's life, do menial jobs, find himself destitute and abandoned, experience imprisonment, ruin and despair. At the same time Lope was to rise swiftly to dazzling glory, earn—and spend—money by the bucketful, behave as haughtily and munificently as a king; he was to be the favourite of the great, a nobleman among nobles, loved by women, courted by princes, the centre of adulation and applause. The life of which Cervantes dreamed fell like a ripe fruit into Lope's lap. Is it surprising that Cervantes, seeing his lucky rival lording it, while he himself was struggling with sordid misery, should have felt bitter and frustrated?

*

Lope's arrival banished Cervantes from the theatre. Not that Cervantes' plays had met with disapproval; he said himself that they had never earned him "rotten cucumbers or other appropriate missiles". But without having actually failed on the stage, his dramas had not evoked enthusiasm either—nor did they deserve it. As soon as Lope's comedies reached the public, Cervantes and other playwrights were swept aside. It was the end of Cervantes as a dramatist.

His withdrawal from the theatre was a defeat, and he recognized

it as such. Many years later, in 1614, when his *Comedias* appeared in print, he confessed in the prologue: "I left the pen and
the writing of plays; I had other things to do. . . ." With the
bitterness of the old disappointment assuaged, he added: ". . . and
immediately there appeared that Monster of Nature, the great
Lope de Vega, henceforward to rule over the theatre; he established his dramatic kingdom, converted all actors into vassals
under his jurisdiction, and began to flood the world with his
felicitous, well-constructed comedies."

Here Cervantes puts Lope's triumph chronologically after his
own renunciation of the stage. Still clinging to his old illusions,
and considering himself as great as Lope, in some respects even
greater, he did not wish to acknowledge his defeat. Yet Lope's
victory had not merely coincided with this defeat, it had contributed to it, and Cervantes was always acutely conscious of the
fact.

It is impossible to guess at the nature of the "other things"
Cervantes "had to do" after his failure as a dramatist, but we can
guess at the pressing problems he faced. The sky overhead had
darkened—as Cervantes said, "it had turned to bronze". His
last contracts for plays, such as the one with the actor-manager
Gaspar de Porras, were obviously concluded under the pressure
of his financial need. This pressure only grew as time went on.

To make his situation more painful, Miguel lost his father.
Thirty years before, in Valladolid, Don Rodrigo de Cervantes
had been in prison for his debts. Ever since, life had brought him
nothing but trouble. During his last illness, five days before his
death on June 13, 1585, he made his will. He bequeathed all
he had—though there was nothing to bequeath—to his children,
but even in death he relied on his wife to take the final decisions.
He asked to be buried "in the parish or monastery that seemed
best to his wife, Doña Leonor de Cortinas". Masses should be
said for him as selected by her and "wherever she pleased".
And he wanted to be accompanied by "the Cross, and the
priests, and the confraternities and friars his aforesaid wife would
choose, because all this he left to her free will and wish"—which

was no more than he had done in all life's difficulties. The poor old surgeon probably died wondering how he would manage in the Other World without his wife.

The documentary information about Don Rodrigo is scanty, and refers only to his weaknesses. All the same, one is made to feel that his good qualities—true kindness, a Christian spirit, and devotion to his family—made it easy for people to forgive him and remain fond of him. Miguel owed to his father the best and the worst in his own character. In his precarious situation, he felt his loss particularly deeply, but he had not much time for mourning or even sorrow. The needs of the day were too urgent. He had begun to produce a flood of petitions and to spend fruitless hours in the antechambers of those who were in a position, but did not wish, to help him. It was a mode of existence that continued until the end of his life.

Like Dante before him, he learnt "how bitter it is to eat the bread of strangers and wear out the stairs in strangers' houses":

> Tu proverai si come sa di sale
> lo pane altrui, e com'é duro calle
> lo scendere e il salir per l'altrui scale.
> E quel che più ti graverà le spalle
> sarà la compagnia malvagia e scempia
> con la qual tu cadrai in questa valle;
> di tutta ingrata, tutta matta et empia
> si farà contra te. . . .

You shall find out how salt is foreign bread,
  And find out too the going up and down
  An alien stair, how hard it is to tread.
But what shall weigh your shoulders most with sorrow
  Shall be the vile and vicious company
  That tumbles with you down into that hollow;
For mad, unjust, ungrateful shall they turn
  Against you. . . .[1]

---

[1] English version by T. W. Ramsey, Hand and Flower Press, 1952.

Passing through a similar ordeal, Cervantes was to put the same bitter lament into different words: "Fortunate he whom Heaven grants a piece of bread for which he is not forced to thank anyone but Heaven itself."

He, too, was to suffer from the ingratitude, envy and malice of the company he had to keep in "that hollow". But perhaps because he was less conscious of his spiritual nobility than the Florentine, less self-contained and less fiery, he never rose to such a gesture as the magnificent challenge to the powers-that-be in Dante's final apostrophe:

> ... *ma poco apresso*
> *ella, non tu, n'avrà rossa la tempia.*

"Their cheeks not yours because of it shall burn." ... Not so Cervantes. He was cowed by the ignominy, not exalted by it. And because he was riddled with doubt, his protest has a muffled sound.

24

Rearmament

FOR the second time in his life, Cervantes went to Seville, the beloved home of his boyhood, but now the city's gaiety cast no spell on him. He called it "shelter of the poor, refuge of the wretched", although he himself found, as yet, no shelter there. The purpose of his journey was business: he came to Seville as an agent for several Madrid trading houses, commissioned to collect outstanding debts for them, and soon returned to Madrid.

His short absence, however, somewhat improved his relations with his wife, perhaps because it gave Doña Catalina time to forget about his neglect of their home and their irreconcilable differences of temperament. The autumn of 1586 found Miguel in Esquivias. On October 25, he and Doña Catalina were godparents at the baptism of the son of Simón Fernández and Maria Romana in Esquivias church. For a short while their marriage seems to have been peaceful; it may have been that sheer necessity obliged Cervantes to adapt himself to his wife's wishes, at least while he was still struggling to find a way out of his critical situation.

It did not last. Before long he was back in Madrid, visiting Esquivias only on rare occasions. From his wife he had little help, and even less, of course, from his own relatives. Since his father's death, Miguel's mother and her daughters were living together again. They may have urged him to stay with them and give up his erratic way of life, but though he may have felt drawn to the idea, there was no rest for him. He had to chase after recommendations for the job for which he had applied—a menial job, for he was now far less demanding. He made the round of his friends in the hope that they might help him to achieve this modest aim. It was a sordid prospect, but the best he could hope for; he was about to descend yet another rung of the ladder, still without touching bottom. His ambitions as a writer were apparently buried—at all events, Lope de Vega reigned supreme, and people had forgotten about Cervantes and his plays.

In this year, 1586, the Spaniards had lost their taste for tittle-tattle because the grave problem of England fully occupied their minds. Philip II's half-hearted, veiled attempts to cow the enemy country had met with strong retaliation, with audacious acts of piracy, with intrigues and provocation. All Spain rose in protest. The grandees advised the King to take action against Queen Elizabeth. Philip, however, delayed a decision which all regarded as inescapable, partly because he had an innate reluctance to resort to arms, and partly because he was influenced by the maxim of his father, the Emperor Charles V: "Never lose England's friendship"—this friendship being necessary, if France was to be kept isolated. But England was heading the league of Protestant Powers, not so much for reasons of faith as for reasons of political expediency. Catholic Mary Stuart—Mary, Queen of Scots, who had been the remote goal of Don Juan's dreams—was still a prisoner, but from her castle she continued to write letters to the King of Spain in which she solicited his country's support in her struggle for liberty. This was a strong incentive for Philip: success on Mary Stuart's part, though admittedly becoming an ever more shadowy possibility, would have meant friendship between Britain and Spain, and an immense gain for the Catholic world. For Philip himself, as Don Juan had pointed out, it would have meant an immediate settlement in Flanders. It might have signified peace in Europe.

During recent months, the small island of which Philip II had once been King, through his marriage with Mary Tudor, had carried its audacity to intolerable lengths. English volunteers had gone to Flanders, with the connivance of their Government, and were fighting against Spain under the banner of the Prince of Orange. England had offered asylum to the Portuguese pretender, the Prior of Crato; promises and encouragement from England were fanning the resistance in Portugal. And from England—this was the hardest blow—Hawkins, Drake and their associates sallied forth to plunder the Spanish galleons. Their rich booty filled the coffers of the Queen of England and her ministers. Spanish complaints were countered with endless excuses, vague explanations, and declarations of goodwill by the Queen herself, which were at once nullified by new acts of piracy. In the judgment of one historian, "no other king would have shown so much patience as Philip II". This patience, however, only increased the pride and daring of England.

All this constituted a dark menace, comparable to the storm/ cloud that had threatened from the Orient in the days before Lepanto, and even more dangerous, since there was behind it the drive and energy of a young, rising nation, while Spain had no great generals to put in the field. Philip had every reason to ponder over his one/time subjects, the people of England, whose character had always been an enigma to him. Long past were the days when he and Mary Tudor had knelt in the transept of Winchester Cathedral and the congregation had called down God's blessing upon them; when after Mass the herald had pro/ claimed: "Philip and Mary, by God's Grace King and Queen of England. . . ."

Another memory came to haunt Philip, that of a pale, quiet young princess, even then an adept at hiding her feelings. He had saved her from the scaffold. When Dudley's conspiracy was uncovered—that plot to assassinate Mary and Philip and put Elizabeth on the throne—her death would inevitably have fol/ lowed, had he not intervened in her favour. This he had done in the hope of finding in her an ally who would help him to realize his future plans. It had been a false hope. She and her country were now forcing him into the most fateful decision of his life.

Tardily Philip decided to act. He sent for the Marquis of Santa Cruz, listened to his report on the state of the armed forces, and studied their potential. Then he set the old war lord the task of creating a fleet strong enough to sail against England. Preparations were to be carried out in the deepest secrecy. To the King the enterprise seemed comparatively easy, and the reports about the first English reactions to his rearmament, when spies brought news about it to London, confirmed him in his opinion. This grave miscalculation led to one of the greatest reverses in history.

Some people see in the disaster of the Great Armada the cause of Spain's fall from power. I cannot share their point of view. Spain's decline was a process, the defeat of the Armada was an incident. An incident, it is true, that accelerated the nation's fall, and was a national tragedy marking the dividing line between two periods in Spanish history. It marked the end of Spain's greatness, but this greatness had already been on the wane. Just as the battle of Lepanto did not cause, but only hastened, the ruin of Ottoman power, so the disaster of the Great Armada did not cause, but only accelerated, the ruin of Spain.

The main causes of Spain's setbacks in the Mediterranean area had been lethargy, lack of foresight, and negligence. They had grown into national weaknesses. Abroad, people began to say, "If death has to come to you from Spain, you have still many years to live". In every field, muddle and incompetence were rife. The Marquis of Santa Cruz, perhaps the only Spaniard to understand the full significance of the coming military action, spent his whole energy battling in vain against profiteering on the part of purveyors, corruption in the army, and the general carelessness over the planning and implementation of rearmament. When Santa Cruz went to Lisbon to inspect the supplies, he found that the purveyors had delivered faulty goods, that work was proceeding desperately slowly, and that the naval squadrons could not possibly be ready by the required date.

The King, who had taken so long to come to a decision, now began to show a feverish impatience otherwise foreign to him. He bombarded Santa Cruz with orders to launch the fleet at once, blamed him for the delays, and went so far as to appoint the Count of Fuentes special commissioner for the purpose of inspecting and investigating the state of the fleet in the ports. This was a bitter and undeserved humiliation for the old Marquis, who had given a lifetime's devoted service to his country. Then came new orders for the squadrons to sail, whatever their state of preparedness. These were followed by renewed reproaches in the harshest terms. Amid all this confusion, Santa Cruz died, worn out by the excessive strain or, in the words of a chronicler, "eaten up by so much sorrow". He was fortunate: he did not have to witness the expedition's end.

While the Spanish preparations progressed at a sluggish pace, measures against the threatening invasion were taken in England with great dispatch and in an upsurge of patriotic zeal, as soon as the Queen and her ministers realized that nothing could stop Philip from pursuing his plan and that the moment for diplomatic appeasement was past. It was the old, old story of David and Goliath—the giant, over-confident of his strength, who takes up the fight without circumspection, and his little adversary, who puts every ounce of energy into the struggle because he knows that his life is at stake. Only, in this instance the people of Spain believed that God was with Goliath, and that the outcome thus would reverse the Biblical story.

In 1586, when preparations for the naval expedition were well advanced, the Spanish Navy appointed a number of commissioners or commissaries who were to requisition food supplies for the ships' crews and the fighting contingents who were to go with the fleet. One of these commissaries was Cervantes. It was a shabby, inglorious job, in keeping with the prevailing atmosphere, but he accepted it as a lesser evil: the life he was leading was shabbier still. On one of the last days of the year, or it may have been one of the first days of 1587—we have no exact information—he departed again to take up the post he was to occupy for eight years. His mother and sisters remained in Madrid; Doña Catalina stayed in Esquivias with her own relatives. Miguel set out alone, to tackle "the most odious, difficult and thankless task of his life".

On his arrival in Seville, Cervantes took lodgings at the inn

L

in the Calle de Bayona where he had stayed during his last visit. He had known the landlord, Tomás Gutiérrez, in Madrid at a time when the latter was an actor and impresario. Gutiérrez had given up his theatrical activities and was devoting himself to running the highly successful inn he had established in Seville. It has been assumed in some quarters that Cervantes could afford to live at a hostelry which was considered one of the best in the city because the landlord was an intimate friend of his, their common love for the theatre constituting the bond. From a few words of gratitude written by Miguel it has been inferred that Gutiérrez was his protector and benefactor. Words of praise expressed by Cervantes, however, can never be accepted at their face value, for we know how lavish he was with eulogies. Gutiérrez did guarantee a ridiculously small sum, which Cervantes borrowed, but this can scarcely be taken as proof of a particularly close friendship. On the other hand, it is certainly true that Miguel's salary would not have been sufficient to pay for his board at a fashionable inn in Seville at the usual terms. In the absence of other evidence, I incline to the view that the ex-actor, wise to the ways of the world, took Cervantes in on easy terms because he hoped to benefit from his lodger's current employment—a hope that would have been justified in most instances, but not in Cervantes' case. When his situation became precarious, Cervantes had to move elsewhere. For a start, however, he made Gutiérrez's inn his headquarters. It was a good place from which to observe the life of Seville; it was situated between two popular centres, Las Gradas and Compás, abounding in hawkers, ruffians and street-walkers, but it was also frequented by many of the important travellers who came to Seville.

As soon as he had settled in, Cervantes reported to Diego de Valdivia, deputy to the Purveyor-General, Don Antonio de Guevara, to receive his instructions. And, one day, at the crack of dawn, the new commissary set out for the Andalusian country-side, astride an old nag in the manner of Don Quixote.

His first assignment took him to the town of Ecija. It was the commissaries' task to collect local contributions towards the large stocks of olive oil and grain which were needed for the impending expedition against England. Every township had been assigned its quota by royal decree. The Government, however, had fixed the official prices for nearly all commodities at a level below the current market prices. Moreover, the State paid—if at all—only after great delays. Such payments were made with gold from the Spanish possessions in America, if and when a ship with bullion managed to elude the English privateers.

Before a commissary was sent to a town, its authorities were notified as to the proportion of their quota in oil or grain that was expected from them on this occasion. It was their duty to collect the relevant quantities from the householders and have the total ready for the commissary to take over on arrival. But in practice things worked out differently. The constant demands and the uncertainty about payment exasperated the local people. A town might be ordered to deliver a fresh quota at a time when its last delivery was not yet paid for. Municipal administrations, not wishing to make themselves unpopular with the townspeople and not always above corruption, were wont to accept delivery of whatever they could obtain without pressure—which was very little—and to leave it at that. In these circumstances the office of a commissary became unpleasant and thorny for those who took their duties seriously. They were bound to come up against resistance, which sometimes developed into rioting. More than one commissary came home with a broken head.

If a commissary found on his arrival that the stock collected by the local authorities fell short of the quota, he would have to go from house to house with his clerk and a constable. They had the legal right to break into the domicile of anybody who had infringed the decree, to open all locked doors, to arrest and imprison anyone who offered resistance, and to search his premises, while the whole neighbourhood would look on and hurl abuse—or worse—at the officers.

In some instances civic or ecclesiastical bodies were themselves offenders, hiding and hoarding stocks they had bought on their own account, with a view to selling them at higher prices later on. This they were able to do by virtue of their official status; in the case of the clergy, the people feared excommunication if they raised any protest. In such cases a commissary had to resort to diplomacy, cajolery and negotiation—the velvet glove technique. Actually, most commissaries came to an arrangement with the authorities concerned. This suited both sides, the authorities because they were left to their devices, and the commissaries because they had their rake-off; to complete the quota, they then squeezed the ordinary people, on the proverbial principle that "cries from the humble are not heard in Heaven".

There were many protests against these evil practices. Counter-measures were attempted, without result, and at a later stage the King himself intervened. In a royal missive of 1593, Philip II spoke of "preventing the damages and extortions which the commissaries and constables of the purveyors to My galleys habitually inflict on vassals and peasants in Andalusia, in the course of requisitioning wheat, barley and other commodities needed for provisions, and which so far it has proved impossible to abolish in spite of many legal proceedings and stern sentences".

It was indeed a shabby job Cervantes had accepted. A commissary's pay was a pittance—most of them had their own ways and means of eking it out—and it was paid at irregular intervals, sometimes years after it was due. Apparently the Spanish Treasury took it for granted that commissaries would do something to help themselves, as in fact they did.

This was the situation into which Cervantes had blundered— he, with his honesty and good faith, his patriotism, his belief in his good name and honour, and other such outworn, old-fashioned ideas. He was foolish enough to want to do his duty, to act justly and fairly. To his first assignment he brought a severe code of conduct that was truly quixotic. Almost at once he found himself embroiled in difficulties.

Among the stocks of grain that Cervantes sequestered was a quantity belonging to the clergy. The King's decree had been explicit on this point: "The commissary will sequester any quantity of the said wheat or barley, and take it from whomever has it in his possession, regardless of his station and position, *whether ecclesiastical or otherwise.*" This sentence contained a hint of possible danger from that quarter, perhaps an indirect warning to proceed with caution, but Cervantes took it literally.

It happened in Ecija. Certain stocks of bread, wheat and barley belonged to the parish of Santa Cruz, other lots to the Dean and Chapter of Seville. Cervantes, carrying out his instructions to the letter, seized them.

The scandal that followed was unprecedented. The people interpreted the attitude of the ecclesiastical authorities as a defence of their own interests and as an opportunity to attack one of the hated commissaries without fear of the consequences. Cervantes was lucky not to be stoned. The Archbishop of Seville's steward excommunicated him and instructed the vicar of Ecija to expose Cervantes' name to public disgrace by exhibiting it on the bulletin-board outside the church door.

Cervantes found himself compelled to hurry back to Seville, where he explained to his superiors everything that had happened and made great efforts to obtain an annulment of the excommunication. It was only granted after the confiscated grain had been restored to its owners and, no doubt, after Cervantes had promised to act in future with more discretion. Maybe this was the first occasion on which, in his own words, he "was struck with bewilderment on seeing that the shepherds were wolves and, instead of guarding their flocks, tore them to pieces". Or, like the poor dog Berganza in his *Dialogue of Two Dogs,* he may have asked himself, "How can they understand and talk so much about God, and yet act so much like the Devil?"

It was not long before Cervantes, carried away by zeal and indignation, roused the anger of the clergy once more. This time he confiscated wheat belonging to a priest in Castro del Río. When the sacristan interfered, Cervantes ordered his arrest. The angry outcry this provoked was still worse than in Ecija. People hardly trusted their eyes when they saw what the commissary had dared to do in his "madness". From Cordova came orders to

excommunicate him, and once again Cervantes' name was pil/
loried on the church door. For the second time he had no
choice but to return the confiscated grain, to defend his actions,
and to travel post/haste to Seville to extricate himself from his
quandary.

Fortunately the documents relating to these episodes have been
preserved. They reveal the essential Cervantes, his kindness,
which nobody ever denied, and his honesty in surroundings
where honesty had become an empty word. On both occasions
he was praised by his superiors for his firmness and probity. His
functions were extended soon afterwards. Furthermore, he had
not made himself personally disliked, although his acts as an
official provoked the resentment of people who saw in him the
man responsible for enforcing the hateful decrees. Take the
example of Ecija, where he so often applied the full rigour of the
law and was so often showered with insults. When the Pur/
veyor/General, Don Antonio de Guevara, received funds to pay
for the quotas of the last requisition, the same peasants of Ecija
who had cursed Cervantes got together and authorized him to
collect on their behalf the sums due to them at the office in
Seville. Another document shows us that a plenary session of
the Ecija town council rejected an accusation levelled against
Cervantes. But moments such as these, when he felt himself
recompensed, were rare.

For most of the time he was entangled in disputes with recalci/
trant peasants and in skirmishes with local authorities; facing the
women's tears, the men's threats, and the insults of both; lost in
a maze of figures and papers and in endless bickering with clerks.
The Spanish essayist Ramiro de Maeztu summed up Cervantes'
problem when he said, "If he was hard on the contributors,
farmers or tenants, he had to see them suffer; if he relented
towards them, he was in danger of losing his post." For a man of
his disposition, it was a most unenviable job, but—it kept the
wolf from the door.

At the beginning of 1588 he was entrusted with the milling
and haulage of the grain and oil he requisitioned; a little later,

another chore was added, that of turning into biscuits the flour which his district produced under quota. It meant hurrying to and fro, covered in dust, measuring, checking, filling casks, tasting, dealing with farmers and supervising his assistants. His office had gained in importance, but its difficulties had also increased. Cervantes had to rent a store-house in Ecija and find more collaborators. No sooner had things begun to improve for him than a letter from a certain Cristóbal de Torres, an attorney, advised the Corregidor—the magistrate—of Ecija to "check on certain quantities of barley which were taken from the town by the commissaries". This was obviously aimed at Cervantes. He heard of the matter, and took immediate steps to refute the indirect accusation.

Although he was aware that the municipal authorities had disregarded Torres' demand, he wanted a clarification of the issue. On September 26, 1588, when the town council met in session, the clerk Trapel, Cervantes' assistant, turned up there and demanded in the name of his chief that the aldermen should investigate the denunciation. In the following session, on 30th September, the whole council from the Mayor, Garci Lasso de la Vega Galindo, down to the last alderman, put on record a protest against the insinuation, and their appreciation of the commissary's rectitude and fairness.

Soon, however, another sneaking accusation was levelled at Cervantes, again in Ecija, and this time by a member of the town council itself. The man started a whispering campaign to the effect that the commissary had seized higher contributions of grain than the quota had allowed for. A statement written in Cervantes' own hand is our only source of information, both of the accusation and of Cervantes' reaction to it. It shows that he had lost nothing of his old fiery energy when it came to defend-ing his good name: "And so that the truth may be seen and verified, I beg and implore this city to let it be proclaimed by the town-crier in the market place and other public squares that everybody from whom I have collected wheat or barley shall come forward to lay witness,"

Occupied with petty worries of this kind and with endless paper-work, interrupted by short trips to Seville, where he seems to have had few friends and little leisure, Cervantes spent a restless summer during 1588.

One day the news spread that the Great Armada was about to sail. Two recent events had roused the Spaniards and the King himself to fever pitch—if this term can ever be used of Philip. One was Drake's bold raid on Cadiz, when he sailed up to the roadsteads, sank eighteen ships, and carried off six others that were already equipped with cannon and ammunition. This exploit had a far greater significance than was at first apparent. It gave the English exact information about the disposition of the Spanish fleet and its purpose, and about the armament of the ships. The Spanish fleet was thus placed at a disadvantage even before it went into action. England was in a position to organize her naval squadrons in the light of the newly acquired facts, and to equip them with stronger artillery—a superiority that was to be one of the factors in the defeat of the Armada.

The second event that influenced the Spanish nation was the execution of Mary, Queen of Scots. Her death sharpened the antagonism the Spaniards felt toward Queen Elizabeth, and weighed heavily in Philip's sudden final decision to launch his attack without further delay. An aggravating factor was that Leicester, the Queen's favourite, had joined the rebels in the Low Countries at the head of six thousand English soldiers. Yet, in the last analysis, nothing shook the Spanish people so much as Drake's "singeing of the King of Spain's beard" at Cadiz. It was the first time in living memory that a Spanish city had been at the mercy of an invader. A wave of chauvinism swept the country. The Cortes passed violent, warlike resolutions, which were, however, less easy to put into effect. As usual, the Exchequer was short of money. So as to be able to concentrate all material efforts on preparations for war, Philip suspended work on the Escorial, which was a supreme personal sacrifice for him. To gain time, the fleet was being equipped in the most careless fashion, quite apart from the fact that every move was known to the English. The Spaniards hoped that prayer and Divine aid for the enterprise, to them a sacred one, would make up for defects in their military armour: "God guides them. . . ." When all was over, it was the other side which struck a medal claiming that "God breathed and they were scattered".

The alarm was raised throughout England. To unify the nation, the darkest rumours about the Spaniards and their King were put into circulation. The sack of Brussels, the Duke of Alba's harsh measures in Flanders, the conquest of America, the Inquisition—everything was recalled, and everything was painted in the most lurid colours. There was no lack of extravagant atrocity stories: it was said, and even believed, that the Spanish soldiers had orders to kill with their knives all men, women, and children over seven, and brand all infants, who would grow up to be slaves. It was also said that the Spanish galleons would have aboard thousands of wet-nurses for the orphaned English babies, and that they would carry cargoes of instruments of torture for the use of the Inquisition in conquered England.

Such tales fanned the will to resist the would-be foreign invaders. Threatened with the fate of an occupied country, the English closed their ranks around their Queen. Never had Elizabeth been so genuinely popular as in those days. And Philip II had no inkling of the truth when he imagined that his soldiers would find an easy prey in a doubt-ridden, divided people. His young kinsman, Prince Alessandro Farnese, who was stationed with troops in Flanders, waiting to ferry them across the Channel under the protection of the Armada, was more clear-sighted; urgently he warned the King that the enterprise had little hope of success. Philip paid no attention to this warning.

After many false starts and mishaps, which included a severe gale, the Spanish squadrons were at last assembled in the harbour of Corunna. On July 22, 1588, they set sail for England.

The fleet, the greatest that had ever sailed, consisted of 130 ships with an armament of over 2,400 pieces of artillery; they carried roughly 20,000 soldiers, 8,000 sailors, and 2,000 men on the rowing-benches. It was the best part of Spain's armed forces.

The *San Juan* had aboard, as a simple soldier, Spain's most renowned poet, Lope de Vega. He celebrated the fleet's departure in a sonorous poem which begins: "Glorious Armada, all ablaze with banners", and describes the "masts of the Faith, where a white pennant flutters on every spar".

As in the days of the Turkish menace, the fleet took with it the thoughts and anxious wishes of the whole Spanish nation. But this time there was no Don Juan of Austria, no Marquis of Santa Cruz among the commanders. There were gallant captains and officers, there were good fighting men, but inspiration and enthusiasm were lacking. The Grand Admiral and Commander of the Armada, the Duke of Medina Sidonia, was a timorous man who suffered badly from sea-sickness.

They sailed on July 22; eight days later they sighted the coast of England. Although some fishermen had volunteered the information that the English navy was concentrated in Plymouth, Medina Sidonia did not seize this opportunity to take the enemy by surprise and destroy the bulk of his fleet. Refusing the advice of his captains, he decided to sail up the Channel, to the relief and amazement of the English leaders who had feared to be caught in a trap. Now they, in turn, sailed from Plymouth in pursuit of the Spaniards.

The Great Armada was an awe-inspiring sight and resembled a floating city. With its forest of masts, over which rose the towering poops of galleons and galliasses, it "gave cause to wonder whether this was a campaign at sea or on land". Ranged in an immense half-moon, the ships advanced in slow, stately motion, as if too heavy for the wind even when all sails were filled.

As soon as the English squadron appeared, the Spanish fleet moved into battle formation. This, however, proved useless. The English commanders refused an open battle but harried the slow Spanish ships from afar with their superior artillery, avoiding the danger of being grappled and boarded, and escaping because of their lighter, faster ships. In the skirmishes, the bulky Spanish vessels came off worse. By the time the Armada reached Calais, many of its capital ships were crippled, much of the ammunition spent, and two of the best galleons lost. From one of them, *Nuestra Señora del Rosario*, the captain and 650 men had been taken to London as prisoners-of-war—the first trophy.

Then came the night of August the seventh. The Armada was anchored off Calais, waiting in idleness for the arrival of Farnese's troops and boats, which were to be escorted across the Channel. Farnese was delayed in Dunkirk. At midnight, Spanish sentries saw a number of flaming objects rapidly approaching from the English coast. The enemy, making good use of the favourable wind and current, had launched fire-ships, buoyant ships impregnated with tar, filled with inflammable material and explosives, and set alight. It was by no means a new expedient. Julius Caesar and Plutarch had described it; and in Brussels the Flemish insurgents had recently used the device against the Spaniards. The impact on the Armada was nevertheless tremendous. If the old Marquis of Santa Cruz had been there, he might have known how to counter this move, but Santa Cruz was dead. With him the spirit of discipline seemed to have deserted the Spanish navy. The sentries who raised the alarm also spread panic from ship to ship. Medina Sidonia lost his nerve. Though some Spanish historians—Cabrera, for instance—have tried to explain his subsequent actions as deliberate tactics, the fact is that the order to weigh anchor was given in unreasoning, panicky haste. The advice of more courageous and far-sighted officers was disregarded in the confusion, and there was no attempt by the command to appraise the situation calmly.

The supreme commander could not have come to a worse decision. The whole manœuvre was carried through haphazardly, without a plan, and when attempts were made to remedy matters it was too late. The current was sweeping the Spanish ships into the open sea, on a pitch-black night. There the English lay in wait and at once opened fire. A gale began to blow, accompanied by thunderstorms and cloudbursts. Slowly the Spaniards were carried towards the sandbanks of Dunkirk. In the dark the Spanish ships crashed into one another, with the pilots unable to control the rudders. The officers' commands were either not heard or not obeyed. From time to time a Spanish gun was fired at random, but the English cannons were busy all night long.

By daybreak the Spanish fleet was in a state of chaos. The ships left unscathed by the storm and the enemy gunners were no longer a force strong enough to tackle the English, but they went into action nevertheless. The worst came on the following day, the ninth day of August. A north-westerly wind brought violent squalls, and the Spanish ships were driven towards the shallows of the coast of Zeeland. "We saw ourselves lost," said Luis de Miranda in his report, "either captured by the enemy, or the entire Armada wrecked on the shoals. It was the most dreadful day ever, because all the men had despaired of a good outcome and expected to die."

Suddenly the wind changed and made the heavy Spanish war-ships veer slowly northwards. They were short of ammunition, food and water, their crews were totally exhausted, but when the Duke of Medina Sidonia gave the final order to break off the action and sail home, old captains cursed him for it, weeping with rage.

They had drifted to the northern extremity of the Channel. To make their passage home through the narrows would have been to court destruction, for the English ships, though their ammunition was spent, were close enough to their bases to replenish all their supplies. Therefore the Spanish command decided to run up to the North Sea, round the British Isles to the west, and then set course for Spain.

The gale had grown even fiercer. Giving up the pursuit, the English ships left their enemy to the elements and returned to port —and to their triumphs. After four grim days of ceaseless battle with the gales and the Atlantic rollers, the Spanish ships, or such as were left, staggered homeward. First their food ran out, then their water. The horses had to be killed. A number of them, about a hundred, were thrown overboard without having been stunned or killed first, so numbed were the men by their own suffering and danger. Many of the galleons already crippled by the English cannon sank in the open sea, broken up by the waves; others foundered on the rocks, along the west coasts of Ireland and England. Those Spaniards who were able to reach the shore alive were slaughtered by men who hunted for shipwrecked enemies. No quarter was given.

On September 23, 1588, Medina Sidonia reached the port of Santander with twenty-two ships. Forty-four more came limping in later. All the others were lost. Of the 30,000 men who had embarked, about 10,000 came back.

*

Cervantes was in Seville, struggling to defend his good name against both insidious accusations and officials out for his blood, when the first rumours of the naval disaster began to circulate in Andalusia. He forgot about his private concerns in the upsurge of his feelings. The old soldier of the Tercios stirred in him. Though in his heart he may have known that the bad news was only too true, he refused to accept it. Without waiting for more definite information, he felt driven to express his anxiety for his country in verse, thus breaking the silence of years:

> *Bate, Fama veloz, las prestas alas;*
> *rompe del Norte las cerradas nieblas;*
> *aligera los pies, llega y destruye*
> *el confuso rumor de nuevas malas,*
> *y con tu luz esparce las tinieblas . . .*

> Hasten, O Fame, bestir your ready wings
> to cleave the serried fogbanks of the North,
> be fleet of foot and tarry not, to end
> vague murmurs that foreshadow evil things—
> dispel the darkness, let the light shine forth . . .

"Fame" was swift indeed, and the darkness, the fog of uncertainty, was soon dispelled. When the shattering news arrived, leaving no room for doubt, Cervantes raised his voice once again.

His verses, an apostrophe to Spain, were clumsy: "Mother of men valiant in war, archive of Catholic soldiers . . ." But at the same time they expressed a deep and genuine emotion. He asked Mother Spain not to think it a disgrace that her sons came back having "filled the ocean with their misfortunes". It had not been the enemy's strength that had turned them back, he claimed, but the implacable gale, the sea, and Heaven that "permits the enemy to raise his head a little".

Blinding himself to the facts which he must have known, Cervantes in his poem went on to forecast revenge. The return of the fleet could be nothing more than the evasive tactics of a bull in the ring when it swerves before returning, with deadly effect, to the attack. He ended with an appeal to the King to gather his forces and resume the fight:

> March on, then, Philip, master, lord and King,
> Second in name, and man second to none . . .

Philip II heard the news in his Escorial. There he had once received the report of Lepanto, the greatest victory of his reign. Men who had observed him on both occasions found little difference in his demeanour then and now. This time he only repeated words his father, the Emperor Charles V, had used when Maurice of Saxony's treachery had forced him to flee from Innsbruck: "It was not God's will." Charles V, however, had begun at once to prepare for revenge; Philip suppressed his grief and turned to his customary duties. The echo of public clamour did not penetrate the thick walls of the Escorial.

The Spaniards were stupefied by the news of the disaster. Refusing to accept the truth, they blamed the defeat on the gales alone and would not admit that the greater fleetness, the swifter manœuvring and superior gunnery of the English ships, but above all their resolute action in the face of Medina Sidonia's inept, vacillating leadership, had carried the day.

Eight years later one of the victors over the Great Armada, Lord Howard, led a naval squadron into the port of Cadiz. His

men, Englishmen and Dutchmen, sacked the city and burnt all
ships at anchor. Their bold exploit met with no resistance and
they set sail, their ships laden with rich booty, without having
suffered any serious loss. And this was at a time when the
Spanish people were still dreaming of avenging the Great
Armada!

This time Cervantes did not join in the general patriotic outcry, at least not by expressing his fury at the humiliation the
enemy had inflicted upon his country. Other happenings had
roused his indignation. On the eve of the English raid on Cadiz,
soldiers of the National Militia, a unit formed for the defence of
the Spanish coast, had paraded through the streets of Seville,
beplumed and beribboned. It was a sort of civic guard, consisting of householders and commanded by illustrious gentlemen of
the region. They drilled and practised in the Campo de la
Tablada, as part of the summer fairs, as it were. The day after the
English landing, the Militia marched into Cadiz with the Duke
of Medina Sidonia at their head, ready to avenge the outrage.
They found the town in ruins, the English far out to sea. Heroics
turned into farce, and as such Cervantes saw it. He wrote a
crudely satirical sonnet, full of local allusions, in which he compared the Militia with the effigies carried by religious confraternities in procession during Holy Week: "They frighten, not
the English, but the mob." The name of the captain of the
detachment was Becerro, which means Calf, and Cervantes made
the obvious pun: "Bellowed the Calf and put them into file . . ."
The earth resounded with their steps, the skies darkened and
promised ruin to the enemy, but

> . . . *y al cabo, en Cádiz, con mesura harta*
> *ido ya el Conde, sin ningún recelo*
> *triunfando entró el gran Duque de Medina.*

And finally into Cadiz, a good while
After My Lord had gone, entered in glory
the great Duke of Medina without fear.

It was meant to sound farcical, but it is not difficult to sense what rage lay concealed beneath the travesty. Cervantes' bitterness was such that he, usually so discreet and respectful, referred to the men he was mocking by their real names. The years after the defeat of the Great Armada had wrought their change in Cervantes.

25

Mirage of America

FOR a while a battlefield remains shrouded by smoke and fumes; when they lift, reality stands revealed. This experience Spain as a nation and Cervantes as an individual shared.

He continued in his post for a short time after the return of the remnants of the Armada. But the gale that had scattered the fleet also swept the commissaries away. Requisitions for the Navy were suspended. Cervantes had not been paid the money due to him. As a penniless supernumerary he stayed on in Seville, trying to raise funds and partly living on his friends' kindness. He was in a worse plight than at that time in Madrid when he had failed as a playwright. Then he had at least been able to turn to the life of a public servant. Now he had failed in this too. He began to think of America, "the refuge of those who despair of Spain", and to settle his affairs accordingly. Whether or not he had definitely decided to depart, the tone of the documents of that period suggests that Cervantes thought of the American solution as in the nature of a death warrant, for he actually drew up papers amounting to a last testament.

So we find him submitting an expense sheet for the milling at Ecija: "All this I swear by God and the sign of the Cross I have spent on milling and many other things I have not recorded, and I sign it with my name on this day, the 6th of February, 1589."

Soon afterwards he was paid back fifty ducats he had lent to Juan Cervantes, possibly a kinsman, at a time when he himself had not been quite so hard pressed. Then, again, on June 26, he signed a paper by which he acknowledged a debt to Tomás Gutiérrez, the innkeeper, and transferred in payment a debt owed to him, Cervantes, to Gutiérrez's name. By this means Cervantes wiped out his debt, but at the same time he declared that he was leaving the inn. This is one of the documents which show both Miguel's fecklessness and his kindness: he had helped a friend with money although he himself was owing money.

He spent the rest of the summer and autumn of 1589 on paper work, preparing and submitting to the Treasury auditors his vouchers for grain and oil, but did not obtain their final acceptance. The Spanish Treasury failed to pay its employees regularly, yet on the other hand it expected them to render impeccable account sheets; and Cervantes' accountancy was never beyond reproach. How he subsisted during all this time is not clear. He probably undertook small commissions and asked his friends to lend him money on account of the arrears due to him. During the winter he continued his arduous work of putting his accounts in order, settled his personal affairs as best he could, and when everything seemed provided for, wrote a petition, no doubt after having found out through friends where vacant posts were to be had overseas.

The petition was formally directed to the King, but in reality applied to the Council of the Indies, and reads as follows:

"Sire: Miguel de Cervantes Saavedra declares that he has served Your Majesty for many years, in campaigns at sea and on land, such as fell to his lot in the last twenty-two years. Specifically he took part in the Great Naval Battle, where he sustained many injuries, including one from an arquebus which cost him one hand; in the following year he served at Navarino and later in Tunis and La Goleta. Journeying to this capital with letters from the Lord Don Juan and the Duke of Sesa, which recommended him to Your Majesty's favour, he was taken prisoner on the galley 'Sol' together with his brother, who had also been in Your Majesty's service during the same campaigns. Both were taken to Algiers, where they exhausted, for the sake of their ransoms, all their property, as well as the property of their parents and the dowries of two unmarried sisters who were reduced to penury so as to ransom their brothers. After their release they were in Your Majesty's service in Portugal and the Azores, under the Marquis of Santa Cruz, and at this moment they are still in Your Majesty's service: one brother as ensign in Flanders, while the other, Miguel de Cervantes, after having carried letters and instructions to the Alcalde of Mostagenem, has been in the employment of the Navy at Seville under Antonio de Guevara. All this is confirmed by documents. During the whole time Miguel de Cervantes has never been granted any favour. Now he humbly begs and requests to be given, if Your Majesty sees fit to confer it upon him, any one of four vacancies at present existing in the Indies, viz. the auditor's office in the new Kingdom of Granada, the Civil Governor's office at Soconusco in Guatemala, the account-ancy for the galleys stationed in Cartagena, and the Magistrate's office in the city of La Paz. Any of these offices with which Your Majesty would favour him he is willing to accept, being a man of skill, with sufficient merits to warrant Your Majesty's favour, because it is his desire to continue always in the service of Your Majesty and in that station to end his life, as his forefathers before him, which would signify a great boon and mercy for him."

Miguel sent off this petition in May, 1590. On July 14 and 31 of the same year, while waiting for a reply, he granted powers of attorney respectively to his wife, Doña Catalina, and to his sister, Doña Magdalena. He authorized them to cash, in his name, any money credited to him, and any debt in kind owed to him, with full powers to litigate if necessary. Moreover, he made a sworn declaration about the accounts concerning his various assignments, a document which is extremely obscure and which caused the Exchequer to harass him endlessly. This is hardly sur-prising, for did not an earlier expense account he submitted con-tain the tell-tale phrase, "And many other things I have not re-corded"? This turn of speech reveals the muddle there was in his ledgers—a muddle which corresponded to the lack of order in his personal existence.

Apart from these attempts at straightening out his affairs, there is not a document to show us how Cervantes spent the summer and autumn of 1590. He seems to have wandered aimlessly about the streets of Seville. When the cold season came and they grew deserted, he needed warm clothes but had no money to buy them. He did purchase five yards—five-and-a-half *varas*—of a coarse cloth in the shop of Miguel de Caviedes and Co. on November 8, but the ten ducats they cost were beyond his means. Instead, he signed a document in which he undertook to pay the sum within three months, and Tomás Gutiérrez, his former landlord, stood as guarantor. Taken together with his application to the President of the Council of the Indies, the terms of this promise of payment define Miguel's position that winter. He was forced to appeal to the innkeeper from whose hostelry he had moved so as to be able to buy winter clothing. It is left to our imagination to decide whether Gutiérrez, feeling sorry when he saw Cervantes shivering in thin summer clothes, proposed such a solution, or whether Cervantes himself approached his old crony after much doubt and heart-searching.

He was still counting the days until the official answer to his petition should come. He did not know that it had long ago been dealt with and filed away. A few words, scribbled at the foot of the paper by the *rapporteur*, a Dr. Nuñez Marqueño, decided that this ultimate attempt at escape from misery should be doomed to failure: "Let him find something over here, which may be granted to him. Madrid, the 6th of June, 1590."

26

Retribution

In 1590, at a time when Cervantes was too deeply immersed in his own problems to respond to public events, the case of Antonio Pérez took a new turn, the consequences of which affected the whole structure of the Spanish State.

The investigation had dragged on for years, and at times it seemed to hang fire, but in reality it was relentlessly pursued by the King, who let nothing deter him from the course he had set for himself. One day, Pérez found that he was deprived of all liberty of movement and that his emoluments were suspended. Evidence of his disloyal handling of the Flemish question was produced. For the first time he fully realized what the King intended to do with him. When he was about to be arrested in his home, he jumped out of a window and tried to make his escape through the streets of Madrid. With his pursuers hard on his heels, he sought asylum in the church of San Juan. The monks admitted him. But on the King's orders the doors of the sanctuary were forced and Pérez was dragged from the corner behind the altar where he cowered among dust and cobwebs. He was sent to the fortress of Turégano, while his wife and seven children, several of them infants, were thrown into prison.

It turned out that certain papers relevant for the prosecution had disappeared. When Pérez refused to say where they were hidden, he was put on the rack. Eight times the screw was tightened. Few had resisted this degree of torture, and when the pain became unbearable, Pérez, too, promised to confess all. But when he came to make his statement, he accused the King of complicity in Escobedo's assassination.

Pérez was weak and ill, his health shattered by the torment and the incessant strain. In his desperation he devised a plan for escape. He begged his gaolers to let his wife stay with him and nurse him, and in view of his condition the request was granted. One night he escaped from the fortress, disguised in his wife's clothes. A horse was waiting for him and he rode, accompanied by a group of friends, thirty leagues without ever resting till he reached the border of Aragon. There he dismounted and kissed the Aragonese soil. It was said to be his native country, but at that moment Pérez was moved to tears because this was the only part of the Spanish realm where he could expect to be safe from per⁄ secution by the King. The *Fueros*, the ancient constitutional privileges and laws of Aragon, established the independence of the judiciary and so barred the King from direct intervention at the Courts. Pérez, however, was soon to find out that not even the *Fueros* could ward off Philip's fury.

In Saragossa, the Aragonese capital, Pérez was detained and put into a prison under the authority of the Chief Justice of Aragon. This was in reality a form of protection, for within this prison the King himself could not exercise any form of jurisdiction over the prisoner. Across the border, in Castile, Antonio Pérez's wife and children were immediately gaoled once more, as soon as his flight was discovered. Philip sent instructions to Saragossa that Pérez be brought back to Madrid, alive or dead. A trial at which the King's evidence against Pérez would have to be sub⁄ mitted to the Court of Law was stopped by Philip himself, because it was clearly too difficult to secure Pérez's conviction. Instead, the Inquisition instituted proceedings against him, on the grounds of blasphemous words he was alleged to have uttered on the rack. Agents of the Inquisition arbitrarily took Pérez from the Chief Justice's prison and carried him off to the dungeons of the Holy Office in a closed carriage. This grave infringement of their *Fueros* infuriated the people of Saragossa. Supporters of Pérez ran through the streets shouting against the "Antifueros"— the enemies of the *Fueros*—and cheering Liberty. Tumults grew into a mass insurrection. The officers of the Inquisition found it wiser to take Pérez back to the city prison, but then the Holy Office formally demanded his extradition. The climax was reached when the Saragossans wrecked the stronghold of the Inquisition and released Pérez from his cell, to carry him through the streets in triumph.

Philip sent an army under Alonso de Vega against Aragon, to restore public order and re-establish the King's authority. It met with comparatively weak resistance and the rising was soon suppressed. This marked the end of Aragonese autonomy. Pérez, however, eluded the grip of the Inquisition and escaped in shepherd's disguise across the Pyrenees into France. Almost a year later, in September, 1592, thirty-nine Aragonese nobles were led to the scaffold in Saragossa. As always, Philip had taken care to strike at people in high positions. There were few prosecutions of humble men, but the King had insisted that the young Chief Justice, Juan de Lanuza, should pay the penalty. The executioner raised Lanuza's head, severed by a stroke of his axe, for all Saragossa to see. At the end of the procession, behind the men sentenced to death, guards had carried Antonio Pérez's effigy. It was night by the time the executioner had finished his task, and the torches were lit. The effigy of Philip's former secretary went up in flames.

Philip had to be satisfied with this symbolic vengeance and with keeping Antonio Pérez's wife and children walled up in a fortress for eighteen years.

The guilty man himself was free, but he had little joy of his liberty. He spent the rest of his life separated from his country and his children, whom he sincerely loved, busily plotting against the King and currying favour at the French and English courts with his slanderous tales. At first he was treated like a prince, but once he had been squeezed dry, he was discarded by those in power in either country. His old age was dismal, sordid and miserably poor. He never ceased to long for his return to Spain. When King Philip II died, Pérez begged to be permitted to go back, but the heavy hand of the dead sovereign whom he had betrayed still weighed on him, a terrible burden. Antonio Pérez died in exile.

The Princess of Eboli died shortly after Pérez had fled to France. Dragged from prison to prison, she had lost her inflexible pride and learnt to beg for mercy. She was a sick woman when the King deigned to relax the conditions of her captivity to a certain degree. She was kept a prisoner in her own palace at Pastrana, under strict guard, but she was allowed to see her children and even to give festive little parties for her intimates. Then her former lover suddenly escaped to Aragon, and at once the Princess was deprived of the small privileges she was enjoying, although she had had no contact with Pérez since her first imprisonment.

One day masons came to her room, accompanied by her warder, Don Alonso de Castillo, and "with the least possible noise" blocked up doors and windows, leaving a single door open for communication with the outer world. And at this door a guard was posted.

Little was heard of the Princess from that moment on. She was so ill that she could scarcely move from her bed, and was nearly blind. A young daughter of hers refused to leave her mother and was walled up in her room with her. Only a few despairing words, or rather cries, came through the impenetrable walls of Pastrana Castle. They were recorded by a scribe, Torrontero, who, at the Princess's request, had been allowed to her room. "From behind a screen that hid her bed he heard the said Princess, who was lying on the aforesaid bed, cry out, weeping and sobbing: 'What lying slander has put me and my daughter into a prison that is death? I have never offended against my King and Lord. God in Heaven, help us, for Thou art All-seeing and All-merciful, and I trust in Thy succour! Daughter, pray to God that He may not fail us, as He has never failed anyone. You be our witness, Torontío, that they have put us in a dark prison, where we lack air and breath to go on living. It cannot be that His Majesty wishes and allows such a thing to happen!'"

It sounds like an echo of Don Carlos' cry: "Kill me, Your Majesty, but do not imprison me . . ."

The Princess had no more luck with her plea than the King's son, young Don Carlos. She died in that room.

27

Light and Darkness

CERVANTES had not yet given up hope of receiving an answer to his petition, but he no longer counted on it. Still unaware that it was buried in the official files, he was already clutching at another straw. Requisitions for the Navy were being resumed. Guevara had been succeeded in the office of Purveyor-General and Chief Auditor by the Basque Pedro de Isunza, who was an old acquaintance of Cervantes' from the Madrid days. Isunza arrived in Seville in March or April of 1591, to Miguel's immense relief. The only thing Isunza could do for him, however, was to secure Cervantes' reinstatement in his previous job. It meant going back to all the vicissitudes of requisitioning, but Miguel must have regarded it as akin to a return to the fleshpots of Egypt. He felt like a prisoner released from his cell who raises his eyes, and finds spring is there again, with trees and flowers in bud.

When Isunza reported to the King on the appointment of Cervantes and a few other commissaries, he had written that they were all "honest and most reliable men". No other office was available for Cervantes "over here", as the official of the Council of the Indies had stipulated in his marginal note to Miguel's petition. And it had, after all, its compensations. Those wearisome journeys on horseback meant for Cervantes a healthy life in the open air and the sun; it toughened him so that he arrived at old age with all his faculties unimpaired. Also, despite the renewed petty worries and quibbles, Cervantes was gaining fresh experience and came to see villages and landscapes he had not known before. He scoured the arid slopes of the Sierra Morena or rode to Cordova along the pleasant banks of the Guadalquivir.

And he met the other Spain, the Spain of the open roads of Andalusia, peasants and shepherds, carriers and mule-drivers, beggars, pilgrims, and confidence tricksters. He acquired a sharp eye for the parasites who descended on the villages like locusts, straining their wits to escape the necessity for hard work. "All of those vagabond folk", he was to write, "are useless and shiftless, they drink like sponges and are gluttons for bread. To earn one's meals by doing nothing is an art which has many greedy prac-titioners. Therefore we have in Spain so many mountebanks, so many who exhibit puppet shows or hawk trinkets and printed ditties, so many people who never leave the tavern all year round..."

*

In the following year, 1592, Cervantes experienced a great though fleeting joy. Rodrigo Osorio, the famous Madrid im-presario, came to Seville. He had, so it seems, once put at least one of Cervantes' plays on the stage and therefore was an old friend. Miguel hastened to call on him at Gutiérrez's inn. We can readily picture them talking of the theatre, of popular authors and plays new and old. Cervantes' mercurial spirits rose under the stimulus of the other's enthusiasm. After his long intellectual inertia, he felt ideas surge within him, enlivened by the vivid impressions of the past year, during which he had absorbed life in all its crude, colourful actuality. It was like a homecoming: this, after all, was his true profession. Here we have the essential Cervantes, a man with a lasting sense of his vocation as a writer, but who also had his perpetual ups and downs, with long periods of despondency and flashes of an intense ardour; a man who did not always see clearly what he wanted in life and sometimes did not see it at all, but never lost his latent creative impulse.

In his poetry—for he continued to write laborious verse—these changes of mood are most frankly expressed. One day he was given to unashamed self-advertisement:

> *Yo el soneto compuse que así empieza*
> *para gloria inmortal de mis escritos . . .*

> The sonnet I composed which thus begins,
> to the immortal glory of my pen . . .

Then, in a moment of dejected insight, he would confess to failure through lack of genuine poetic gifts:

> *Yo que siempre me afano y me desvelo*
> *por parecer que tengo de poeta*
> *la gracia que no quiso darme el Cielo . . .*

> I, who must ever strive and sleepless try
> to make it seem I own a poet's gift
> which to me Heaven chooses to deny . . .

Only to say, in a sudden access of pride, of his *Galatea*:

> *Yo corté con mi ingenio aquel vestido*
> *con que al mundo la hermosa Galatea*
> *salió para librarse del olvido . . .*

> I fashioned with my craftsman's skill the dress
> that Galatea donned, to show the world
> her lovely self, saved from forgetfulness . . .

Upon which boast he went on to complain that *La Galatea* had never been popular and to blame this on the envy of his contemporaries. And yet, shortly before he wrote these verses, he had —in a passage of *Don Quixote*—accepted the general verdict and admitted his own dissatisfaction with the romantic pastoral novel of his younger years!

Nobody ever took the trouble to rescue Cervantes from his doubts and strengthen his self-reliance, with the result that he oscillated between arrogant confidence and abysmal dejection.

On this occasion, he was swept off his feet by a rush of optimism. Talking with his friends, listening, no doubt, to Osorio's flattering remarks, he relived the successful first night of one of his dramas—and promised himself to resume his work for the stage.

On September 5, 1592, Cervantes signed an agreement in which he committed himself to write six plays for Osorio. The fee was to be fifty ducats per play, and the plays were to be delivered "as soon as possible". Twenty days after the delivery of each script, the play was to be performed. And then, "if it appeared to be one of the best dramas performed in Spain", he was to be paid his fifty ducats. Further on in the agreement, Cervantes repeated with even greater insistence this ambitious clause, which betrays his feverish exaltation: ". . . and if, after the performance of each play, it should appear that it is not one of the best in Spain, you are under no obligation to pay me anything for the play concerned, for such is my agreement and understanding with you . . ."

It is not known whether Cervantes ever started to write any of the commissioned plays, or whether, once the intoxication had worn off, his doubts returned and he drifted back into the mono-tonous rhythm of his everyday existence. However that may be, the agreement was never implemented. Something utterly different happened to Cervantes and affected his whole outlook.

He was sent to prison. It happened two weeks after he had signed the agreement with Osorio and while he was in Castro del Río on business connected with the current requisition. Behind his prison spell there lies a complicated story.

The new office of "Commissaries' Judges" had been introduced shortly before, as other measures against the requisitioning abuses had been ineffective. Judge-Magistrates were appointed, who had to keep track of all the commissaries' transactions and investigate complaints, especially from the big landowners, who had been most vocal in their indictment of the commissaries. No longer was it safe for a requisitioning official, armed with the appropriate decree, to enforce delivery of the quota. The "Commissaries' Judges" had the right to endorse or nullify a commissary's acts as they saw fit, to lift embargoes, order the return of sequestered goods, and even to imprison the commissary himself.

The remedy was worse than the ill. Before, it had been the commissaries who abused their powers; now the judges did so. The wretched, harassed commissaries were caught between demands from above, resistance from below, and suspicious vigilance on the part of their special judges, so that they did not know which way to turn. Cervantes had repeatedly complained about the new system, but without success. The machinery of the Exchequer was becoming increasingly complicated and cumber^ some. In the domain of public finance there were hundreds of prominent officials of Medina Sidonia's stamp, and if they were in no position to lead the State into a spectacular defeat such as that of the Great Armada, they let Spanish economy drift like a rudderless ship, with which the clerks and magistrates were continually tampering.

One of the Treasury's new watchdogs was Francisco Moscoso, not only a "Commissaries' Judge" but Town Magistrate of Ecija as well. He received denunciatory advice to the effect that Cervantes had illegally seized 300 *fanegas* of wheat in store at Ecija. Without even attempting to investigate the truth behind the accusation, he ordered Cervantes to return the grain or its value in cash, and in addition to pay a very high fine and the cost of the legal proceedings. Meanwhile Cervantes was to be im^ prisoned.

From this indecent haste and harsh treatment we may assume that Moscoso felt a personal animosity against Cervantes, perhaps since the time when he had acted as commissary in Ecija. Miguel attempted to defend himself, but the prejudice against a commis^ sary was too great; he was taken to the local prison of Castro del Río, no doubt a squalid, evil^smelling hole as all prisons in small country towns were at the time.

That this was a trumped^up charge, or at least that the sentence was out of proportion to the offence may be deduced from the fact that after a short time Cervantes was released on bail.

All the same, the effect upon him of this first spell in a Spanish prison cell cannot be stressed too much. It is not difficult to imagine Miguel's feelings. He must have been convinced that he was being unjustly treated, he must have resented his helplessness and the malicious enjoyment with which people had watched the spectacle of a commissary taken to gaol. But the wound must have gone deeper still. He had been in prison before, but that was in Algiers, when it had been an honour to be maltreated by the enemies of Spain and, as he put it, the enemies of mankind. To be gaoled in Spain was a very different matter. It meant dis- honour, a disgrace to him and his family, a stain on the name of which he was so proud. He kept silent about his true feelings, but they can be detected in his writings. The bitterness which he had first betrayed during his last stay in Madrid grew more pro- nounced. Poems with a sardonic or insolent twist became more numerous.

Yet Cervantes did not flee the world like Timon of Athens, nor did he turn into a ruthless cynic. He was saved from this, we like to think, by his power of irony, his zest for life, and his in- vincible goodness of heart—his quixotry.

Scarcely out of prison, he gave another proof of his generosity and eagerness to help others. Again, this is a highly involved story. In the previous year, one of Cervantes' own assistants, Nicolás Benito, had been denounced as having sequestered a large quantity of wheat and barley in the town of Taba, although the granary belonged to the Army. The original complaint was lodged against the subordinate commissary, but Isunza himself became the real target; he was being held responsible for the sum owed to the Army. If his adversaries had achieved their objective with their litigation, it would have cost him his post, at the very least.

Cervantes, who had already been interrogated about the matter soon after it arose, came to his chief's aid when the situation became dangerous. In December, some weeks after his own arrest and at a time when he could not yet have shaken off his sense of injury, he wrote a letter to the King, through the channel of the War Council. He claimed that he, Cervantes, was alone responsible for his assistant's act. One of Cervantes' biographers says that the letter reads like a page out of the Romancero, where a vassal demands justice from his overlords.

". . . And it is not just that the said Purveyor or I should be the object of such slander, nor that the said Purveyor should be un- justly molested. And to show this to be the truth, I offer to render account at the capital or wherever it be Your Majesty's pleasure, and to produce due and proper surety and bond, apart from those I owe to the said Purveyor, so that the sum stipulated by any Court sentence shall be paid. And may it be Your Majesty's pleasure that, provided I furnish the aforesaid surety and bond, and render account as I am proposing, the said Purveyor should not be molested either in his person or in his property, since he owes nothing, and therefore I beg that justice shall be done."

Cervantes' letter did little, if anything, to improve his protector's situation. Rather, his interference—arising from the same impulse which had earned him admiration in Algiers—was dismissed with scorn. In the eyes of the gentlemen of the War Council, Miguel de Cervantes was an underling who defended his chief because he was afraid of losing his own job.

Isunza died soon afterwards, maybe because he had not the strength to stand the pressure and worry this imbroglio inflicted upon him. His death alone saved him from a tangle which might have led not merely to his disgrace in the eyes of his superiors, but also to imprisonment under a very severe sentence. Cervantes' letter had no other result than to compromise its writer.

28

In the Mire

WHEN Isunza fell ill, his office was temporarily filled by the auditor Miguel de Oviedo. Under the new chief, Cervantes remained in his post in spite of the incidents in which he had been involved. He was, however, employed elsewhere, mainly in the western districts of Andalusia. A series of small townships—Paterna, Almonte, Ruciana, Bollullos, La Palma, and so on—figure in the receipts and vouchers he signed during these sum‚ mer months of 1593, when he was on the road again, hurrying from one place to the next.

In the late autumn, probably at the beginning of November, his mother died in Madrid, in a shabby house in the Calle de Leganitos which she had rented for the yearly sum of fifty ducats. Only her daughters, Magdalena and Andrea, were with her. Her son Rodrigo was in Flanders (where he was killed in action in 1600), while Miguel had disappeared from her ken as com‚ pletely as if he had gone to a foreign country. The active, tem‚ peramental Leonor de Cortinas died a quiet, lonely death.

Miguel's long absences from his parental home and his restless existence after his return from Algiers had loosened the bond between him and his mother. And yet, she had remained one of the few beings on whose steadfast affection and loyalty he could always count: her passing left him with a deepened sense of isolation.

In the spring of 1594 he went to Madrid, presumably in con‚ nection with Treasury business. The accounts he had submitted for his various requisition assignments had not yet been approved. There is no evidence to show what else he did in Madrid. He may have seen his little daughter Isabel, officially the child of Ana Franca's husband Rodríguez, but it is not even known whether her stepfather and her mother were both alive at the time. For, five years later, she was an orphan, and Miguel's sister Magdalena engaged her as a servant under a formal contract in which she assumed responsibility for the girl's upbringing and training in housework. Meanwhile, it may well be that Cervantes began to dream of finding in this child a companion for his old age, and that he was attracted by the little household set up by his two sisters, together with Andrea's daughter Constanza. Certainly his matrimonial situation showed no improvement; if he went to see Doña Catalina in Esquivias, it only served to sadden him. There is, in fact, nothing to indicate that he was seeking to make a permanent home either in Madrid or Esquivias. Miguel was still the solitary vagabond.

He was about to return to Seville and his post, when he heard that the institution of naval commissaries had been suppressed. In future, supplies for the Navy were to be differently organized. This was bad news for Cervantes. Without having settled his accounts pending with the Treasury, without having been paid the arrears of salary and expenses due to him, he was once again a supernumerary, among a host of others in the same plight. He could either slink back to his wife and live in Esquivias, where he felt stifled, or he could stay with his sisters, who earned a scant living by taking in needlework. Alternatively, he could try to obtain help from his friends or petition people of influence. There was no other prospect in the overcrowded capital. To live a hand-to-mouth existence in Seville had been hard enough, but to live in misery in Madrid, among his family who had once shared his optimistic hopes, was worse because it was a confession of complete failure. What Cervantes did was to call once again on all the influential people he knew, though he had to swallow the impertinences of secretaries and lackeys on his endless round of the houses of the great.

After a while he was lucky enough to be given a so-called sinecure. His patron was an auditor called Augustín de Cetina,

N

who had dealt with some of Cervantes' official accounts in
Seville. It is ironical how many bureaucrats' names have been
preserved for posterity solely because they had some connection
with Cervantes—usually this meant no more than that they
had treated him in an overbearing manner—and how many
names of public figures and great aristocrats Cervantes saved from
oblivion by virtue of his fame, although they scarcely deigned to
receive him. There was, for instance, His Grace the Duke of
Bejar, Marquis of Gibraleón, Count of Benalcázar and Bañares,
Viscount of La Puebla de Alcover, Lord of the Townships of
Capilla, Curiel and Burguillos—all these titles are duly enumerated on the first page of *Don Quixote*—who never even acknowledged the dedication, without which nobody would have
remembered his existence. And Don Augustín de Cetina
belongs to the lower ranks of this company.

When Cervantes sought him out in Madrid, Cetina was no
longer a simple auditor but a member of the Supreme Council of
Auditors. He had risen so high above the ex-commissary that,
as Cervantes expressed it, he had nearly lost sight of him. Nevertheless, Cetina did listen to Miguel's case and was good enough
to look round for a job "over here" which might satisfy this stubborn supplicant. There was. In the administrative district of
Granada, the collection of the Sales Tax and other royal taxes
was in a state of chaos; the Exchequer could make nothing of the
accounts, let alone extract the overdue money. Cetina offered
this commission to Cervantes. Heartfelt thanks, sir! A moment,
please—there is first a small formality to attend to . . .

If Cervantes was to be appointed *recaudador*, tax collector, he
had first to satisfy the auditing department of the Treasury that
they would be able to recover the whole amount of tax arrears
entrusted to him: he would have to produce some sort of surety.
The taxes he was to collect represented, on paper at least, a very
considerable sum, two and a half million *maravedis*.

This problem might have been solved quite quickly, since
Doña Catalina's landed property was valuable enough. Yet the
way in which Cervantes handled it throws light on the relation-

ship between him and his wife. Sooner than ask her this favour, Miguel turned to a man of rather doubtful antecedents, Francisco Suárez Gasco de Tarancón, who some years before had been accused of having poisoned his wife, and was to declare himself insolvent not very long after his transaction with Cervantes. That Miguel was willing to accept such a man as his guarantor with the Exchequer can only mean that he was unable to find a guarantor of better repute and was prepared to go to any length rather than appeal to his wife. However, the auditor with whom the decision lay considered Suárez Gasco's bond insufficient, either because the man was not trustworthy, or because the sum he had guaranteed before a notary was much below the amount of the tax arrears Cervantes would have to collect.

Cervantes argued hotly that the bond was adequate, and then fell back on his personal standing, "because I am well known, my credit is good, and I am a married man in this place"—for which purpose he gave his address as Esquivias. In the end, when it became clear that the auditor would be satisfied by nothing less than a guarantee signed by both Cervantes and his wife, in addition to Suárez Gasco's bond, Cervantes gave in. Somehow, by painting his situation in the blackest colours, or by promising to mend his ways, or simply by throwing himself on her mercy, he obtained Doña Catalina's assent. On August 21, 1594, in the presence of the scribe Jerónimo Félix, Doña Catalina de Salazar y Palacios and her husband signed a guarantee which included all their property, present and future, and all Doña Catalina's private estate, which by Spanish law would otherwise have been exempted from her husband's obligations.

Two days later Cervantes received the Royal letter confirming his appointment. He left for Andalusia at once.

To collect taxes, above all the *Alcabala* or Sales Tax, was an even more dismal assignment than to requisition goods for the Navy, as Cervantes found out when he came to Guadix early in September. A substantial part of the arrears he was supposed to collect had already been cashed; it had been used to line the

pockets of cashiers and clerks or been paid out in the form of
salaries and per diem allowances, and goodness knows what
besides. Part of the money, too, had been collected, but not yet
liquidated. It cost Cervantes endless trouble to sort things out
and cash whatever there was to cash. When he went on to Baza,
he discovered an even greater muddle. He overstayed his allotted
time and, from Vélez-Málaga, wrote to Madrid asking for an
extension of twenty days, which was granted. On December 9
he finished his task in Ronda. Burdened with the tax money
and a load of worries, he crossed the Sierras in bitter winter
weather. First he went to Seville, and from there he expected to
go back to Madrid to report on his mission. But although he had
extracted as much of the arrears as humanly possible, the total
fell short of the target worked out on paper. Moreover, the
accounts were so confused that they would have needed a wizard
to unravel them. Cervantes knew how difficult it would be to
convince the auditors that, in spite of the chaotic accounts, he
had done his best; all the more so as those old requisition vouchers
of his still had not been passed and liquidated.

Actually things turned out even worse, all because Cervantes
took a step which seemed sensible enough at the time. Instead of
taking the whole sum in cash to Madrid, which entailed a long
journey on horseback, he deposited the greater part of it with a
Sevillan banker, Simón Freire, who had an agent in Madrid.
Having obtained from this man a cash receipt and a letter of
credit, he set off with these in his pocket. But before he arrived in
the capital, he heard that Freire had not only gone bankrupt but
had fled the country. Cervantes hurried back to Seville, only to
find that Freire's assets had been put under embargo by the
Courts. Nor had Freire's agent in Madrid enough funds to
honour the letter of credit. To cap it all, Cervantes received a
letter from the Accounts Tribunal at the Treasury, threatening
sanctions if he failed to recover his deposit with Freire. These
sanctions would have involved his two guarantors, one of whom
was his wife. With immense effort, pulling every possible string,
journeying to and fro between Madrid and Seville, spending his

scant money on it, and getting embroiled in disagreeable disputes, Cervantes at last got out of the hole: the tax money, being
property of the State, was finally released from the embargo. He
did not land in a debtor's prison as he had feared he might—at
least not for the time being.

Cervantes ought to have gone to Madrid to hand over
the balance of the collected taxes and straighten out his
accounts with the Treasury once and for all. His presence there
was urgently requested by the officials. Instead, he stayed in
Seville. It may be that he had used up some of the tax money,
because his fee and per diem allowance had not been paid and the
complications arising from Freire's bankruptcy had cost him dear.
Though it was not a great sum he still owed the Exchequer, it is
possible that he was in no position to pay it then and there. On
the other hand, it is also possible that he failed to see the necessity
of going to Madrid, since he was familiar with the snail's pace
usually adopted by the Spanish Treasury and did not expect it to
move any more quickly over such an insignificant amount.
Whatever his reason, by not going to Madrid to wind up his
assignment, Cervantes put an end to his career as a public
servant. The Treasury had in any case lost confidence in his
reliability, while he, on his part, gave up the struggle and lapsed
for the first time into complete apathy.

For the next few years, Cervantes lived in Seville, and the
scanty relevant documents that have been preserved all testify to
his dire poverty.

In 1595, at a time when he was still battling for the tax money
to be released from Freire's frozen assets, he entered for a literary
competition, but one in which normally no poet of standing and
experience could have been interested. The Dominicans of Saragossa wished to celebrate the canonization of St Hyacinth by
several "poetical tourneys" for which invitations were sent to all
Spanish cities. For one of these contests Cervantes entered a poem,
and it won the first prize—three silver spoons. Had these been
enough to tempt him? Or was it a queer sense of vanity which
made him enter for the competition? His verses were as bad as the

occasion warranted, or worse, and the rhymes which were improvised at the festival in Saragossa in praise of his achievement
were no better.

Hereafter, practically nothing is heard of Cervantes for several
years. There are some faint indications to suggest that he earned
a little money now and then as a commission agent, that he
hawked cloth, incurred debts, hobnobbed with hack-writers, and
was at home in the underworld of Seville. He is even said to have
written ballads for blind beggars to sing.

"Hunger drives talents to do things which are not on the map",
he said on one occasion, and he knew what he was saying.

*

When Cervantes emerged from the shadows eight years later,
he had nearly finished his immortal *Don Quixote*, the book
which encompassed all he had seen and all he had dreamed. Even
while passing through his most wretched years, he must have been
living an intense life of the spirit. It may all have begun as he rode
home at dusk one day, still deeply stirred by an act of injustice
or of callous cruelty he had witnessed—or suffered. The figure of
the Mad Knight, the Knight Errant who is always defeated by
practical people, suddenly assumed shape in his imagination, and
it was as if this image set him free.

The central character, he decided, was to be a defeated Amadis
of Gaul, and the book was to be a novel to end all novels of
chivalry. His hero would have to be "mad", extravagant and
ridiculous; it could not be otherwise with a man who, like
Miguel himself, was ready to sacrifice his life for a high ideal and
who reaped scorn instead of glory without letting it daunt him.
The Knight would have a companion, somebody to look after
him as a guide looks after a blind man, somebody with both feet
firmly planted on the ground. This companion would serve
as the vehicle for all Cervantes' hard-won worldly wisdom. Thus
the picture would be complete. The Knight and his Squire
would constitute a new Order of Knighthood, and in creating

them he, the poet, would purge his soul of all his accumulated bitterness against a corrupt world.

Maybe, somewhere in a corner of his memory, he came across the figure of an old Hidalgo he had known, a bony, shrivelled old gentleman, stubborn, gruff and a little ludicrous, one of the breed of those "who always have a lance in the rack, an ancient buckler, a gaunt horse and a greyhound for coursing". Cervantes would model his Knight Errant on him. He would boot and spur him, put a rusty helmet on his head, and send him out into the hostile world, with a shrewd, mischievous squire at his heels . . .

But even while Cervantes was beginning to live this new life of the imagination, his everyday existence remained unchanged. He was still pursued by magistrates and scribes, no matter whither he sought escape.

On September 6, 1597, Vallejo, the Magistrate of Las Gradas in Seville, was instructed to demand from Cervantes payment of a bond for the Sales Tax arrears he had not yet liquidated; Cervantes was to go to Madrid and submit his accounts immediately; should he fail to do so, he was to be taken to Madrid under arrest. Presumably as a preventive measure, because it was feared that he might disappear and evade his obligations, he was gaoled in Seville.

From this prison, Cervantes wrote to the Accounts Tribunal. The sum he still owed was so small, he argued, that his release might be graciously conceded, all the more so as otherwise he would not be able to consult and check his accounts. After three months he was released.

His stay in the Seville gaol was not a long one, but together with other spells in the same prison during subsequent years—of which we have no precise information, but credible hints—it was enough to give him a very intimate picture of life in this institution, one of the largest of its kind in Spain. There were over two thousand people within its walls, imprisoned for every kind of offence. Aristocrats who had killed their opponents in a duel, brutal murderers, ruffians and sharpers, and poor tax-gatherers like Cervantes, were all herded together. Cervantes has left us a vivid picture of it in his playlet *Seville Gaol*.

The gates of the prison remained open till ten o'clock at night; unhindered by the guards, crowds of people would arrive with parcels, baskets of food and bundles of ragged clothing for the prisoners, so that there was a perpetual coming and going. Every night a hundred and fifty to two hundred women entered the precincts: the wives, mistresses and friends of convicts. The noise in the building was deafening, and it never ceased.

Every day tragic and farcical scenes were enacted within the prison walls. There the inmates celebrated weddings, christenings and Saints' days, heedless of the gloomy setting. There was dancing and singing, love, jealousy and bawdry. Knives and daggers came out on the slightest provocation. In the basement vaults, people gambled and shouted blasphemies; brawls, bullying and cheating were the order of the day. But sometimes, in the midst of all this turmoil, a man would raise his voice in a nostalgic song.

The prisoners had their own religious confraternity of flagellants. During Holy Week they would run along the passages, their backs bare, and scourge themselves mercilessly while they bawled the *Via Crucis*. On the Church's great feastdays the most famous preacher of Seville would give a sermon in the prisonyard, and the men would listen, absorbed, while he spoke of the Redemption. There were processions, too, at which the worst bullies would devoutly escort the image of Our Lady. If a man was sentenced to death, the others would come to him with lighted candles in their hands during his last night, and stay with him until the dawn, intoning litanies.

It was an experience Cervantes absorbed fully, as he did all other human experiences, in a manner which finally enriched his understanding and creative powers. Though transfigured, the traces are there in his work. But, when he first emerged from prison, he took refuge in silence. Apart from his imprisonment, the records for the year 1597 contain no information concerning Cervantes, though a sonnet on the death of the poet Herrera, whom

Miguel had admired in his youth, is attributed to him and was written at about that time.

Two documents from the autumn of 1598 serve to shed a little light on Cervantes' mode of existence nearly a year after coming out of prison. In September, he had again to buy winter clothing—eleven *varas* of duffel cloth—and to find a guarantor because he could only pay for it by instalments. The man who stood surety for him was the Licentiate Francisco de Aguila, and Cervantes promised to pay the merchant, Jerónimo de Molina, within three months. Then, on November 4, he signed a document in the chambers of the actuary Gabriel Salmerón, which records that he bought on credit two quintals of ship's biscuits from a certain Pedro de Rivas, at six ducats the quintal. His bondsman was Jerónimo de Venegas, solicitor at the Court of the Board of Commerce in Seville. Did this peculiar transaction mean that Cervantes bought on credit so as to be able to sell retail for cash? Or that he acted as ship's agent, exploiting his contacts from the days when he was a commissary of the Purveyor's office? Whichever was the case, the fact remains that he had to make a precarious living.

And yet, in this year he found relief, as he later said, by taking paper and pen as soon as night fell. Both in the inferno of Seville Gaol and in the wonderful stillness of his room at the inn, he went on creating scene after scene of *Don Quixote*.

29

The King Dies

ON June 30, 1598, King Philip II was taken from his castle at Madrid to the Escorial in a litter, with infinite precautions, because he was a dying man.

The King's physicians had been against the journey, but Philip wanted to die in the Escorial where his loved ones were laid to rest: "his much-loved father and lord", his "much esteemed and beloved wife Isabel de la Paz", and the young children he had lost. He had grown intimate with death and was now impatient to reach the place where he had chosen to die.

Bad news came to the Escorial from all corners of the Spanish empire. The revolt in the Low Countries continued to gain ground. English ships were roaming the Spanish Main and threatened Spain's possessions overseas. But sombre though the external situation was, the picture in the interior was still darker. The coffers of the Exchequer were exhausted, Spanish economy ruined. Greedy officials were squandering the property of the State. The fields were left untilled, the cities were shrinking, a host of beggars, adventurers and rogues plagued the villages and country towns.

Philip tried to do his best, as he had always done. He signed a peace treaty with France, although it was almost a humiliation for Spain, and he transferred the sovereignty of the Netherlands to his daughter, the Infanta Isabel Clara. He was blind to neither the gravity of the situation nor the insufficiency of his son and heir. In other matters Philip might delude himself, but in this he saw clearly. "The Prince," he said, "has no talent for administration; he is only the shadow of a King; he is more fit to be governed than to govern." These terse words were an apt description of the listless, mean-spirited young man who, though afraid of power, was soon to be the sovereign of the Spanish empire. It was not the least of Philip's sorrows on the eve of his death that he had every reason to fear the turn which Spanish affairs would take under his son's rule.

Philip was confined to his bed in an agony of pain. His whole body was covered with purulent sores and he was racked by violent attacks of gout. Surgeons had tortured him in vain with their so-called cures. A man who had seen him during those operations wrote that the King had only once complained that he could not bear any more; on other occasions he had merely asked them to stop for a while, or to handle him gently. Fever gave him a burning thirst, but his physicians would not let him take so much as a sip of water or any other liquid. Sometimes when, on wetting his scorched lips, he inadvertently swallowed a little water, he would glance at the doctors as though asking their forgiveness. Their surgery only increased his suffering. New festering sores appeared and the stench of the pus became unbearable. It was as if all the suppressed ills of his mind were breaking through his skin, in a terrible vengeance of nature on the man who had wanted to be as impervious as bronze or granite.

On 1st September Philip was given the Last Sacraments. After the ceremony all but his son left the chamber. The King called the Prince to his bed and—according to the King's own account—said to him: "I should have preferred to spare you this scene, but I wished you to see how it all ends."

Philip's last agony continued for twelve more days. He had always been fastidious, not tolerating an ink blot on a paper, the slightest dirt stain, or the least sign of disorder. Now his bed was covered with unspeakable filth. The bed linen had not been changed for forty-seven days so that, in his own words, his back and buttocks had begun to rot. The pain the slightest touch or movement cost him was so excruciating that nobody dared to tend him. The physicians had given up all attempts at treating his illness. Sitting by his bed most of the time, however, was a friar who read to the King passages from the Gospels, in which he found consolation. And from time to time a young woman would step softly to the bed: Clara Eugenia, Philip's favourite, the eldest daughter of Isabel of Valois, who was never far from her father during his last illness. She would take over the sacred books from the cleric and go on reading aloud from them. Her presence and sweet voice would cause a glimmer of pleasure to light up the King's pain-racked face. It was at Clara Eugenia's birth that Philip had ordered all the bells in Spain to be rung, from Gibraltar to the Pyrenees.

But the end was in sight. The King's body began to putrefy while he was still alive. He groaned in his brief moments of sleep, but when he was awake his dignity and composure never left him. He had still the strength to speak to the people near his bed, to give advice and comfort, and to repeat again and again the words: "Fiat voluntas tua!"

To the last his brain was clear and his will unshaken. He expressed his wishes for his funeral: they were to pass a cord round his neck, with a wooden crucifix which should rest on his chest; they were to lay him in a plain tin casket and solder the joints so that no stench should come from it; this casket was to be put into another coffin, lined inside with heavy white satin and covered outside with black-and-gold cloth, a great cross embroidered on it. Thus everything was arranged. The towers of Philip's Escorial, his life's work, would rise above the Castilian uplands, defying the ravages of time, while he himself would rest within the tomb that had been opened near to where lay those most dear to him.

At four o'clock in the morning of September 13, 1598, the King seemed free from pain, a last mercy for which he had been praying. His ashen face was serene. In one hand he clasped the crucifix the Emperor, his father, had held in his last hour; the other held a candle which had been blessed in the sanctuary of Montserrat. It was lit, "to lighten him on his dark journey". King Philip kissed the image of Our Lady stamped into the candle wax, and kissed the crucifix; then his head slumped forward. The friar who had been reciting the last prayers fell silent. It was as if all those present had ceased to breathe when the King breathed his last.

In the adjoining chapel, young choristers of the Seminary intoned the chants of First Mass.

*

Spain had waited for the news of Philip's death, but when it came it was regarded as a national disaster. Hated by the outside world, this stern King had captured the imagination and affection of his people. Perhaps the Spaniards felt that with him a whole era, great in spite of all its faults, had come to an end.

It was inevitable that Cervantes should have shared the feelings of his countrymen, being at all times sensitive to public events which affected his country. Whatever his personal opinion of his King, and whatever mental reservations he might have had, Philip's death affected him profoundly, although he was absorbed in his own struggle with adversity.

In Seville, solemn funeral rites were staged to honour the dead King. The traditional "tumulus", the symbolic funeral mound erected in the Cathedral, was the biggest and most elaborate in all Spain. Great architects, sculptors and painters had contributed to it. Among the verses dedicated to the occasion was also a poem by Miguel de Cervantes.

The culminating ceremony, however, was delayed for two months because a violent feud about the order of precedence had arisen between the Law Courts and the Holy Office. The new King's intervention was needed to end the dispute.

Ariño in *Sucesos de Sevilla*, his chronicle of Seville, says: "Orders came from His Majesty that the last honours should be rendered on Tuesday, the 19th of December . . . and on that day, when I was present in the Cathedral, there came a brash poet and recited a stanza of eight lines on the subject of the grandeur of the tumulus." The stanza was a sonnet, the brash poet who was unknown to Ariño was none other than Cervantes.

There was in Seville at this time a so-called Academy, a sort of artistic centre, whose meetings were held in the studio of the painter Pacheco. Following Madrid's example, the leaders of Sevillan intellectual life met together and Pacheco painted portraits of many of them. Contrary to charitable legends, however, Cervantes never belonged to this company. Neither his mood, nor his duffel coat, nor his poetry qualified him for a place in so conventional a gathering. He was more at home in the slums and among unsuccessful, unknown bohemians who applauded him, gave him the sympathy he needed, and appreciated his biting satires. If he read the first chapters of *Don Quixote* anywhere at that time, it was not in an Academy but among his fellows in misfortune. A man like Ariño had not yet any reason to take notice of him.

Shortly after the memorial service for King Philip II, Lope de Vega arrived in Seville for the beginning of the theatrical season. With him came Micaela de Luján, a beautiful actress who held his affection for more years than any other woman and was the mother of several of his children. Lope was at the height of his popularity and fame, but even so there were dissident voices. In certain quarters he was bitterly attacked for his conduct. One such attack, an anonymous sonnet couched in aggressive language, greeted him on his arrival in Seville—and it has been attributed to Cervantes.

Internal evidence certainly points to Miguel being the author. The sonnet is in keeping with what we know of his temper and circumstances at the time, and it bears a close resemblance to the sly digs at Lope which appear in various chapters of *Don Quixote*, though, not being anonymous, they are there somewhat more restrained in tone. It must have infuriated Cervantes to watch Lope's triumphal journey through life at a time when his own journeys all led to the Accounts Department of the Treasury, with the prison-house looming up as the next port of call.

Lope countered the sonnet with an equally scathing little poem, and promptly forgot about it. Cervantes, however, remembered. When he was no longer quite so bitter and his natural generosity got the upper hand, he doubled back in his tracks, so to speak, and gave due praise to his rival.

*

Apart from these isolated incidents, of which there is some documentary proof, Cervantes' life for several years seems to be hidden in complete obscurity. The gap has been filled by a legend.

In the village of Argamasilla de Alba, a small place in the Mancha—Don Quixote's home country, as well as that of his squire Sancho, and his dream lady, Dulcinea—it was traditionally believed that Cervantes wrote his *Don Quixote* while in prison there. According to one version, he had gone to Argamasilla to collect tithe arrears on behalf of the Priory of San Juan; the inhabitants rioted, and he was gaoled. A second version has it that Cervantes worked for a saltpetre and powder mill in Argamasilla, and that he provoked the people's anger because the mill exploited the waters of the river Guadiana which they needed for irrigating their plots of land. Yet a third version of the legend sets Cervantes in prison in El Toboso, Dulcinea's birthplace; the reason was supposed to be that he had offended a female member of a vengeful family.

In modern times, this Argamasilla tradition has been discounted. All the same, only a century ago, the people of Argamasilla de Alba were convinced of the truth of the story, passed on from father to son, that the "Casa de Medrano" was the building in which Cervantes had been imprisoned. It was part of this tenaciously held tradition that Cervantes had appealed to a kinsman in Alcázar de San Juan, by name of Juan Barnabé de Saavedra, to come to his rescue; the words of Miguel's letter were actually quoted. Its opening sentence was: "Long days and dismal nights are besetting me in this prison, or I should say, this hole . . ." The vague hint in *Don Quixote* that the novel was written during a prison spell was taken to refer to Argamasilla.

In the absence of documentary evidence, it is impossible to come to a definite conclusion. I, however, feel inclined to think that there is a core of truth in the Argamasilla legend. The intimate knowledge of this district which Cervantes displays in his *Don Quixote* is striking. He knew the villages of the Mancha inside out—much too well to have been there only on hurried journeys as collector of bad debts. Also, the fact that Cervantes chose this region for Don Quixote's home is surely significant. For reasons which we can only surmise, he transferred recollections of his wife's uncle, Alonso Quijano—whose name, and possibly whose features as well, he borrowed for his Don Quixote —from the Toledan landscape of Esquivias to the Mancha. It is by no means unlikely that the discredited legend of Argamasilla will one day be resuscitated on the strength of irrefutable evidence.

Be this as it may, whether *The Adventures of Don Quixote de la Mancha* was written in the solitude of a small country lock-up; in Seville Gaol, "where every discomfort has its refuge and every noise its abode", as Cervantes seems to suggest; in his room at a shabby inn in Seville; or piecemeal in all those places, the fact remains that Cervantes carried the almost completed manuscript of *Don Quixote* with him when, emerging from the darkness of his worst years, he returned to Madrid.

30

A New Start

CERVANTES came back to Madrid in 1603 or thereabouts. The Accounts Department was still out for his blood because of his old, never liquidated accounts, and his journey was no doubt partly concerned with this everlasting incubus. Even so, his main purpose was to find a publisher for *Don Quixote de la Mancha*. The novel had acquired fame long before it was cast in its final mould, let alone published. In literary circles, and by no means only in third-rate writers' sets, some of its passages were freely quoted. Cervantes had read the most important chapters to his friends in Seville, and their provocative novelty had captured his hearers' imagination. The exploits of the gaunt Knight from the Mancha had established themselves by word of mouth, so that the success of the publication was assured in advance.

The publisher with whom Cervantes made an agreement was Francisco de Robles, bookseller to His Majesty the King, and the son of the man who twenty years earlier had published *La Galatea*. The original contract is lost, but it appears to have included an advance of money which enabled Cervantes to rid himself of his most pressing financial worries, to face his family with some degree of self-respect, and to revise his unevenly written text in a more quiet frame of mind.

Of his family, only Miguel's sister Magdalena was living in Madrid at that time, leading a withdrawn existence. She had long outlived her former propensity for sentimental affairs in which tenderness was inextricably mixed with practical considerations, and for endless matrimonial projects. Miguel's daughter Isabel was by now living with Doña Magdalena, nominally as a servant—a pretence which may have served to conceal the girl's real status from Doña Catalina, who sometimes would visit her sister-in-law. What rôle Cervantes played in this arrangement is one of the many details of his life of which we have no record.

Inevitably, Miguel's homecoming was fraught with emotion, especially when he came to explain to his sister that he wanted at long last to have a fixed home and to unite all the remaining members of his family under one roof. A plan was conceived whereby brother and sister were to move house to Valladolid, the seat of the Court in those years and therefore the most suitable place for a writer who badly needed contacts with the people who counted. Andrea, Miguel's other sister, had already settled in Valladolid. Together with her daughter Constanza she worked as seamstress for some of the great houses, thanks to her old connections. Andrea's consent to the plan of setting up a joint household was never in question: Miguel could be sure that she would be at least as pleased as Magdalena. But there still remained the problem of Miguel's relationship with Doña Catalina, his wife. He set himself the task of bringing about a reunion with her as well.

His newly won self-confidence made it easier for Miguel to go to Esquivias, and in the manor he found the atmosphere less icy. Rumours of *Don Quixote* had spread even to a remote place like Esquivias. Miguel's brother-in-law, the priest Don Francisco de Palacios Salazar, deigned to speak to him. A little later, he journeyed to Toledo in Miguel's company, an unheard-of occurrence, and in the end went so far as to pay a visit to the Cervantes in Valladolid. Success is an effective peacemaker.

Doña Catalina herself had been very lonely. The big old mansion was silent and gloomy. Much as she loved her house and her quiet existence close to her relatives, the failure of her marriage had slowly turned everything to dust and ashes for her. When her mother died in 1604, her ties with her childhood home were loosened and she was no longer so averse to a change.

Thus, Doña Catalina fell in with her husband's wishes. She agreed to go to Valladolid, where she would share the house not only with his two sisters and his niece, but also with the girl who now began to be known as Isabel de Saavedra—Saavedra being a surname which Miguel had adopted. The pretence had been dropped: Doña Catalina knew that Isabel was her husband's illegitimate daughter. She accepted it, as she accepted a way of existence foreign to her old self. And—up to a point—she stood the test.

*

Valladolid, the seat of Philip III's Court since 1601, was in a state of ferment. Under the new regime, favours, privileges and sinecures were redistributed; one festivity followed the other. Everyone was out for himself, and all together were bent on having a good time.

Philip III was, as his father had said, the shadow of a king. One of the innumerable wits who flocked to the Court called him "the painting of a king". He was delighted to leave the cares of government in the hands of his favourite, Don Francisco Gómez de Sandoval, Duke of Lerma. The Duke manipulated the King as he pleased, while he himself was being manipulated by one of his pages, a young man of obscure origin who started with the name of Rodrigo Calderón, became Count of Oliva, later Marquis de Siete Iglesias, with a fantastic annual income—and ended on the scaffold.

These two men ruled Spain for many years. Under their sway Valladolid was a gay and dissolute town, and a centre of malicious gossip. But the gossip's main target, the royal favourite, was in an almost unassailable position. Don Francisco was Grandee of Spain under two titles, that of Marquis of Denia and that of Duke of Lerma. He was a Gentleman-in-Waiting, General of the Spanish Cavalry, and that was only the beginning of his list of honours. Having amassed a considerable fortune, he placed his whole family in prominent and lucrative posts. His wife was First Lady of the Queen's Wardrobe; his uncle, Cardinal Sandoval, was Primate of Spain and Grand Inquisitor; one of his brothers was Viceroy of Valencia; his father-in-law was Viceroy of Naples; and the rest had been favoured with titles and offices in keeping. Obviously, the Duke was a loyal family man. Moreover, he was resourceful. The posts he did not wish to reserve for his relatives he sold to the highest bidder. He let himself be handsomely paid by the interested people of Valladolid for his trouble in securing the transfer of the Court to this city. Five years later, he let himself be paid even more handsomely by the interested people of Madrid to secure the Court's return there. Even the tragedy of the Moriscos, the descendants of the defeated Moors in Spain, provided good business for His Grace. He was an ardent supporter of their expulsion from the country, and when they had been expelled, he kept the greater part of their property for himself. Though the Duke of Lerma came to a bad end, he lived a prodigal life, feared, flattered, and at times even blessed by the people.

Under the Duke's wing, Spanish society in general and the society of Valladolid in particular enjoyed unaccustomed freedom. Restraint and decency became outmoded, corruption, venality and licentiousness were taken for granted. And, like toadstools on rotting wood, bad poets, cheap humorists and satirists arose by the score. It kept high society amused. The King was busy hunting, playing ball—*pelota*—and devoting himself to religious exercises; the royal favourite was busy getting richer and ever more powerful. Spain, weakened and impoverished, was rapidly sliding downhill.

It was into this morass that Cervantes stumbled when he came to Valladolid in 1604. In spite of past experience, he decided once again to try his luck at the Court. His attack of optimism did not last; he had no more luck than on previous occasions. "O Court," he wrote at about that time, "you endorse the hopes of bold applicants and shorten the hopes of shy deserving ones; you amply sustain shameless rascals, and starve honourable but timid men to death."

Apparently Cervantes obtained an audience with the Duke of Lerma. Since he had neither the money to purchase a post nor the luck to belong to the clan of the Sandovals, the outcome was a foregone conclusion. The Duke, moreover, had been informed of Cervantes' difficulties with the Exchequer, but not of his ser-vices as a soldier and public servant. After the usual two months of cooling his heels in the Duke's ante-chamber, Cervantes was received by the great man for a few moments; he left no wiser than before. It was alleged that the Duke had treated him with contempt. If so, Cervantes never mentioned it; in public he was full of praise for the Duke. By this time, however, Miguel had learnt to tread warily. In matters of the wicked world, the scep-tical Sancho in him had become his guide, not the visionary Don Quixote.

*

On July 21, 1604, Cervantes was back in Esquivias where his signature was needed for the act of partitioning his mother-in-law's estate between Doña Catalina and her brother. The result-ing document is illuminating.

Since Doña Catalina and Miguel had resumed their life together, it might have been expected that henceforth all they possessed would be joint property. Now Doña Catalina had inherited landed property which she was prohibited from giving away or selling by a clause in her mother's will. In her declara-tion about the division of the estate between herself and her brother, and again in a later document in which she ceded certain parts of her own share to her brother, Doña Catalina explained, somewhat gratuitously, that the clause in her mother's will intended to make sure "that her aforesaid husband should not be able to make use of this property". This bald statement shows that the latent dichotomy between Miguel and Doña Catalina— between his bohemian shiftlessness and her inborn thrift—per-sisted in spite of appearances. The gulf was never bridged, not even by the years they spent together in seemingly close com-panionship.

*

In August, 1604 Cervantes travelled to Toledo with his brother-in-law, to look after the sale of some of his wife's farms. On this occasion, and during subsequent visits to Toledo in 1604 and 1605, Cervantes crossed Lope de Vega's path again.

There had been a slight rapprochement between the two writers. At least, the 1602 Madrid edition of Lope's epic poem, *La Dragontea*, included eulogistic verses dedicated to the author by Cervantes. That these verses were written in the same year seems unlikely, since at the time Cervantes was larding his *Quixote* manuscript with quips directed against Lope. Possibly Lope had accepted or invited the flattering verses during a previous encounter, and more to confer an honour upon Cervantes than to procure a testimonial for himself. In any case, the improvement in their relations was short-lived.

The two years during which Cervantes had occasion to go to Toledo coincided with Lope's residence in the city. Lope kept two households and divided his time between his newly-wedded wife, Juana Guardo, who had brought him a fortune, and his mistress, Micaela de Luján, whom he had established in Toledo as well. Now over forty, he had passed his zenith. The complications in his private life and an incipient decline in public favour made him irritable. During Cervantes' sojourn in Toledo, his name may have been mentioned with pointed praise in the presence of Lope, who could not fail to know, at first by hearsay and later by reading them in print, about Cervantes' attacks on him in *Don Quixote*. The outcome of it all was a letter Lope wrote to a friend in Valladolid. The words pretend to be humorous, but a certain bitterness breaks through:

". . . And what shall I say of the poets? Oh, this poor century of ours! In the coming year many of them will make their start, but *not one of them is as bad as Cervantes, or idiotic enough to praise 'Don Quixote'*. . . . I shall not say more, or I would follow the example of Garcilasso who said, 'Satire I am approaching step by step'—which is something I hate more than Almendárez hates my tales or *Cervantes hates my comedies* . . ."

This may have been an outburst of bad temper, but it probably reflects a sincerely held opinion. Lope cannot have felt great enthusiasm for *Don Quixote*, for much in it would not be to his taste. Moreover, he was wont to think of Cervantes as a bad versifier and colourless writer, from whom nothing striking could be expected. If Lope's aggressive remarks were written after the publication of *Don Quixote*, as some modern scholars deduce, and not, as has been generally assumed, in the year before, it seems probable that Lope had only skimmed through the book. In this case, he would have taken in nothing but the first few "funny" episodes which, while they ensured the immediate popular success of the book, were in reality only its superficial shell, not its core. Lope's tumultuous, self-centred life left him little time for anything that did not further his own interests. He would not have troubled to penetrate beyond the surface of a novel in which, into the bargain, he was attacked. And Lope always reacted violently against attacks and criticism.

Finally, there may have been a grain of envy in Lope when he hit back at Cervantes. Just as Cervantes always hankered after a success as a dramatist which would make him Lope's equal, so Lope could not bear to see Cervantes outshine him as a novelist. *Don Quixote* must have been a thorn in his side, for which Lope de Vega never quite forgave Cervantes.

3 1

"The Adventures of Don Quixote"

EARLY in January, 1605, *The Adventures of the Ingenious Knight Don Quixote de la Mancha* appeared in print.

It was a red-letter day in Cervantes' life when he turned the pages of the first copy. This constituted a bulky volume, though in its proportions more pleasing to the eye than the current novels of chivalry. The lettering of the title, the author's name, and the dedication were finely balanced. In the centre of the title page was an emblem of the publishing house, an armorial shield with the motto *Post tenebras spero lucem.* It showed in the background a lion couchant on a hillock, in the foreground a raised arm, its fist bearing a falcon which seemed ready to take off in flight. Motto and emblem fitted Cervantes' life so well that we cannot but believe them to have been his personal choice. "After the darkness I hope for the light"—he had always done so.

The book's success was tremendous and immediate. Cervantes tended to let his imagination run away with him, but on this occasion reality exceeded his wildest hopes. Within a few days of publication the novel had achieved an astounding circulation. People were seen reading it in the streets; copies found their way into palaces, roadside inns and modest private houses. Clearly its publication had come just at the right moment to fulfil the needs of the public. Soon *Don Quixote* was known throughout Spain. Several reprints were called for. As early as April 11 Cervantes signed a document in which he confirmed that he had sold to Francisco de Robles the right to print the book in Portugal, Aragon, Valencia and Catalonia. On the following day he signed another document granting Robles full powers to prosecute

those responsible for unauthorized editions printed or in preparation in Portugal.

This was fame and glory indeed, though it had come in a less
spectacular manner than Cervantes had once dreamed. Instead of
being crowned poet laureate to the applause of an admiring
crowd, he earned the more sober and quiet homage of countless
readers who loved his book. He was aware of this and it gave
him deep satisfaction; but at the same time something seemed to
be lacking. What he had most hoped for, the acclaim of the
arbiters of literature—the official hallmark, so to speak—was
denied him.

At first *Don Quixote* caused a certain stupefaction in the literary
sets. Nobody was willing to believe in the genius of this author
whose earlier works, *La Galatea*, the poems and dramas, were
buried in oblivion, with a few phrases of tepid praise for epitaph.
There followed something like a tacit agreement to ignore the
whole inexplicable phenomenon of *Don Quixote* and its creator.
But this could not last, and finally Cervantes began to be an
object of professional envy. One day he received an envelope for
which his niece paid the carrier a *real*; it contained an anonymous
sonnet "which was bad, spiritless, devoid of elegance and wit,
but full of vituperation for *Don Quixote*". When Cervantes
later told the story, he insisted that the only thing he resented
about it was that it had caused him to squander a *real*. Actually
it was a sign that the recognition he so ardently wished for was
coming his way, that his work was no longer ignored. All the
same he felt hurt. Among the clique which jeered at his novel
were people he had looked upon as friends, and he was not yet
sufficiently sure of himself not to mind. Also, he longed to be
famous, and if ever a writer was willing to sacrifice everything for
this end, it was Cervantes; through all his writings we can detect
a note of plaintive nostalgia for that pre-eminence in the world of
Letters which he failed to achieve.

Every author, poet and artist, however great, needs encouragement. He wants to see how those who feel and think like him
respond to his work—to see himself reflected, as it were, in a

perfect mirror. This is necessary if he is to continue to believe in himself. "My conviction is incommensurably strengthened as soon as another human soul shares it," said the German poet Novalis. Cervantes had striven hard to win the acclaim of the best minds among his contemporaries when he wrote his dramas and poems—which were least worthy of their approbation. Now, when he had created Don Quixote, he still met with indifference on their part, or with strictures which made the taste of popular success turn bitter in his mouth. He may have had one of his detractors in mind when, in *Persiles*, he let a malicious defamer succumb to an arrow which pierces his tongue. And he may have recalled a personal experience when he made his Don Quixote raise the vizor of an attacker, only to recognize the face of his best friend.

Nevertheless, it was not all a matter of ill will; many at the time failed to understand the deeper implications of Cervantes' work. It is far easier to assess the quality of a genius when distance lends it perspective. A close-up can be confusing through the very power and originality of genius, which causes petty fault-finding and uncomprehending jealousy to creep in.

Cervantes had to be content with his popularity. If it did not raise him to literary eminence, it completely changed the outward pattern of his life and aroused people's interest in him.

The Duke of Bejar, however, to whom Cervantes had dedi- cated this first volume of *Don Quixote*, showed no sign of interest. The author was not fulsome enough to enlist the Duke's sym- pathies, and not important enough to flatter his vanity. It has even been said that the Duke at first refused to accept the dedi- cation and only acceded after Cervantes had implored him to listen to his reading of at least one chapter of the novel. In any case, Cervantes can scarcely have had any illusions about the Duke, even though, as a true son of his era, he always showed the great- est respect for the social hierarchy. He dedicated his novel to this man because it was the fashion to introduce books with pom- pous dedications to some powerful person who posed as a patron of letters, but who did nothing to prevent the greatest writers of their times from dying in miserable poverty. Cervantes has hinted that he took this step on the mistaken advice of a friend, possibly when he was still smarting under a rebuff at the Court. Furthermore, he modelled the dedication closely upon that contained in a book published by another writer years before.

"Relying on the favourable reception and appreciation Your Excellency accords to all manners of books, as a Prince eminently disposed to honour the liberal arts and especially those which are too noble to be abased to the service and gain of the vulgus, I have decided to publish THE INGENIOUS KNIGHT DON QUIXOTE DE LA MANCHA under the aegis of Your Excellency's most illustrious name, begging with all the respect due to such greatness that you may graciously receive him under your protection . . ."

Cervantes must have written this in one of his moments of devil-may-care cynicism, when he thought—as another great writer of this period, Quevedo, was to put it some years later—that "he who is in need would be foolish to stint compliments". Be that as it may, the dedication to the Duke of Bejar, while it cost him little, brought him nothing. The Duke did not react to it, and Cervantes never mentioned him again, nor did he dedicate any other work to him.

32

Cloak-and-Dagger Drama

IN 1605, Valladolid celebrated with great pomp and festivity the birth of the King's first-born, the future King Philip IV. The date coincided with the arrival of the English envoy, Admiral Lord Howard, Earl of Nottingham, who came with a glittering retinue to put the seal on the peace treaty which had been signed shortly before in London. Valladolid gave the Ambassador a magnificent reception. The Constable of Castile, himself recently returned from London, wished to "pay for the many courtesies he had received there", as the chronicler of those days, the Portuguese Pinheiro da Veiga, recorded.

The English reached Valladolid in the early evening. Shortly afterwards the town-crier announced that no woman was allowed to go out at night unless on her husband's arm, "so as to avoid traffic with heretics". Heavy punishment was in store for anyone infringing this decree. For many days, the people of Valladolid watched curiously as the six hundred gentlemen of Lord Howard's suite passed through the streets, "fair-haired, tall, with flowing locks". An old woman, seeing their gallant bearing, sighed and said: "And to think they will all burn in Hell!" With amazement the Spaniards observed the men who had been their arch-enemies in the days of the Great Armada and the sack of Cadiz. The chronicler describes the Ambassador himself as a "thick-set man of about sixty, elegant and well-mannered, with a large face, a very tall figure, and apt for his mission"; adding, "he is better than our own Constable, who at his side looks like a sickly sacristan".

It had been Lord Howard who, together with Essex, had made

the audacious naval raid on Cadiz in 1596, when the town was laid waste and the Spanish ships at anchor were set on fire. He came wearing a halo by virtue not only of that bold exploit, but also of his generous behaviour towards the people at his mercy, a generosity which he had known how to defend with verve when he was accused of showing excessive weakness in the English parliament.

Now he arrived on a peace mission, at a time when Spain's already lowered prestige had been further damaged through two hapless expeditions against England which the Duke of Lerma had launched. And the Spaniards were tired of war. Lord Howard was fêted, feasted and cheered. He received munificent presents and was the guest of honour at sumptuous feasts. The King displayed his courtly grace and skill at games; the Spanish gentlemen appeared in splendid attire; the ladies adorned their most exquisite dresses with "so many jewels, ribbons and trinkets that some of them looked like saints' images covered with medals", according to the Portuguese chronicler.

No comment on the English visitors was made by Cervantes; at least, none is recorded. We may, however, imagine him at one of those noisy public functions, hovering in the wings, in the discreet shadows, and watching the Englishmen enjoying their festive gala. He always cherished a certain admiration for the northern enemy, whom he contrasted sharply with the barbaric Turk; so much is evident from his later writings. On this occasion, his fair-minded appreciation cannot have been enough to stifle an inner dismay. Not so very long ago his poems had reflected his nation's common belief that the defeat of Spain would be wiped out and avenged. Now this illusion finally vanished into thin air, like the sparks of the rockets and catherine wheels let off in honour of the victors. Was it only seven years since Philip II was buried? His days seemed as remote as the deeds in the ballads of chivalry. These crowds were boisterously gay and thoughtless, they did not mind. And we can picture Cervantes leaving the festival a tired, bowed man who felt very old and not a little sad.

Another poet, Góngora, was present at those festivities in
Valladolid, and he gave vent to his feelings in a satirical sonnet.
It begins:

> The Queen gave birth; the Lutheran arrived
> with heretics and heresies six hundred . . .

and it ends:

> We were left poor, the Lutheran grew rich;
> and called upon to write these exploits were
> Don Quixote, Sancho Panza, and his ass.

This twist at the end of a mordant poem does not sound friendly
towards Cervantes, nor could anything but a caustic reaction to
Don Quixote be expected from that man of spleen, Góngora. Yet
it shows that not even he, the intellectual, could ignore the rising
popular author. If the sonnet was intended to ridicule Cervantes
and call the personages of his book vulgar by implication, it mis-
fired. In its way, Góngora's venomous allusion was a gesture
of recognition.

*

Edition after edition of *Don Quixote* flooded the country. For
the first time in many years Cervantes had reason to be hopeful
—and then his hard-won contentment was shattered once more
by an unsavoury scandal.

It was towards eleven o'clock on the night of June 27, 1605.
The women of Cervantes' household (with the exception of his
wife, who was not in Valladolid at the time) had gone to church,
he himself was already in bed. Suddenly the deserted Calle del
Rastro—Junk Market Street—echoed to loud cries for help. But
the people of the neighbourhood were afraid of getting involved
in anything which might lead to a criminal investigation. Some
may have peeped through the shutters, others hastened to close
doors and windows and to put out the lights. More than once a
man had been left in the street, bleeding to death unaided, because
of this general fear—which, it will be seen, was not altogether
unfounded.

It was left to a fifteen-year-old boy, who lived on the same floor as Cervantes, and to Miguel himself, to act as good samaritans. Carrying a lighted candle, the boy, Esteban de Garibay, accom-panied Cervantes out into the dark street where they found, reel-ing almost on their doorstep, a youngish man who carried in one hand a sword, in the other a small shield; he was bleeding pro-fusely. Together, Cervantes and young Esteban—who recog-nized the injured man—helped him upstairs to the rooms of Esteban's mother, Doña Luisa de Montoya. While they bedded him on a mattress on the floor, others ran to fetch a priest, a constable and the nearest surgeon, one Sebastian Macías, surgeon-barber to His Majesty's Mounted Bodyguard. Macías bled and tended the man, who had two deep stab wounds, one in the thigh and the other in the groin, where the peritoneum was found to be perforated.

In due course the magistrate arrived: Licientiate Cristóbal de Villarroel, one of the four Justices of the Peace in Valladolid, accompanied by the constables Francisco Vicente and Diego García. He immediately began his investigation of the case by taking a statement from the victim.

The latter turned out to be one of many young sparks who had flocked to Valladolid to become hangers-on of the high nobility, with no other occupation than swordplay, dancing and wench-ing. His name was Don Gaspar de Ezpeleta, he came from Navarra, and his protector was the Marquis de Falces, Captain of the King's Archers. Don Gaspar was a well-known man-about-town, who was at home in the best society. He took most of his meals at the Marquis de Falces' table, rode the Marquis's horses, and in return kept the Marquis amused by his pranks. His posi-tion was half that of a friend and boon companion, half that of a buffoon. He often took part in jousts and tourneys, sometimes exhibiting considerable bravery, sometimes merely playing the fool. Once he had fallen off his horse during a joust, apparently because he was in his cups, and Góngora had thought it worth-while to ridicule the incident in two ten-line stanzas.

Juana Ruiz, the landlady of an inn in the Calle de Manteros, gave evidence that, in the three months Don Gaspar had lodged with her, he had slept in his own bed at best fourteen times. Where he spent his nights was explained by his page, who said that his master "entertained amorous relations with a married woman" and used to go to her house, near the Calle del Rastro. In the Duke of Lerma's Valladolid this was not a particularly shocking revelation. To quote Pinheiro da Veiga once more, married women there gloried in their love affairs "because they knew that a woman without a lover is like an untended vineyard". Ezpeleta had not only stayed in that house many nights, but, so the page declared, had expressed misgivings about somebody who lived there and had threatened to kill him.

In addition, the landlady had a strange tale to tell. A gentlewoman with her face muffled in a cloak had called in Ezpeleta's absence and had demanded to see his room. There she had begun to sob and to cry: "Oh, scene of my shame and disgrace! Oh, you wicked traitor, how great a wrong you have done me! By Almighty God, you will pay for it, if it takes a hundred years—I shall be avenged!" This tragi-comedy, so revealing of life in contemporary Valladolid, was told by the landlady with many juicy details. She said she had been sorry for the unknown lady and had tried to comfort her, with the result that she gained her confidence. The lady, after having made Juana Ruiz swear to keep everything a deep secret, had confessed why she wanted to enter Don Gaspar de Ezpeleta's room. She had given him two golden rings, one set with diamonds, the other with emeralds, which had been her wedding present. It was left unexplained whether she had given them to Don Gaspar as a love token or—more probably—so that he could pawn them. But now her husband had enquired about the rings; as she was unable to produce them, he had begun to threaten her and "made her life a misery". Juana Ruiz recalled that the cloaked lady had said, "unless Ezpeleta returned her rings she would deal with him in a way he would never forget; she was not a woman to let anyone make a fool of her, and would take revenge for the trick he had played on her".

By that time the two women had grown so intimate that the lady in the cloak even confided her husband's name: he was the secretary Galván, and lived near San Salvador.

What had happened to Ezpeleta could now be pieced together, partly from his own evidence. On the evening in question he had, as usual, gone to the house of his "great friend", the Marquis de Falces. Not finding him in, he had waited for his return, and then the two men had gone out riding. Ezpeleta had stayed with the Marquis for the evening meal. Later he had sent his page for his sword and buckler, had exchanged his short cloak for his valet's voluminous cape—Cervantes and young Garibay had found it lying on the ground a few steps from their front door—and, so disguised, had gone to keep a date with a lady at the Rastro. Not far from the Marquis's residence, near the Hospital, he had come across a servant girl with a pitcher who was going for water. He had paid her a compliment, the girl had answered back in the manner of her class, and upon this he had gone closer. She turned out to be the servant of a certain Doña Maria de Argomedo (who lived in the same house as Cervantes). He made a grab at her, told her who he was, and asked her to come with him. The girl—this was her own evidence before the Magistrate—had "told him indignantly that she did not want to, and went to fetch her water". The adventurous gentleman had walked on, only stopping for a moment at the sound of music which attracted him. Past the little wooden bridge across the Esgueva, near the Hospital, a cloaked man had stepped up to him and asked where he was going. Ezpeleta had answered that it was none of his business; but, sensing that this was not a man to be fobbed off with mere words, he had drawn his sword and buckled his shield. Then the other had lunged and, in Ezpeleta's words, "they had a very good fight". Neither before nor after their encounter had he been able to identify his attacker—or so Ezpeleta maintained to the last.

All clues, then, pointed in the same direction. Juana Ruiz had produced the name of the cloaked lady's husband; the Justice of the Peace himself found a note in Ezpeleta's pocket, a fact which

P

leaked out although he did not use it in the evidence; the constables had surprised the cloaked lady during a second visit to
Ezpeleta's room, on the day after the fatal incident; subsequently
she had seen the Magistrate in his private house, without witnesses—something which Villarroel did not mention during the
proceedings. Finally, the servant girl whom Ezpeleta had accosted
made another important statement. She said that on her way
home, near the wooden bridge and before coming to the Hospital, she had seen a man "who was small, dressed in black, with
his cloak sliding from his shoulders, and was in the act of sheathing
a sword; he wore no collar but a neckband and his doublet was
buttoned the wrong way". He had passed her in a great hurry,
as though running away, so that she had not been able to see him
very clearly. But she had the impression that his face had been
round, his beard newly trimmed, and of a reddish colour, and
"that she would recognize him if she met him again".

This should have been enough for the man who had stabbed
Ezpeleta to be traced, but the Magistrate knew better. And his
treatment of the case involved Cervantes, whose sole connection
with the incident was an act of simple human kindness.

On the morning of June 29, Don Gaspar de Ezpeleta died,
still in Doña Luisa de Montoya's room. Several attempts were
made, one of them at the very last moment of his life, to wrest
from him the name of his assailant, "to relieve his conscience".
But if Ezpeleta was a parasite and rogue, he was also a gentleman.
He refused to say more than that the other had met him face to
face, as an honourable man; he neither knew him, nor wanted to
know who he was—he only wanted to be left in peace. And
with these words he died. Doña Magdalena de Cervantes, who
had nursed him devotedly all the time, was at his bedside.

Villarroel, the Justice of the Peace, had no doubt started off
with the intention of using the obvious key figure, the lady in the
cloak, to track down the guilty man. Very soon, however, he
dropped this line of investigation, either because it led to the
secretary Galván, or because it would have involved another and
more important person. Instead, Villarroel made a *volte-face* and

transferred his attentions from the house where the crime had its origin to the house where the victim of the crime had found shelter.

The tenement house in which Cervantes lived was one of the newly built houses near the Junk Market. It was not exactly a temple of virtue; the motley crowd of tenants was typical of Valladolid, where overcrowding had led to a great housing shortage and families took rooms wherever they could find and afford them. On the ground floor there was a tavern. Above it was the floor which was occupied on one side by the Cervantes' household, on the other by Doña Luisa de Montoya and her two young sons; she was the widow of Esteban de Garibay, chronicler and usher to His Majesty. The next floor, too, was occupied by two different tenants, one a certain Doña Mariana Ramírez, and the other, Doña Juana Gaitán, widow of Cervantes' old friend, the poet Pedro Laínez. Doña Juana had taken in lodgers: Doña Maria de Argomedo with her sister and niece, both young and unmarried, and a married couple, Rodrigo Montero, an old retainer of the Duke of Lerma, and his wife Jerónima. Finally there lived in the garret, all by herself, an old widow, Doña Isabel de Ayala. She was a *Beata*—not only devout but also bigoted and intolerant in her religious attitude—and would have no truck with any of the people in the house "because she had always been shocked and scandalized by their excessive social life". Doña Isabel's pious zeal was so great that she found it necessary to watch the comings and goings of the whole household. When the Justice of the Peace interrogated her, she gave him a long, circumstantial and angry description of her neighbours' way of life.

There was that Doña Maria Ramírez: she was notoriously living in sin with a married gentleman of Valladolid called Miranda. Then there was Doña Juana Gaitán: two or three times the Duke of Pastrana and the Count of Concentaina with their servants had called on her. This was in fact true, and Doña Juana, when taxed with it, explained that the two noblemen had come to thank her for the dedication of one of her deceased husband's books. Three formal visits for the sake of a dedication sounded somewhat far-fetched; but similar visits were received by many families in Valladolid, without the excuse of literary business, and nobody took umbrage. Still, Doña Isabel de Ayala was not only shocked by what she saw but convinced that nameless orgies were going on in that household.

And then there were the Cervantes. They had many callers, such as Don Hernando de Toledo, who was the squire of Higales, the Genoese contractor Augustín Ragio, and the young Portuguese Simón Méndez. Mostly they were Miguel's acquaintances from his days in Seville, who came to discuss business and bring him commissions, but some of them may also have come to see his daughter or his niece, Andrea's daughter. According to Doña Isabel de Ayala strange gentlemen came and went, by day and by night: "they have parties, and gentlemen are admitted to their rooms whom this witness does not know, all of which gives offence and causes gossip". She was more definite about Simón Méndez—he "was the illicit lover of the writer's daughter".

Clearly most of her allegations were inspired by malice, but this does not necessarily mean that Isabel de Saavedra was blameless. There is no real proof either way. Simón Méndez—a married man—had once given her a costly present, but the girl explained this away by saying that he had simply done it as a good friend of the family, and her two aunts backed her up. For old Doña Isabel de Ayala, however, the present was conclusive evidence that the relationship she suspected was a fact, and as such she represented it to the Justice of the Peace. Simón Méndez tried in vain to deny the allegation. It suited Villarroel to treat it as the truth, for he was busily building up a new case based on the assumption that Ezpeleta had had relations with one or the other of the young women in the house.

Doña Magdalena, of all people, furnished him with what he considered to be a clue. Cervantes' younger sister had retired from mundane affairs and took an interest only in her religious duties; not many years later she was to enter a religious Order. But

Don Gaspar de Ezpeleta had been so grateful for her nursing that he had willed her a gown made of "silk of her own choice". This aroused Villarroel's suspicions. A silk gown for an elderly *beata*, a devout churchwoman, who always dressed in serge? Was it not more likely that the dress was in reality destined for one of her young relatives?

The statements of the various tenants of the house, including Doña Isabel de Ayala's, had brought nothing to light which could explain Ezpeleta's death, and very little which had any bearing on his person at all. But the Justice of the Peace was determined at all costs to avoid involving Mr Secretary Galván or the cloaked lady, and therefore Doña Isabel de Ayala's dark hints at immorality presented him with a welcome alternative.

"In view of the result of these investigations, the Justice of the Peace Don Cristóbal de Villarroel decrees and orders the arrest and subsequent transfer to the royal prison in this city of the following persons: Miguel de Cervantes and Doña Isabel, his daughter; Doña Andrea and Doña Constanza, her daughter; Doña Maria de Argomedo, her sister and her niece; Doña Maria Ramírez; and Don Diego de Miranda. This is my instruction and order."

And so it came to pass. Miguel de Cervantes, his daughter, his elder sister Andrea and her daughter, were taken to prison while neighbours in the street gaped at them and said ugly things behind their backs.

They were all detained for a couple of days, just long enough to inflict a bitter and undeserved humiliation on them, and to deflect suspicion and attention from those others Villarroel wanted to shield. When the prisoners were set free, the decision of the four Justices of the Peace of Valladolid contained several almost equally humiliating injunctions. Cervantes himself was released on his own bail—he had not once been interrogated during his arrest—but all the women were confined to the house, and the magistrates forbade any further contact between Simón Méndez and Isabel de Saavedra. They were even more severe with Doña

Maria Ramírez and Diego de Miranda—all in the name of public morality. With Valladolid society in the state Pinheiro da Veiga described, this by-product of the investigation into Gaspar de Ezpeleta's death was a fantastic farce.

*

The injustice had been glaring, yet Cervantes was past the stage when his peace of mind could be disturbed by the arbitrariness of judges or the rudeness of constables. He had never learned how to avoid the pitfalls of life, but he had at last learned to take them philosophically. In his *Persiles* he was to explain that it is unwise to relax when the tide of events seems favourable; rather one should be on one's guard, for the "current of evil starts from afar". It was hard to have an act of decency repaid with gratuitous insults, the more so since Cervantes was an ageing man, and had hoped to bask in the sunshine of his belated success. But the blow was not crushing. This time the pettiness and pitiful cowardice of others only served to throw his character into bolder relief.

Cervantes' integrity was, in the end, undeniable. Not one of his many opponents, brutally outspoken as they often were, ever quoted the Valladolid incidents—or for that matter any of his spells in prison—against him as something of which he had reason to be ashamed. And it was not as if he had tried to cover them up; on the contrary, he almost paraded them like so many trophies. On the very first page of *Don Quixote* he said, to all intents and purposes, that his novel was "engendered in prison". This was not a plea for clemency towards the possible defects of the book—though the statement is part of such a plea—but a challenge. Similarly, he never apologized for his excommunication, but made it clear, through a passage in *Don Quixote*, that he felt pride in the actions that had brought it upon him. There Don Quixote speaks of the Cid's excommunication by the Pope in person, after he had smashed the chair of the French King because it had been placed above his own overlord's seat at the

Papal Court. "And on that day", says Don Quixote, "the Cid behaved as a very honourable and valiant knight."

Cervantes had ultimately won an inner poise which no adversity could upset, for it enabled him to transmute each trial and sorrow into an enriching experience.

33

Last Return

THE Court moved back to Madrid, and Cervantes with his family followed suit.

They found rooms in the popular quarter of Lavapiés, in the Calle de la Magdalena at the back of the Pastrana Palace. There, Miguel was near Cuesta's printing shop where the latest edition of *Don Quixote* was in preparation, near the bookshop of his publisher, Robles, and near the "whispering gallery" where people of the theatre used to meet. There were old threads to pick up and new literary aspirations to pursue. But he was also near two centres of spiritual life which began to attract him more and more as he grew old: the monasteries of the Mercedarian and Trinitarian friars. In the first, his father was buried. The second harboured the friars of the Order of Father Juan Gil, the Redemp, torist, who had once come aboard the Bey of Algiers' galley to restore life and liberty to Miguel. Memories of his captivity and of bygone wars assumed a different hue when he recalled them now, for, to use his own words, "it is very sweet to speak about past torments in quiet, and about the dangers of past wars in peace".

In Madrid Miguel was at last at the centre and hub of Spain's intellectual life. Even though all his troubles were not over, he was able to devote more time to his writing, and this in itself was restful, a relief after prolonged frustration. Six editions of *Don Quixote* had been issued, the seventh was in print. He was working on a second part of the novel and had begun another book. While he could not afford to give up the small-scale business activities by which he eked out a living, it is reasonable to assume that he entered a period of relative ease. He had in-fluential friends willing to help him, like Don Juan de Urbina, administrator of the estates of the Priory of San Juan, and power-ful protectors, such as the Count of Lemos and Cardinal San-doval. Life, it seemed, had grown tired of loading his weary shoulders with fresh burdens.

Soon after their arrival in Madrid, Miguel's daughter, Isabel de Saavedra, married Don Diego Sanz del Aguila. What little is known of this episode points to its having been a marriage of con-venience. Cervantes' friend Juan de Urbina was an intimate of the bridegroom—and possibly Andrea had been at her match-making again. She had never been one to yield to sentiment, and the dismal result of her interference in Miguel's own case will not have deterred her from arranging the future of her niece in what she considered the most practical manner.

Isabel's husband was of noble descent, a gentleman of the Knightly Order of Alcántara, and a man of some means. The couple settled down in a house in the Calle de Jardines, where their only daughter was born at the beginning of 1608 and christ-ened Isabel. While we like to think that Cervantes took delight in the first smiles of his little granddaughter, Isabel Sanz del Aguila, his happiness—as so often before—was short-lived. Don Diego died before the first year of his marriage was over. Almost at once a new suitor for Isabel appeared on the scene. He was Luis Molina, a businessman whom Cervantes had known in Valla-dolid and who was by now a frequent guest in his home.

As a penniless girl, Isabel de Saavedra seems not to have inter-ested Molina, but things took on a different complexion when she became a widow whose attractions were enhanced by the pro-perty she had inherited from her husband and the connections he had established. Molina was still young, a pleasant com-panion, shrewd and enterprising; he was a spendthrift, liked to cut a good figure, and allowed nothing to stand in the way of his vanity and expensive tastes. Though he sounds as if he might have been a congenial husband for Isabel de Saavedra, herself no pattern of virtue, he was not a son-in-law with whom Cervantes could live in harmony for long. And even Isabel, who parted ways with her father for Molina's sake, ended by living separated from her husband.

At the time of his marriage, Luis Molina was leading a busy life. Apart from his own business—he may have used Cervantes as a commission agent at some stage—he was secretary to the Italian bankers Carlo and Antonio Trata. On his return from Italy in 1598, he had been carried off to Algiers by Turkish pirates. It was after he had been ransomed that he settled in Valladolid. Perhaps his Algerian experiences made Cervantes warm to him in the first place. Molina's charm and liveliness certainly succeeded in winning him Cervantes' affections, though this was not difficult, as we have seen.

Once the marriage had been decided upon, Cervantes wanted to give Isabel a dowry fit for a gentlewoman and a *grand seigneur's* daughter. Molina may well have dropped a hint, but Cervantes' own love of reckless generosity is sufficient explanation. As usual, he greatly overrated the improvement in his circumstances which, soberly regarded, were still somewhat precarious. The great sales of *Don Quixote* had brought its author little benefit because he had signed away his rights; nor did his publisher show him any particular liberality, and Cervantes owed him at that time 450 *reales*. But in his imagination, Cervantes was about to become a rich man.

On August 28, 1608, Cervantes signed a marriage contract in which he undertook to pay his future son-in-law, within three years, two thousand ducats in cash as his daughter's dowry. Don Juan de Urbina signed as his guarantor, "for certain reasons which moved him to do so", as the document stated somewhat mysteriously. In a similarly mysterious fashion, the house in the Calle de Jardines which Isabel de Saavedra and her first husband had occupied appeared in a clause of the contract. It was described as the property of Isabel's little daughter, in the event of whose death it was to go to Miguel de Cervantes, her grandfather. At the same time, Juan de Urbina was committed to the payment of all taxes and duties on the property. It was, as other documents prove, generally assumed that Urbina was the real proprietor of the house. In a later will, however, Isabel de Saavedra maintained that her first husband had had a claim to it. Cervantes' own title to it, such as it was, was meant to serve as collateral security in respect of the dowry.

It is impossible to guess what lay behind this complicated arrangement. Isabel de Saavedra later insinuated that the whole transaction had been a manœuvre of Urbina's, who had abused her father's good faith. Some have maintained, on the other hand, that Urbina had simply acted as a disinterested, generous friend. But were there not quite different motives behind it all? We know for certain only that after Cervantes' death, when his granddaughter too was dead, Juan de Urbina went to court to reclaim the house as his property from Isabel de Saavedra.

As far as Molina was concerned, Cervantes was sadly mistaken if he expected his son-in-law not to make an issue of it, should circumstances delay or prevent the payment of the dowry. Molina must have known upon what shaky foundations Cervantes' hopes of affluence were built, but he had Urbina's signature. And Don Juan de Urbina was a wealthy landowner from the Mancha, he had a substantial income from his post with the Priory of San Juan, his grain, timber and charcoal contracts, his mills in Tembleque and his real estate in Madrid. It is highly probable that Urbina had undersigned the marriage contract at Molina's suggestion. He himself may have thought that Cervantes' prospects were good enough, but certainly Molina considered Urbina's signature the real asset.

On September 8, 1608, the solemn engagement ceremony was performed in the Church of San Luis, and six months later the wedding itself took place in the same church. Cervantes and his wife were the "godparents" of the bride. Thus Doña Catalina gave away her husband's illegitimate daughter and contributed her share to the happy event—which fulfilled the hopes of none of the participants.

34

Growing Solitude

IN April, 1609, Cervantes joined one of the many religious con-
gregations which sprang up in Madrid during those years. They
were founded to resist the rising tide of Protestantism, but they
also served as havens of rest for sensitive people who sought a
refuge from the saddening spectacle of everyday life. The congregation Cervantes chose was one to which many other prominent men belonged; it called itself the "Congregation of the
Unworthy Slaves of the Most Holy Sacrament", had been
founded by Fray Alonso de la Purificación the year before, and
was attached to the monastery of the Trinitarians.

Miguel often went to the sanctuary. Only there did he find
perfect peace; in the latter part of his life, he returned to the child-
like faith he seemed to have lost during the stormy years of his
struggle. No other member visited the monastery so frequently
and carried out his duties with so much fervour as he did.

Some of his old friends, and some who were by no means his
friends, belonged to the same brotherhood. There was, for
instance, the novelist Espinel, whom Cervantes distrusted, seeing
in him a "Zoilus", a potential libeller—after Miguel's death,
Espinel in fact tried to blacken his name. There was the great
satirist Quevedo; and there was Lope de Vega. Cervantes' chief
rival had also grown weary of his ceaseless battle with mediocrity
and jealousy, and of all the trouble his impulsiveness caused him.
He, too, began to feel isolated, and his poetry became tinged with
melancholy. No doubt he and Cervantes occasionally met in
this retreat and exchanged a few words. But, much as we should
like to think that the two poets whose names are linked in the

history of Spanish Letters were able to bury the hatchet, the differences between them were too great to be bridged in amity.

Cervantes frequently rode to Esquivias, ostensibly to look after his wife's farms or to inspect the new vineyard on the road to Seseña, which held a special attraction for him. In reality, how-ever, he was glad to have a pretext for roaming the countryside; the old vagabond spirit was still alive in him.

At night Cervantes worked on the second part of *Don Quixote*, but progress was slow. Life in its autumn mood was so sweet in spite of everything; long talks with understanding friends were so welcome; the twilight hours when he rode toward the first lights of Madrid on his return from Esquivias were so entrancing—Miguel was not inclined to press on with his *Quixote*. Sometimes he followed the impulse to write in a different vein. Thus, he completed the collection of stories which were published in 1613 under the title *Exemplary Tales*, breaking off this task, in turn, to prepare eight dramas and eight dramatic sketches for publica-tion in a single volume. But even though he took his time over it, *Don Quixote* remained the true centre of his life, and became ever more clearly the story of his own spiritual journey. The second part reflected the calm wisdom to which Miguel had attained, yet it also betrayed that the old hurt at finding himself disregarded was still rankling, and that he was beginning to fear a new disappointment, not the last in store for him, against which he had to steel himself.

At the beginning of the second part, Cervantes sends the Knight of the Doleful Countenance out on his quest again. But first Don Quixote has to obtain the blessing of his lady, Dul-cinea—"grave without arrogance, tender with chastity, pleasant out of courtesy, courteous through good breeding, the most divine creature God sent into this world"—whom he has never yet seen. Don Quixote knows that he is riding towards the most perilous adventures of his life, but also that, if he is hallowed by Dulcinea's blessing, there is no obstacle he cannot overcome.

Astride Rocinante and accompanied by Sancho on his ass, Don Quixote sets out for El Toboso, where his adored mistress

has her palace. The night is calm and dark, and seems to hold
strange mysteries. Cervantes conveys in comparatively few words
that his Knight rides, not towards a prosaic village in the Mancha,
but to a legendary place, and also that Don Quixote secretly
dreads the fulfilment of his dream, his first encounter with Dulcinea. After midnight he and his squire reach the straggling out-
skirts of El Toboso. Dogs bark, asses bray. In vain Don
Quixote looks for Dulcinea's castle or palace. The night begins
to pale, and once more the world of reality clashes with the world
of fantasy. With the approach of dawn, everything turns crude,
matter-of-fact and vulgar, striking fear into Don Quixote's heart.
He and Sancho make for a shadowy object looming up before
them, which the Knight takes for a castle tower; but instead
they stumble into the cemetery by the village church. A young
peasant with a plough comes singing down the road, driving a
pair of mules before him. With grave kindliness, Don Quixote
asks: "Can you tell me, my friend—and may God grant you
good fortune!—where the palaces of the peerless princess, Dulcinea del Toboso, are to be found hereabouts?" The ploughman
does not know, he is not a native of the village: ". . . It is only
a few days since I came here. In the house opposite live the
parish priest and the sacristan, they will be able to give you information about this princess, sir, because they keep records of all
the inhabitants. For myself, I should say there is no such princess in the whole village. Ladies there are many, grand ones too,
and every one of them may well be a princess in her own home."

"Well, friend, then she about whom I ask must be among
those ladies", answers Don Quixote. Without waiting for
further questions, the young peasant urges on his mules: "That
may be. And good-day to you, the sun will soon be rising."

The graveyard into which he had blundered, and the factual
remarks of the peasant which shattered his self-absorbed enchantment, strike Don Quixote as bad auguries; he vacillates. Has it
all been a dream, will he never see his Dulcinea—will he meet
death instead, or the defeat he fears more than death? But Sancho
Panza tricks his master, rescuing him from his doubts, and Don

Quixote rides on without the blessing of his lady which would
have made him invincible.

*

Miguel's life in Madrid was not destined to remain peaceful.
The first blow was the death of his sister Andrea. In June, 1609,
simultaneously with Doña Catalina, she had "taken the habit"
which made her a lay sister of the Third Order of St Francis.
Four months later she died. Her death left a vacuum which no
one was able to fill. It had been Andrea, with her gift of compromise, her vigour and her warmth, who had kept the household together. Now she was gone, a quick succession of events
led to the virtual disintegration of the family. A few months
after Andrea's death, Miguel's wife took a step which to a certain extent marked her withdrawal from her husband's home;
almost exactly a year after Andrea's death, the remaining sister,
Magdalena, died after a lengthy illness, at the beginning of which
she, too, had taken the habit of the Third Order of St Francis;
and in the course of the same year the latent disagreements
between Cervantes and his son-in-law over the payment or,
rather, non-payment of Isabel's dowry became acute. In the end
it came to a break between father and daughter.

On June 16, 1610, Doña Catalina appeared unexpectedly,
and without her husband's knowledge, at the office of the
scrivener Baltasar de Ugena, like herself a native of Esquivias, to
make her will. In this she may have followed the advice of her
brother, for whom she always showed great affection, and of her
other relatives in Esquivias; she maintained close contact with all
of them. In her will, Doña Catalina left practically everything
she possessed to her brother Francisco de Palacios, with the
exception of small bequests to her husband, his niece Constanza,
her other brother, who was a monk, and to her maid.

To her husband, Doña Catalina bequeathed the usufruct of a
few small pieces of land, among them the vineyard on the road
to Seseña; upon Miguel's death, this usufruct was to go to his

niece, Andrea's daughter Constanza, for two years, after which the property was to revert to Doña Catalina's brother.[1] For as long as they enjoyed the revenues from those plots of ground, Miguel or his niece, as the case might be, were to arrange for four masses a year for Doña Catalina's soul. She also willed to her husband the bed in which she would die, the bedclothes, and a few other pieces of furniture, "for the sake of the great love and good fellowship we have had together".

While this will shows a marked degree of stinginess towards her husband, which must have been apparent to Cervantes—though it may have been less painful to him than has been alleged—it demonstrates above all this luckless woman's profound loyalty towards her land and her own kin. Seen in this light, it is a touching and pitiable document.

Doña Catalina had fallen among people whose habits were utterly different from hers and whose conduct was contrary to that which she had always accepted as right. Can we wonder that her thoughts dwelt incessantly on the past, on things as she had known them? Her dead parents, her living relatives, her country house, her fields and vineyards—everything called to her. In her will she stipulated that "my body shall be taken to the village of Esquivias . . . and I shall be buried in the tomb of Fernando de Salazar Vozmediano, my father, which is in the choir of the church of the aforesaid village, next to the Main Altar, and has its own stone slab . . ." She wished to be reunited in death with her father and mother, as though to ask their forgiveness for the act of disobedience she had committed when she married.

And yet, before she died, she altered her will again. We may assume that the last years of her life together with Miguel had swept her narrow mind clean of every resentment at old wrongs, and that ultimately she only remembered his kindness and the tenderness he showed her at the end. She had learned to know

---

[1] Two years after this will, Doña Catalina changed the clause about her bequest to Miguel so that the usufruct of the pieces of land should go directly to her brother —perhaps because she thought that Miguel was in any case unlikely to survive her. (Translator's Note.)

and understand him better in those last years, and to love him more. After his death, her own loneliness and other people's praise of him may have ennobled Cervantes in the eyes of his widow, and so melted the ice in her heart. On October 20, 1626, ten years after Miguel's death, when Doña Catalina was living together with her brother Francisco in the Calle de los Desamparados in Madrid, she went to the notary Alonso de Valencia and asked him to amend the burial clause in her will: she wished to be buried in the Trinitarian convent where her husband was laid to rest.

Shortly before Doña Catalina made her first will, something occurred which threw Cervantes into such a state of excitement that he was prepared to cast everything overboard and begin a new existence abroad. The Count of Lemos, who had shown interest in Miguel's writings, was appointed Viceroy of Naples—needless to say, he was one of the Duke of Lerma's family. The post of Viceroy was greatly coveted because the Kingdom of Naples—then under Spanish rule—was "one of the most suc⁄ culent and most highly valued sinecures", as the Marquis de Rafel says in his book on the Count of Lemos.

A *littérateur*, politician, man of the world, connected with the oldest of Spain's aristocratic families, married to the Duke of Lerma's daughter, the Count of Lemos enjoyed considerable popularity. It was (again in the words of the Marquis de Rafel) only to be expected that a man of his social position, and connected as he was with Lerma, should be honoured with the highest offices. Of moderate intelligence, he was kindly, open⁄ hearted and generous, qualities which Cervantes would have appreciated in any man, let alone in the Count whom he had a right to consider his patron and protector. Lemos was genuinely interested in Letters—he wrote poetry and plays himself—and liked to have the most famous writers in his entourage. Lope de Vega, Góngora and many other prominent authors each acted, at some stage, as his secretary. But he was also surrounded by a whole crowd of smaller fry who, jockeying for posts and favours, readily lauded his indifferent verses to the skies.

Q

The Count's appointment caused a great flutter in all the literary dovecotes. Every poet, great or little, dreamed of joining the retinue which was to accompany the new Viceroy, and of scintillating at his future court in Naples.

While the preparations for the journey were under way, the Count's secretary died. Faced with the necessity of finding a successor without delay, the Count remembered Lupercio Argen-sola, a brilliant poet—and brilliantly clever at flattering the Count's person and family as well. Argensola, who lived in Saragossa, eagerly accepted the post which was offered to him, and he and his brother immediately set off for Madrid. These two men began to engage the personnel which the Count would take to Naples.

The Argensolas were besieged by applicants. They jostled one another outside the door, and letters poured in upon the brothers. Every possible string was pulled, for one and all wanted to go to Italy. Among the most important candidates for a post was Góngora; and, in the rear, though with equally great hopes, came Cervantes, trusting in the friendship the brothers Argen-sola professed for him, and in verbal promises they had given him.

Miguel, now sixty-three, was living with his wife, sister and niece; he had good friends; and though trouble was never far off, his days passed in comparative quiet. Here in Madrid he had the manuscripts on which he was working, he had his *Don Quixote*. He was at home in its streets, and he had the company of his regular cronies. Nevertheless, he was possessed by an irresistible impulse to leave all this. What a hold it obtained over his mind can be gauged by the intense effort he put into his application for a post, and by the acute disappointment and sorrow which characterized his utterances when he met with failure. Some-thing more than the simple urge to get away or the wish to live at ease and play a rôle at the court of Naples is behind Miguel's insistence; or so it seems to us. Had the thought of Naples awakened some distant memory—conjured up the vision of a long-lost hour of blissful happiness? Was he overcome by the wish, almost the obsession, "to see if there are any birds left in the nests of yesteryear"?

It was fortunate for Cervantes that the Argensolas, being better courtiers than friends, left him behind in Madrid together with the best of the poets, with Góngora, Suárez de Figueroa and the rest. The two brothers had no wish to engage anyone who might steal their thunder at the Count's court, so they selected suitable mediocrities, discreet and prudent men without the least brilliance. Cervantes was by no means the only one to protest, but his complaints were couched in restrained terms—he suppressed the anger he clearly felt. While he could not help wondering whether the Count of Lemos was aware of his new favourites' methods, he knew that a favourite's sympathy or antipathy may have an enormous influence on his master. Therefore he addressed to the Argensolas, in a passage in his *Journey to Parnassus*, only a few plaintive verses tempered by eulogy, and for the rest decided to dedicate his next published work to the Count himself, as a kind of test which would tell him whether he had grounds for hope in the future.

Regret at having been denied the opportunity to return to his beloved city of Naples was the main emotional inspiration of the long poem, *Journey to Parnassus*. So fervently had he hoped to revisit the paradise of his youth, so vividly had he visualized the people he would meet there, that he had to undertake an imaginary journey to make up for his loss. In imagination his ship calls at the port of Naples, he walks through the streets of the town, and he embraces a young soldier who calls him father, whom he calls son. Thus did Cervantes give expression to his longing for Naples, which remained with him till his death. But he stayed in Madrid, in growing solitude.

*

On October 11, 1610, Doña Magdalena de Cervantes, "being ill in bed with a malady Our Lord had decreed she should suffer, and fearing death, as is natural in any living creature," wanted to record her last wishes.

She, like her brother, was hard pressed by poverty; there was virtually nothing in the house to bequeath. All the same, it was necessary for her to make a last will, and the scrivener Jerónimo López was called to her sickbed, together with witnesses.

This will of Doña Magdalena's reveals strange aspects of her life, which was not without its secrets. There is in existence another document dating from her youth, in which a certain Juan Pérez de Arcega undertakes to pay her three hundred ducats in compensation for failing to carry out his promise to marry her. And another obscure affair emerges from her last will, again concerned with something like a breach of promise.

Doña Magdalena stated that a married man named Fernando de Ludeña owed her three hundred ducats, which she had lent him while he was still a bachelor. According to her story, she had gone to his house after his marriage and had demanded her money back from him in the presence of his wife, Doña Ana María de Urbina. Don Fernando, "not wanting to upset his wife", had denied that he owed her money. When she had come to his house a second time, he had "repeatedly threatened her, saying that she would not get a cent from him unless she gave him a document with the confession that he owed her nothing". When they were left alone, however, he had "promised to pay her an allowance during his lifetime and, in case she survived him, to leave her enough for her livelihood". On this under-standing she had given him the document he demanded. But now she declared "on her conscience" that Ludeña still owed her those three hundred ducats. She willed this debt to her brother and niece jointly, and added that they should get the money from him or "at least tell him about it, as a burden on his conscience, for he knows it is true, and this is my will."

She also bequeathed her niece two small rents—so-called bread-and-water allowances, usually given to old retainers—which she, Magdalena, had been granted by Don Enrique de Palafox, a Knight of the Order of Calatrava, who "had it in his power to give them, owing to His Majesty's grant of 'bread-and-water allowances' to the aforesaid Knights", and who had empowered her to transfer them in her will. Finally she left to her niece her own share in the soldier's pay still due to the heirs of her brother Rodrigo, killed in the battle of Nieuport in 1600— a debt which it was beyond human power to cash from the Exchequer.[1] It was, in short, a testament in the true style of the Cervantes family, leaving the "heirs" nothing but debts and tangles, empty phrases and requests to have Masses read for the soul of the deceased.

Doña Magdalena died three months later. Neither her brother nor her niece had the means to pay for her funeral. It cost twelve *reales*. The expenses were defrayed by the Sisters of the Third Order of St Francis, in whose convent she was buried.

---

[1] Cervantes signed a document bearing the same date as Doña Magdalena's will, in which he ceded his share in the "inheritance and soldier's pay" of his brother to his niece Constanza. That he did not cede it to his daughter Isabel is evidence of the state of their relations, even though there was little hope of anyone ever getting the full amount of the pay arrears. (Translator's Note.)

35

Fortitude

Now Cervantes was left alone with his wife and his niece. The break between Miguel and his daughter was as complete as if she had died. One day Molina, Isabel de Saavedra's husband, went to court because the contractual dowry had not been paid within the set time limit of two years. Don Juan de Urbina, who had signed the document together with Cervantes, was forced to pay, since Cervantes was destitute. Neither Miguel's literary success, nor the occasional help of patrons, nor the money he earned as an agent for businessmen, had been enough to keep him afloat. He was in debt with his publisher, Robles; he was still in debt with the Exchequer in respect of his accounts as tax-gatherer; he was in debt with Don Juan de Urbina, and with others, whose names have not been preserved. A letter from Lope de Vega, taken together with Cervantes' own remarks in *Journey to Parnassus*, furnishes proof of his plight.

A new "academy" or literary circle had been organized in Madrid. It was called "Selvaje", The Forest—a pun on the surname of Don Francisco de Silva, who acted as host at its gatherings; the intellectual élite of the capital, with Lope de Vega at its head, belonged to it. In the letter in question, Lope de Vega first pokes fun at the academy and then refers to Cer-vantes in terms which betray an irrepressible animosity. His remarks make it clear that Cervantes was passing through another critical period in his financial affairs, and that he still made a bad impression by his attire and general appearance. Lope de Vega, for instance, gibes at Cervantes' spectacles, which he had bor-rowed for a moment, saying that "they looked like badly cooked poached eggs". On the other hand, there is a scene in *Journey to Parnassus* in which the poet is left without a seat in a gathering of brilliant Men of Letters—an obvious reference to a humiliating incident at the academy; when he is told by Apollo to fold up his cloak so as to make a cushion of it, the poet reminds the god that he possesses no cloak. And towards the end of his poem Cervantes tells us that, on coming back to Madrid, he repairs to his "sad and dreary lodgings". In grim reality—though not in the poem—he had to move from his lodgings soon afterwards, probably because he was unable to pay the rent.

With so many sorrows and vexations to harass him, we might expect to see Cervantes despairing and rebelling against his lot. He did nothing of the kind. As he lost, through death or estrangement, one after another of the human beings who had lent his home what attraction it possessed, the drab misery he had thought was a thing of the past weighed upon him once more, and brought him the inevitable share of neglect and disregard. But Miguel still would not give in. A tremendous inner conviction filled his being, there was mounting faith in his own work; and this new pride expressed itself in his writings.

We have conclusive proof of the change in him when we compare the dedication to the Duke of Bejar of the first part of *Don Quixote*, with the dedication to the Count of Lemos of the *Exemplary Tales*, which he had just completed. In the one, Cervantes humbly and timorously begs a favour; in the other, he makes a plain statement. Instead of requesting an honour as before, he now almost confers one, when he says, "May Your Excellency take note that I am dedicating to you, without more ado, twelve tales which, had they not been tooled in the workshop of my intellect, would claim their place among the finest." Then follows a prologue which contains a passage full of a creator's pride and satisfaction: "To this end I am applying my skill, hither my bent led me, and all the more so as I understand (and it is indeed a fact) that I am the first teller of such tales in the Castilian language; for, the many tales which may be found in print in this country are all translated from foreign languages,

while these are mine, neither copied nor stolen. My mind engendered them, my pen gave birth to them, and now they grow
lustily in the arms of the printing press." This is almost a counter-
attack against the neglect as a writer under which he had been
smarting.

Through his renewed belief in himself, Cervantes seemed to
gain in stature. He worked incessantly, new projects crowded his
mind. His activities as commission agent stopped almost completely; at such times as he did not take part in the meetings of
actors or writers, make brief excursions into the country, or get
involved in heated discussions, he wrote page upon page with an
enthusiasm which was miraculous at his age. Even while he put
the finishing touches to the *Exemplary Tales*, he continued with
his *Don Quixote*, wrote the *Journey to Parnassus* and prepared his
plays for the book edition—they were plays which had never
been performed, and the new Entremeses, eight gay dramatic
interludes which Cervantes added to eight full-length dramas,
were in their own way quite brilliant. *Seville Gaol*, which I
unhesitatingly attribute to Cervantes (*pace* the contrary opinion
of several scholars), is as fresh a masterpiece today as when it
was written. At the same time he seems to have begun to
draft the first chapters of his *Persiles* and to plan a sequel to the
Galatea, as well as a work called *Weeks in the Garden*. Between
1600 and 1610 he wrote more than in all the previous years of his
literary life; during the following six, from 1610 to his death, his
output exceeded even that of those fertile ten years. What is more,
he had never written with such pithiness, clarity and fluency.
One might be inclined to speak of a second youth, were it not
for a faint sadness in all the works of his old age, a sadness
reflecting the harsh conditions of his existence and the loneliness
in which he lived.

36

Journey to Parnassus

VIAJE DEL PARNASO, *Journey to Parnassus*, did not appear in print until 1614, but in it Cervantes' earlier acute disappointment about the frustrated journey to Naples finds expression. It also mirrors the petty irritations which he refrained from introducing, even obliquely, into the second part of *Don Quixote*, a work on an altogether higher plane. Furthermore, it presents us with many personal details concerning Miguel's life, which are invaluable to the biographer. *Journey to Parnassus*—written in triplets—is a poem which often takes on a polemic aspect; it speaks of Cer-vantes' poverty, of the jealousy which dogged his career as a writer, and of his low standing in the literary hierarchy. But, above all, it is pervaded by Cervantes' faith in his own genius. He was aware of the shabbiness of his appearance; he was equally aware of his colleagues' arrogant silence or of their mockery. His answer to all this was to express his deep inner contentment in the clearest possible terms. His verses show his pride in every-thing: his writings, not excluding those of least merit, his life, his character, his struggle with adversity, and his very poverty.

The occasions when he had been slighted, in the Academy "Selvaje" or elsewhere, were not forgotten; but in the *Journey to Parnassus* the god Mercury serves as his avenger. Mercury invites Cervantes to a gathering of the greatest Spanish poets, allots him a place in the first rank, and acclaims him, though first voicing his concern over Cervantes' attire:

> ¿ *Oh Adán de los poetas, oh Cervantes!*
> ¿ *qué alforjas y qué traje es éste, amigo,* . .

O Adam of the poets, O Cervantes,
What saddlebags, what garb is this, my friend . . .

The "Adam of the poets" offers no apology, but says:

> *Señor, voy al Parnaso y, como pobre,*
> *con este aliño mi jornada sigo.*

> I go, sir, to Parnassus, Being poor,
> I travel on in this habiliment.

Thereupon Mercury assures him that he has no need for osten‑
tation and external honours:

> *. . . que, al fin has respondido a ser soldado*
> *antiguo y valiente, cual demuestra*
> *la mano de que estás estropeado.*

> *Bien sé que en la naval dura palestra*
> *perdiste el movimiento de la mano*
> *izquierda para gloria de la diestra.*

> *Y sé aquel instinto sobrehumano*
> *que de raro inventor tu pecho encierra*
> *no te le ha dado padre Apolo en vano.*

> *Tus obras los rincones de la tierra*
> *llevándolas en grupa Rocinante*
> *descubren y a la invidia mueven guerra.*

> *Pasa, raro inventor, pasa adelante . . .*

For, after all, you once obeyed the call
And were a valiant soldier, as the sight
Of your disfigured hand does prove to all.

I know that in the bitter naval fight
You lost the use of your left hand and wrought
By this the greater glory of your right.

I also know, the rare inventor's thought
and superhuman instinct in your breast
Father Apollo gave you, not for nought.

Already countries east and north and west
Discover your works, your Rocinante's load,
And leave embattled jealousy distressed.

Pass on, O rare inventor, on your road . . .

Cervantes is concerned lest any, in good or bad faith, should confuse him with the herd of flatterers who spend their lives fawning on the great and powerful:

> *Tuve, tengo y tendré los pensamientos,*
> *merced al cielo que a tal bien me inclina,*
> *de toda adulación libres y exentos.*

> *Nunca pongo los pies por do camina*
> *la mentira, la fraude y el engaño,*
> *de la santa virtud total ruina.*

I had, I have and I shall have a mind
Free and exempt from base blandiloquence,
For Heaven's mercy has me thus inclined.

Nor do I enter in the places whence,
To ruin all that holy is and good,
Lies sally forth, deceit and fraudulence.

He attacks the hypocrites who, in mock modesty, belittle their own poetry even while they secretly thirst for praise; in criticising them, he upholds the different attitude he himself adopts:

> *Aquel que de poeta no se precia,*
> *¿ para qué escribe versos y los dice?*
> *¿ Por qué desdeña lo que más aprecia?*

Jamás me contenté ni satisfice
de hipócritas melindres. Llanamente
quise alabanzas de lo que bien hice.

He who esteems himself no poet, why
Does he write verse, why read his verse with pride?
Why does, what he most values, he deny?

I never was one to be satisfied
With small hypocrisies. For work well done
I want applause, and this I do not hide.

Then Cervantes defends himself against the reproach of having
been too prodigal with his eulogies of others, tilts at the bad poets,
but without mentioning more than one name—only to relapse
into his old vice which he has just forsworn: he heaps praise on
a number of poets, most of them obscure, in the same manner
and with the same lack of true poetry as in *La Galatea*.

After this, the poem goes on to describe his landing in Naples,
where he finds his way back to the "streets he had once trod for
more than a year", and meets his mysterious son. In talking to
him, he recalls his lost youth:

En mis horas más frescas y tempranas
esta tierra habité, hijo, le dije,
con fuerzas más briosas y lozanas . . .

"In my most youthful and my freshest hours,
I lived, my son, here on this soil," I said,
"When livelier yet and brisker were my powers" . . .

The poet attends a brilliant tourney, which provides him with
an opportunity to laud some of the noblemen who take part.
Then, tired of fighting and writing, he returns home, and enters

Into Madrid clad in a pilgrim's garb,
For it is useful to appear a saint.

Thus the poem ends in a gently satirical vein.

Though *Journey to Parnassus* is highly interesting as a psychological document, as a work of art it adds nothing to Cervantes
stature. It contains, no doubt, the best poetry he wrote, but also
some of the worst; and his worst was very bad. Where Cervantes
does not express a strong personal feeling, he falls back on com-
monplace and padding, relieved by occasional lyrical passages of
a certain beauty, as when he speaks of his lost illusions which,
carried away by light winds, "scattered their seed in them, and in
the sand".

He offers us profound ethical reflections, and some of his lines
echo with the thunder of grand rhetoric. But then follow barren
stretches of verse which were best buried in oblivion as one of the
aberrations which, in a genius like Cervantes, are so often
encountered.

The great Spanish thinker, Don Miguel de Unamuno, resented
this. It caused him to make a sharp distinction between Don
Quixote and his creator, because to him the creator seemed unworthy of his creature. Unamuno found it impossible to understand that a man who had written so much mediocre stuff, and
so much that was simply and frankly bad, should at the same
time have been capable of writing *Don Quixote*. He even went
so far as to hint, though very discreetly, that Cervantes may have
drawn on somebody else's writings. In my opinion the problem
is precisely the opposite: it was strange, though by no means
inexplicable, that the man who wrote *Don Quixote* should at the
same time have produced such undistinguished work.

Cervantes—and this cannot be stressed too strongly—was
before all and above all the author of *Don Quixote*. If one has
followed Cervantes' life, sincerely and humbly listening to his
pulse, as it were, then the force which moved him to create Don
Quixote becomes evident.

There is no need to scent a mystery behind Cervantes' use,
as the frame into which he puts the tale of Don Quixote's
adventures, of the fiction that a Moor whom he calls Cide Hamete
Benengeli wrote the original chronicle, while he himself was only
the translator and adapter. His source was no other than his own

life and experience, his passions and feelings, hatred and love, thought and soul. Cervantes poured it all into the mould for Don Quixote, so completely that there was hardly anything left for him to say in his other writings.

*

Cervantes' *Exemplary Tales*, with their dedication to the Count of Lemos, had been published shortly before the *Journey to Parnassus* appeared. These are twelve stories which seem to have been conceived at different stages of his development, and written almost to while away time. Most of them are based on anecdotes of which he had heard tell, or incidents he had witnessed, during his years of wandering. Often they are set in one of the cities he knew at first hand. It is quite possible that Cervantes had originally written them with the purpose of interpolating them in the second part of *Don Quixote*, a device he had used with other stories in the first part. He refrained from doing so; if this was on the advice of a friend, it was, in my opinion, good advice.

Compared with Cervantes' greatest work, the *Exemplary Tales* have many blemishes. The dialogue nearly always is stilted, the situation conventional, the plot full of improbable coincidences. The solution does not so much grow organically from the story as satisfy a preconceived notion; occasionally the "rhetorical colours" of Cervantes' earlier period turn up again. All the same, these stories have their merit within the limits of their genre, and they have been widely translated as well as widely praised. The outstanding story is the picaresque "Rinconete and Cortadillo", with its vigorous narrative and characters seen in the round. "La Gitanilla"—better known as "Preciosa"—is charming and stylistically perfect, the "Dialogue of Two Dogs" has a remarkable worldly wisdom which carries a load of bitter irony. Then there is the story of the "Jealous Husband from Estremadura", with sharply characterized protagonists; its solution of the problem of an unhappy marriage, however, is once again contrived. In "Licentiate Vidriera", Cervantes uses sparkling aphorisms in his observations on the way of the world, influenced, it would seem, by Erasmus of Rotterdam and the philosophy of ancient Greece.

The remaining tales are considerably weaker, but even they are redeemed by the author's amazing vigour, which was unimpaired by his age. The following is his self-description in the prologue to the *Exemplary Tales*, written in 1613, for, when he knew that the world took interest in him, and hoped that posterity would be curious to know what he was like, he more than once found pleasure in describing himself: "This man you see before you—chestnut-brown hair, smooth, broad forehead, merry eyes, a beaked but well-proportioned nose, silvery beard (less than twenty years ago it was golden!), big moustaches, small mouth, with no more than six teeth, and these in bad condition and worse alignment, for not one corresponds to another; neither tall nor short of stature, of vivid colouring, white rather than sallow skin, somewhat bowed, and not exactly light on his feet—this man, I say, is the author of *La Galatea, Don Quixote de la Mancha*, and *Journey to Parnassus*, as well as of many other works which found their way here and there, perhaps without bearing the name of their maker. He is commonly known as Miguel de Cervantes Saavedra. For many years he was a soldier, and for five-and-a-half years he was a captive, which taught him to be patient in adversity . . ."

37
The True Quixote

In the early autumn of 1614, Cervantes interrupted his work on
Don Quixote to write a composition for a literary contest.

On October 12, 1614, the capital was to celebrate the beatification of Mother Teresa de Jesús—St Teresa of Avila—with
great solemnity. All Spain's writers were invited to take part in
a competition for the best verse and prose in her honour, the first
prize being a silver jug. The jury consisted of three young aristocrats, sons of the leading great families and all of them more or
less closely connected with the Duke of Lerma; and Lope de
Vega was their literary assessor.

Again, as years before when Cervantes took part in a competition in Saragossa, is it not easy to understand what moved
him to do so. It meant that, at the age of sixty-seven, he was
vying with beginners and hack writers of occasional verse, and
that he had to submit to the decision of Lope de Vega, the
arbiter in this case. He did, in fact, win a prize for his stanzas
to the Blessed Teresa, and Lope himself read Miguel's verses
to the assembly. Many of Madrid's writers censured Cervantes'
participation in the contest as a deplorable weakness, others
openly jeered. Lope de Vega may have smiled at the other's
inveterate poetic ambitions as he read his prize poem to a select
audience; he must have enjoyed his rôle as sponsor of Cervantes,
especially if he remembered the many occasions when they had
crossed swords. Perhaps it was, after all, a streak of childish
vanity in Miguel which gave his detractors this facile opportunity to feel superior. But it was a matter of no consequence.

During those days, however, another literary event occurred in

Saragossa, that caused Cervantes the last, and by no means the least, sorrow of his life.

Saragossa, also, was celebrating the beatification of Mother Teresa. One of the spectacles was a sort of masque based on characters taken from *Don Quixote*. This was, in itself, nothing new. The novel was so popular that its almost legendary figures put in an appearance at most public entertainments, not only in Spain. By that time, the book had been translated into English and French. In Germany, too, a figure burlesquing Don Quixote appeared as challenger in a tourney at Heidelberg, given in honour of the Elector of the Palatinate and of Elizabeth, the daughter of James I. The crowd of spectators at Saragossa was delighted with the capers of Don Quixote. Only—this Don Quixote was no longer Cervantes' creation. He was the figure evolved by another writer who, under the name of Alonso Fer-nández de Avellanada, native of Tordesillas, had not only furnished the material for the spectacle at Saragossa but had also written what pretended to be the sequel to *Don Quixote* by its real author. This fake Part Two was even then in print in Tarragona.

Avellanada (to give him his pseudonym) was not content with poaching on another's preserves—for whatever private or merely mercenary reason. He also wrote a prologue to this apocryphal second part of *Don Quixote*, in which he grossly insulted Cer-vantes, almost as if he had an old personal grudge against him, and, in doing so, made free use of the name of Lope de Vega.

We do not know when Cervantes first saw a copy of Avellan-ada's book—there can have been little delay, because somebody is sure to have drawn his attention to it—but everything proves that it was one of his bitterest moments. To begin with, he was aghast; then, when he read Avellanada's boorish prologue, this turned to furious indignation. The unknown plagiarist made mock of Cervantes' age, his crippled hand, his unprepossessing figure, and of his very virtues which in this presentation sounded like so many faults; he painted Miguel as an ignorant and can-tankerous man, full of envy, whose character and deportment had lost him all his friends.

R

The author of the bogus *Quixote* was clever at hiding his identity. To this day it is a matter of conjecture, and the strangest conjectures have been voiced. The topical allusions made by Avellanada may have been deliberately misleading, but internal evidence suggests that the man belonged to one of the literary cliques in Madrid over which Lope de Vega was the undis- puted master. The idea of producing a "second part" in parody may well have been conceived there, and Lope himself may not have been altogether innocent. Seen from that angle, there was a grain of truth in Avellanada's biting remarks. Certainly Cer- vantes passed through a temporary crisis which made him keep away from the literary sets. Whenever he turned up at a gathering, at least at a gathering dominated by Lope and his followers, he may have shown himself much as Avellanada describes him— morose, sardonic and mistrustful. He had cause for distrust. He must have known that in those circles he was the favourite target for hostile comment, and that the people around him put down to arrogance and rudeness what was only his way of defending his self-respect in such surroundings.

All this is, of course, mere guesswork. It is safe to assume, however, that the author of that prologue was inspired by envy and jealousy. It is somewhat remarkable that the pseudonym has proved impenetrable. Only the fact that in Spain Cervantes had won little renown as an artist, in spite of the big sales his novel had enjoyed, explains why the perpetrator of the literary fraud was not shown up at the time.

If Cervantes had an inkling of his adversary's real name he kept silent about it. What obsessed him was the event itself, the harm it did him, and the need to protect his name and his work. In his agitation, he even overrated the merits of the book; he feared that it was, in its way, successful enough to lessen his, Cervantes', popularity and to reduce public interest in his own Part Two, which was still unfinished when the spurious one appeared. This filled him with impatience and anxiety, quite apart from his anger.

Reading Avellanada's pseudo-*Quixote* today, we find it

difficult to understand Cervantes' concern, and even more difficult to see why he thought it worth while to change his original plan and make his Don Quixote go to Saragossa. However, if Miguel exaggerated the importance of Avellanada's book, this had a salutary effect on him: it caused him to redouble his creative effort.

Cervantes had already completed a substantial portion of his Part Two. Now he read it through with a critical eye, sharpened by the challenge, and became fully conscious of the meaning of his work. Never had he written with greater intellectual clarity or with greater craftsmanship. He had almost forgotten the line he had followed at the beginning of Part One. He invested Don Quixote with a human quality which irradiated all other beings and all inanimate things. Cervantes now knew and loved the character he had created to the point of self-identification: "For me alone Don Quixote was born, and I for him . . . only we two together are as one", he was to say on the last page of his novel.

This second part incorporates brief nostalgic excursions to the landscapes of Cervantes' childhood, it revives buried illusions and distant memories. There is, for instance, the scene where Don Quixote meets on his way a wagon-load of strolling players. He sees their costumes, a death mask, swords and spears, sceptres and crowns; in his imagination he is about to embark on a dangerous adventure. But when he is told the true facts his warlike fervour evaporates; in a gentle mood, almost with emotion, he dismisses the players: "Go with God, good people, and have your festival. And if there is any way in which I may be of service to you, tell me your request, I shall meet it with good will and pleasure. For, when I was a child I was already fond of pantomimes, and as a young boy I could not take my eyes off the strolling players."

It is no more than a fleeting moment, but in this passage Cervantes himself seems to greet a happy memory with an overflowing heart, even while the company of players drives gaily off, and the Knight relapses into his folly.

Further on in the book, Don Quixote comes across a young soldier "of eighteen or nineteen, gay of face and, it seemed, agile of body", who is going to war, a bundle on his back, and singing dance tunes to relieve the tedium of the road. Here, surely, the aged Cervantes evokes the young man he once had been, marching to war—a song on his lips—along the roads of Italy, after having left a Cardinal's palace "because he would rather have the King as his lord and master than a doltish courtier". He, too, may have felt certain misgivings and have wished for someone who would understand him and strengthen him in his resolve. Therefore he makes the young man tell Don Quixote about his hopes. The good Knight encourages the soldier, gives him sage advice and—invites him to supper: "For the moment I shall say no more to you; but jump on my horse's back and come with me to the next inn, where you will sup with me. And tomorrow morning you can follow your road which God may grant be as good as your way of thinking deserves."

There are many flashes of simple humanity; flashes of anger and satire there are too; but above everything we find a goodness, a loving-kindness, which grows and expands as the book progresses. The style shows an unselfconscious mastery which weaves the two strands of the real and the ideal into a tapestry of sober, solid and marvellously clear colours. And even though Cervantes, like Homer, may sometimes nod, his characters are always people of flesh and blood.

The invisible presence of the man who called himself Avellanada weighed on Cervantes' mind as he wrote the last section of his work, but he went ahead purposefully. The pattern of the narrative was now subordinated to the central idea. Don Quixote loses much of his impulsive candour, Sancho much of his wheedling trickery; against his will, Don Quixote turns a stranger to his own self, while Sancho comes closer to the Knight. Each defends the other, but Sancho defends the reality of life, and Don Quixote the reality of his dreams without which he cannot live. This struggle is ultimately resolved when the two, Don Quixote and Sancho Panza, merge into one.

There comes the moment when Don Quixote must suffer defeat and die. Cervantes, one suspects, rebels against this harsh law, but he knows that it is inevitable because, in truth, Don Quixote *has* been defeated and he *must* die. But it is not the "Knight of the White Moon"—his well-meaning friend in disguise—who vanquishes Don Quixote on the beach at Barcelona; it is doubt, the insidious doubt which had first assailed him when he saw Dulcinea in person, and which had shaken his faith in his dream world when he emerged from Montesinos' cave. At the Duke's court, the Knight had scarcely possessed the strength of faith to resist the indictment of the priest who destroyed the flowers of his imagination as living flowers are destroyed by a hailstorm. Thus, when his friend, Sansón Carrasco, as the "Knight of the White Moon", throws Don Quixote, the Knight-Errant becomes a pitiful, puny figure on whom even his squire Sancho now dares lay a hand without fear of retribution. After this, nothing is left but to acknowledge defeat, go home, and die. Don Quixote makes his last will—not the will he later dictates in bed, for that is only the will of the old country gentleman, Alonso Quixano. No, he makes this last testament while lying in the sand, at the mercy of his conqueror: "Dulcinea del Toboso is the most beautiful woman in the world and I am the most wretched knight on earth. Drive home your lance, sir knight, and take my life, for you have taken my honour."

(Two hundred years after these words were written, their utter hopelessness brought tears to the eyes of a small German boy—who became the poet Heinrich Heine.)

It is the Knight's last adventure. He is finished. But he still rides along the roads of Spain like his own ghost, seeking to recover his self in the person of Alonso Quixano. A herd of swine tramples upon him, he is bruised and humiliated, since "for the vanquished good turns into bad, bad into worse"; even in the palace of his protector, the Duke, he now finds hostility. At last he hurries back to his village, to rest his weary bones in his own bed. His madness fallen from him, he is once again a mild old gentleman who dies peacefully in Christian resignation, true to the spirit of the older Spanish poet, Jorge Manrique:

> Clear and free consent I give
> To my dying, without cry,
> Without sadness.
> For, that man should want to live,
> When God wants that he should die,
> Is but madness.

It is madness, he at last understands, to want to live; but also madness to want beautiful dreams to triumph over truth; to seek for treasure where there is only filth and misery; to hope for un- selfishness in affection, purity in love, loyalty in friendship, peace on this earth. In the end, the men around poor Alonso Quixano, who imagined himself a Knight-Errant named Don Quixote de la Mancha—the normal people like the parish priest, the barber and Sansón Carrasco, Bachelor of Arts—prevail with their terrible common sense.

To Cervantes, their creator, the victory he had to grant them brought a real and personal grief, for he had put all his passions and dreams into that "madness". As though by way of a last protest, he makes Sancho exclaim: "Don't die, my master, Don Quixote, don't die!"—for Sancho has come to believe in Don Quixote.

And indeed it is not Don Quixote who dies, not the mad Knight; so long as he is mad, he is beyond the reach of death. Perhaps this was the reason why Cervantes, to make possible the ineluctable end, gave him back his sanity. The man who dies so meekly in his bed is good old Alonso Quixano. The other, the one who tilted at giants and rode out, by day or by night, in wind and rain, against the cruel mocking world, to defend the weak, the helpless and oppressed—he still rides on.

38

Sunset

AT the beginning of February, 1615, after Cervantes had written the final VALE at the foot of his manuscript, he took the second part of *Don Quixote* to the General Vicariate of Madrid for the censor's approval.

He was ailing, heavier on his feet than when he penned his self-portrait, and his affairs were—how could it have been otherwise?—in as bad a state as ever. He had been obliged to accept the offer of rooms in the house of the priest Marcilla. We cannot be sure what was the nature of his incipient illness, for we are told only of certain symptoms; it may have been a heart disease or diabetes. Cervantes began to suffer from continuous thirst which nothing could slake, not even "all the water of the seas, which he would gladly drink". But he was always ready to crack jokes about his penury, his ailments, his approaching death. At the same time everything he now wrote was suffused with a tenderness which expressed itself in the increasing use of words such as gentle, soft, sweet, dear. And he had small joys, too, which wiped out much bitterness.

The Count of Lemos had failed to acknowledge the dedication of the *Exemplary Tales*, and Cervantes no doubt feared that, through intrigues of the Count's entourage in Naples, he was out of favour with his patron. Then, unexpectedly, he received a communication from Naples, presumably also material help. The original neglect had pained Cervantes so much that he had not dedicated the *Journey to Parnassus* to the Count. Now he was so moved by the Viceroy's spontaneous gesture that he resolved to dedicate to him all future works he would be able to publish.

He said this in so many words in the dedicatory letter accompanying the book edition of his unperformed plays, which at
last came out in 1615: "Whether or not the garden of my short-
lived ingenuity is exhausted by now, whatever fruit it still
yields, at whichever season, must needs be Your Excellency's."
Miguel, who had so often suffered through the ingratitude of
others, knew how to be grateful on a grand scale.

While the manuscript of Part Two of *Don Quixote* was still
with the ecclesiastical censorship, Cervantes had occasion to
learn at first hand that outside his own country he was considered a great artist. A French ambassadorial mission had come
to Madrid, to discuss the question of an alliance by marriage
between the two royal houses. When Cardinal Sandoval made
a return visit to the French Ambassador, there was among the
chaplains of his retinue a certain Francisco Márquez Torres, who
happened to be the first censor of the Holy Office to be concerned
with Cervantes' new work. According to his account of the
conversation, some of the French gentlemen, "as courteous as
they were cultured, and lovers of good writing", asked about the
best current books in Spain. Naturally Márquez Torres mentioned the manuscript he was even then reading. "As soon as
the name Miguel de Cervantes cropped up," he says, "they
waxed eloquent and said great things about the high esteem in
which his works are held not only in France, but also in the
neighbouring realms—*La Galatea*, which one of them knew
practically by heart, the first part of the present novel, and his
Tales." The Frenchmen were eager to hear every possible detail
about Cervantes, his age, profession, station in life, and circumstances, but the censor "saw himself obliged to tell them that
he was old, a soldier, a Hidalgo, and poor". One of the French
gentlemen thereupon remarked, "If it is necessity which forces
him to write, then please God he will never be affluent, so that,
being poor, he may enrich the entire world."

So pressing were the Frenchmen that the chaplain offered to
guide them to Cervantes' abode. When they called on him in
his drab rooms in the Calle del León, Miguel de Cervantes

received from their lips the first homage of the outside world to reach him. And yet, though they happened to come from Paris, they could equally well have brought him the same message from Lisbon or London. In this sense, Cervantes had triumphed.

With all his new mildness, and in spite of his conviction that he would not live much longer, Cervantes was still capable of protesting against the petty annoyances which harassed him to the last. In the prologue to *Journey to Parnassus*, he said: "God protect you, reader, and as for me, may he grant me patience to bear well with all the ill not a few sophisticated and starchy persons will speak of me." He expressed the same sentiment in a terse sentence in the prologue to his plays: "May God give you health and me patience." But once this was said, he quickly returned to the serenity which had become the keynote of his being.

Not even the state of Spain, whose decline was more clearly discernible with every day that passed, any longer roused Miguel to indignation. He had lost every vestige of narrow patriotism. Turks who are friendly, and Englishmen who are not only friendly but brave and chivalrous, figure in his last works. Everywhere he finds good and bad people, heroes and cowards, and everywhere he discovers a redeeming spark of goodness underneath common selfishness and baseness of heart. In the light of this all-embracing insight, Cervantes wrote the very last of his completed works, *The Trials of Persiles and Segismunda*.

It is a fantastic tale. Somewhere, somehow, a group of people are thrown together and pass through an incredible series of dangers and vicissitudes. They come from all countries and all walks of life; among them are slaves and princes; all are united by misfortune and a longing for better things. It had been like that in the prisons of Algiers, but now Cervantes sees the world as one large prison where "all have desires, but no one's desire is fulfilled." As in his old pastoral novel, *La Galatea*, it is a community ruled by friendship; this time, however, the ideal is not confined to a small Arcadia, but encompasses the globe.

In the person of one of the bolder spirits among the group

Cervantes portrays his youthful self: Periandro dreams of becoming "a corsair in the service of good, fighting against the corsairs of evil". He is a Don Quixote of the sea, with a ship in place of Rocinante. On one occasion, when the friends have landed on an island, Periandro calls the fishermen together and harangues them in the best style of the Ingenious Knight. He wants them to leave their heavy, unrewarding toil for brave new adventures: "Forward then, let us pursue them [the enemy's ship], and let us be pirates, not greedy ones like those others, but pirates in the service of justice."

Persiles is a dull and diffuse work; all the same it accurately reflects Cervantes' frame of mind during his last period, when reality meant nothing and fantasy everything. This time we are not in an earthy "place of the Mancha" as in *Don Quixote*; we are somewhere in the North, among the mists of legend and enchantment. Everything is veiled by a gentle twilight. Neither the landscapes nor the virtues of the characters have their counterpart anywhere but in Cervantes' imagination; yet there is a sad sweetness in the matter and style of *Persiles*, as though carried over from the last pages of *Don Quixote*.

Towards its close the story is livened by some flashes of anger and irony. After wandering from island to island, country to country, and after battling with every sort of misadventure, in which mystery and witchcraft play no inconsiderable part, the protagonists land in Portugal and cross into Spain. The goal of their pilgrimage is Rome, the centre of the new humanity; there they hope to find peace, absolution from their sins, and reward for perils surmounted. But even there, and despite Cervantes' gentle twilight mood, their trials are not over. In Rome, too, justice is for sale, taverns and brothels stand cheek by jowl with the churches, and God is mocked by men. When the hopes of the hero are almost shattered in this nightmare of vice, the bitterness of Don Quixote's defeat reechoes through Cervantes' lines. Yet, although he recognizes that Rome is of this world as much as any other place, Cervantes kisses—in the person of his hero— the Holy Father's foot, makes—through the lips of his heroine—

a solemn profession of his Catholic faith, and places his hopes in Heaven. Before he ends the book, however, in its pages he makes a last journey to the city to which he had always felt so strangely drawn: to Naples.

*

The first censor had given his approval to the publication of Part Two of *Don Quixote* on February 27, 1615. It took ten months until the book came out. Printing was slow; the official bodies which had to grant permits, copyrights and the final sanction were even slower. In the dedication to the Count of Lemos, dated October 31, Cervantes spoke of his new work, *Persiles*, which he intended to "finish within four months" and dismissed the "masquerading" bogus *Quixote* with contempt, not mentioning its pseudonymous author's name. Events proved him to be more justified in this than in his previous anxiety: his Part Two was another triumph, and Avellanada was relegated to limbo.

But Cervantes was a sick man. At the beginning of 1616 his physician recommended rest and a change of air. He went to Esquivias. But, however bracing might be the air, however gay and hope-inspiring the countryside in the early spring sun, Miguel was homesick for Madrid. Before long he rode back, back to what he needed: familiar faces, familiar places, even familiar feuds, all of which were alike dear to him. Above everything there was his work, which drove him on. What did it matter if by going back to it he cut a few days from his brief remaining span of life?

By the end of March he was forced to stay in bed. On April 2, when he made his profession as novice of the Third Order of St Francis, whose habit he had taken two years before, the ceremony took place in his room because Miguel was unable to get up.

He was still able to write, propped up perhaps in an armchair near the open balcony, where he could breathe in the spring air drifting across from the nearby gardens of the Prado. *Persiles* was finished, except for the dedication. Though his brain was busy with ideas for new books, Miguel knew that he was a dying man. In the prologue to *Persiles*, written during those last weeks, though we do not know the precise date, he said: "My life is drawing to its end, and, in step with my pulse which will finish its race on the coming Sunday at the latest, I shall finish my own race in life."

On April 18 he received the Last Sacraments, administered by the priest Francisco López. Friends came and went; he had his niece near him, as well as Doña Catalina, his wife.

On the following day—it must have been in the evening, when all was quiet—he asked for pen and paper. He still owed a debt of gratitude to the one powerful man he had known who had given him help without humbling him. Miguel began to write the famous dedicatory letter to the Count of Lemos, in which he offered him his last work:

"I wish the lines of the old, once famous folk-song which begins 'With my foot already in the stirrup' did not fit this letter of mine so well, for I could start almost with the same words, and say:

> With my foot already in the stirrup,
> With the hand of death upon me,
> This to you, my lord, I write.

"Yesterday they gave me the Extreme Unction, today I write this. Time is short, pains grow, hopes shrink, and with all this I keep alive because I want to live. And I wish I could make my life last till I can kiss Your Excellency's feet. Possibly the joy of seeing Your Excellency back in Madrid, fit and well, could give me life. But if it is decreed that this life shall be taken from me, God's will be done. And at least Your Excellency will know what I have wished for, will know that in me you had a servant so anxious to serve you that he wanted to go beyond death to show you his intent. Speaking as if I had a seer's vision, I say: I am glad Your Excellency has arrived, I enjoy seeing people point you out; and I shall be doubly glad if my own hopes come true, magnified by the fame of Your Excellency's many kindnesses. There are still in my mind some vestiges and ideas of *Weeks in the Garden* and *The Great Bernardo.* If by any happy chance, and to my good fortune—but it would be a miracle rather than good fortune—Heaven were to grant me life, you will see these works and moreover the final part of *La Galatea,* in which Your Excellency has begun to show interest. And to continue my wishing, may, when these works come into your hands, God guard Your Excellency, as is in His power.

"Madrid, the 19th of April, 1616."

This done, Cervantes reconsidered the prologue to *Persiles.* There was still something he wanted to impart. True, his *Don Quixote* was a great success, but still only a success as light literature. Most of his readers took the novel for a funny book and enjoyed it as such: round the two figures of the knight and his squire, farces were built to amuse the public. Only a select few penetrated the humorous façade to reach the true substance behind it. Cervantes had come to this sad realization and before his death he felt a need to warn people against the current misinterpretation. With this in mind, he invented—or adapted from an actual experience on his last ride home—for the prologue an incident on the road from Esquivias to Madrid.

He describes there how he and two friends were riding back to town, when they heard somebody calling out behind them. It was a student in rustic garb, clad in grey from head to foot, who was riding in the same direction on a she-ass. He joined them, they began to talk, and the young man happened to hear one of the men address Cervantes by name. Whereupon he jumped from the donkey's back, "so that the saddle-cushion flew hither, the clothes-bag thither", clutched Cervantes' left hand, and exclaimed: "Yes, yes indeed, this is he, the sane cripple, the famous whole man, the merry writer, in short, the mirth-maker of the Muses!"

Faced at such close quarters with this extravagant admirer, Cervantes would have thought it discourteous not to respond.

Therefore he embraced the young student "so that his neck-band came undone". But then—and this is, to my mind, the serious message behind the whole, half-comical, half-touching episode—Cervantes said, "This is an error into which many ignorant dilettanti have fallen. Sir, I am Cervantes, but neither the mirth-maker of the Muses nor any of the other cheap non-sense you just mentioned. Now take your donkey, sir, mount her, and on the rest of our way we shall have some good conversa-tion." It is in the course of this conversation that Cervantes quotes himself as speaking of his "dropsy" and of his death "on the coming Sunday at the latest".

The message in the prologue to *Persiles*, however, was lost on the contemporary public when the book was published after Cervantes' death. Two hundred years were to pass before the pain and sadness behind the seeming jocularity of *Don Quixote* were recognized; it was the German Romantic School that dis-covered it. And yet what Cervantes had written in that neglected prologue is very plain. Perhaps he wanted to say still more, to enlarge upon the theme, but it was too late.

Only once again did he ask for his pen, to add to the prologue, in wavering letters, his farewell to the world: "Good-bye, all that is charming, good-bye, wit and gaiety, good-bye, you merry friends, for I am dying, and wishing to see you soon contented in another life!" These are the last words we have from him.

Miguel de Cervantes died on Saturday, April 23, 1616. He was laid out in the brown habit of St Francis, and the open coffin was carried the short distance to the Trinitarian church, the church of the convent of Carmelite nuns, by brethren of his religious community. As required by the Third Order, his face was left uncovered. His hands were folded across his chest, and into his left was placed, as a last symbol, a cross shaped like a sword.

*

Three months after Cervantes died, the Count of Lemos arrived in Madrid from Naples, greeted by a host of courtiers and hangers-on who noisily extolled his virtues—those he possessed and those he lacked. Amid the chorus of live flatterers, the grandee was unmindful of the voice of the dead Cervantes. He had forgotten all about the man and his work.

Not long afterwards, Doña Catalina de Salazar, whom her husband—thereby differing from her treatment of him—had made his sole heir, sold the rights in *Persiles*. For these rights, and probably for dues accrued from other works by Cervantes, the publisher was soon in arrears for the sum of four hundred *reales*. It was little enough, but sufficient to bring about a reunion between Doña Catalina, her brother Francisco, and the dead writer's son-in-law, Luis de Molina. Molina, the businessman, was authorized by Francisco de Palacios Salazar to act on behalf of the widow in the matter of obtaining the money from the publisher.

Molina may have been adroit, but he was still a spendthrift without many scruples. His testament records that he once took a sedan-chair worth 800 *reales* from his wife's house while she was lying in bed, "very ill", and that he pawned her jewels and other valuables without her knowledge.

Don Juan de Urbina, Cervantes' "great friend", entered on endless litigation against Cervantes' daughter and her husband to regain possession of his house, which he succeeded in doing years later.

Isabel de Saavedra stubbornly defended her amassed fortune against her husband's insatiable appetite and against Urbina's designs. She died a wealthy and a pious woman.

They were all too busy to remember either Cervantes or his grave. They did not even find time—or the means—to erect a gravestone with a simple inscription. There is nothing to mark the spot where he was buried.

We are left to think of him laid out on a plain catafalque before the Main Altar of the Trinitarian church, dim candle-light falling on the brown habit, the calm face, and the cross in the shape of a sword. In the silent shadows of the night—or the dawn—the last Knight-Errant, astride a gaunt nag, rides slowly, wearily, steadfastly, along the road to eternity, carrying with him the dream of the dead man's life.